An Illustrated History of Early Buckinghamshire

An Illustrated History of Early Buckinghamshire

edited by
Michael Farley

With contributions by Lucy Farr, David Radford,
Kim Taylor-Moore, Barbara Silva, Sandy Kidd,
Bob Zeepvat, and Michael Farley

Buckinghamshire Archaeological Society

An Illustrated History of Early Buckinghamshire
Copyright © Buckinghamshire Archaeological Society 2010

Published by Buckinghamshire Archaeological Society
c/o Buckinghamshire County Museum, Church Street, Aylesbury, Buckinghamshire HP20 2QP

ISBN Number 978-0-9558158-4-3

Typeset by Avocet Typeset, Chilton, Aylesbury, Buckinghamshire HP18 9FG
Design and layout by Amberflare, 32, Park Street, Aylesbury, Buckinghamshire HP20 1BX
Printed by Halstan Printing Group, 2-10, Plantation Road, Amersham, Buckinghamshire HP6 6HJ

Contents

Acknowledgements

This book would not have been produced without assistance from a great many individuals and institutions including staff at Buckinghamshire County Museum and Ros Tyrell of the Portable Antiquities Scheme; the County Archaeological Service; the Centre for Buckinghamshire Studies; Milton Keynes Council Conservation and Archaeology Team, and Berkshire Archaeology.

The Society is most grateful to The Francis Coales Charitable Foundation, The Robert Kiln Charitable Trust, Mr Richard Pushman (Chairman of Buckinghamshire County Council), Milton Keynes Council Conservation and Archaeology Team and the National Trust, all of whom made grants in support of the publication. Sir Henry Aubrey Fletcher kindly contributed the Foreword.

The Editor wishes to thank the individual authors, all of whom apart from himself have full-time occupations and yet have somehow made time to complete their scholarly contributions: Lucy Farr has in addition kindly produced many of the maps. The Editor is also grateful to a number of people who commented on draft texts, to Diana Gulland for the laborious task of preparing the index, and Brett Thorn, Julie Wise and Ros Tyrell for other assistance. Thanks also to the book's Steering Committee consisting of Yvonne Edwards, Brett Thorn, Julian Hunt and Sandy Kidd all of whom made most helpful individual contributions towards its production. Geoffrey Farrer-Brown kindly photographed on behalf of the County Museum several objects in its collection.

Thanks also to Paul Medcalf of Avocet Typeset and Lee Upton of Amberflare who freely gave advice on the book's production.

Finally, acknowledgement should be made to numerous toilers in the field; excavators, fieldwalkers, researchers, specialists, members of local societies and others who have carried out the groundwork, often in very difficult conditions, that has provided the raw material for this book.

Individual authors wish in addition to thank:

Barbara Silva: Danielle Schreve for advice on the faunal aspects of Stone Age Buckinghamshire.

Lucy Farr: Andrew Manning of Wessex Archaeology for advice and use of one image.

Sandy Kidd: Kim Biddulph who summarised our current state of knowledge of Neolithic and early Bronze Age Buckinghamshire for the Solent-Thames Research Frameworks Project; Tim Allen (Oxford Archaeology) and Andy Chapman (Northamptonshire Archaeology) who provided images and information on their recent work and Alison Doggett who kindly gave permission to reproduce fig 2.6 from her book *The Chilterns*. My wife graciously tolerated the piles of books and papers which typify a 'work in progress' and commented on the draft text.

Michael Farley: his supportive spouse.

Kim Taylor-Moore: Professor Chris Dyer, who wrote part of the original paper on which this chapter was based, for his advice and support, and for his many helpful comments and suggestions, and Mel Braithwaite for photography and staff of the CBS.

Illustration Acknowledgements and Copyright

None of the images in this book are to be reproduced in any form without written permission from the copyright holders who are listed below. Figure numbers are cited beside the copyright holder

Alison Doggett: 2.6

Barbara Silva: 1.1, 1.5 (top right, bottom left and right)

Bob Zeepvat: 3.4 (upper), 3.8 (lower), 3.15 (lower),

Bodleian Library, University of Oxford. Ms.Laud Misc.636,fol 10: Fig. 4.2

Brian Giggins: 2.22 (upper)

British Geological Survey. Fig 1.3 Reproduced from BGS data at the original scale of 1:50,000, License No. 2002/005 British Geological Survey (c) NERC

Buckinghamshire Archaeological Society: 1.8 (with P. Lorimer),1.15, 3.9, 3.13 (lower left), 3.24, 4.13, 4.15, 5.8, 5.11, 5.19, 5.29 (left). (These images are mainly from BAS publications, further copyright may rest with originators).

Buckinghamshire County Museum Collections: 1.2, 1.4, 2.8, 2.16, 2.17, 2.21, 3.13, (upper and lower right), 3.19 (top right), 3.20, 3.23, 3.27, 3.29, 4.21, 4.22 (bottom left), 4.23, 4.25, 4.31, 4.33 (top), 5.9, 5.18, 5.27, 5.28

Buckinghamshire County Museum and David Parish: 1.6, 1.7

Buckinghamshire County Council: illustrations marked * are of items in the County Museum collections but the images are from slides held by the Historic Environment Record, County Archaeological Service: 1.13*, 1.16, 2.12, 2.19, 2.20, 2.23*, 2.24, 2.25, 2.26 (right), 3.5*, 3.7, 3.12*, 3.14, 3.15 (upper), 3.16, 3.17, 3.25, 3.26*, 4.3*, 4.5, 4.6*, 4.7*, 4.8*, 4.10*, 4.11*, 4.12, 4.14 (top), 4.16 (lower), 4.17 (left), 4.19, 4.22(top right, centre bottom), 4.26, 4.31* (bottom), 5.4, 5.5, 5.14, 5.5.16, 5.20,5.24, 5.26

Centre for Buckinghamshire Studies: 5.1, 5.12, 5.14

Cotswold Archaeology: 3.22.

David Neal: 3.30

Lucy Farr: 1.11 (after Barker 2006), 1.12 (after Darvill 1987), 1.14 (after Simmons 1996)

Marion Blockley: 3.19 (bottom right)

Mel Braithwaite: 5.7, 5.13 (bottom), 5.17, 5.21 (right), 5.22, 5.23,

Milton Keynes Council: 2.14, 2.22 (lower), 3.1, 3.8 (upper), 3.10, 3.11, 3.18, 3.19 (top left and bottom left), 3.27, 3.28, 3.30,

Michael Farley: 1.5 (upper left), 4.16 (upper), 4.20, 4.22 (top left, top centre, bottom right), 4.27, 4.28, 4.30, 5.2, 5.3, 5.6, 5.10, 5.21 (left), 5.25, 5.29 (right)

National Monuments Record, English Heritage: 5.13 (top)

Northamptonshire Archaeology: 2.9, 2.13

Oxford Archaeology: 2.4, 2.26 (left)

Paul Woodfield: 3.3 (from *Archaeological Journal* 146 (1986), 261)

Peter Lorimer and Bucks Archaeological Society: 1.8

Portable Antiquities Scheme: 4.4, 4.9, 4.24, 4.29, 4.32,

RPS: 2.11.

Sandy Kidd: 2.2.

Thames Valley Archaeological Services: 4.17 (right). 4.18,

The Trustees of the British Museum: 2.15, 3.21

The Ordnance Survey. All of the whole county maps in the book listed following are based on modification of Ordnance survey materials with the permission of Ordnance Survey on behalf of the controller of Her Majesty's Stationery Office (c) Crown Copyright. Unauthorised reproduction infringes Crown Copyright and may lead to prosecution or civil proceedings. (c) Copyright Buckinghamshire County Council Licence No. 100021529 2009: 1.10, 2.1, 2.5, 2.7, 2.10, 2.18, 3.2, 3.6, 4.1, 5.30

Wessex Archaeology: 1.9, 2.3

Contributors

Barbara Silva: Royal Holloway, University of London.

Lucy Farr: McDonald Institute for Archaeological Research, Cambridge.

Sandy Kidd: Buckinghamshire County Archaeologist.

David Radford: formerly Archaeological Officer Buckinghamshire County Archaeology Service, now Archaeologist for Oxford City Council.

Bob Zeepvat: Archaeological Services and Consultancy Ltd, Milton Keynes.

Michael Farley: formerly Buckinghamshire County Archaeologist.

Kim Taylor-Moore: postgraduate research student, Centre for English Local History, University of Leicester.

List of Illustrations
(for copyright see page vii)

Foreword

by Sir Henry Aubrey-Fletcher, Lord Lieutenant

Buckinghamshire has few natural boundaries. It extends across a roughly north-south slice through a range of landscape types and abuts six other counties or former counties. The county was created some time in the tenth or early eleventh centuries (the matter is still open to debate) and it survived roughly intact with minor boundary changes for over 900 years until a series of alterations detached Linslade in 1965 and in 1974 Eton, Slough, Horton, Datchet, and Wraysbury. The most recent change took place in 1997 when the Borough of Milton Keynes became a unitary authority.

Earlier writers on the county's early history could not have imagined the enormous increase in information that has become available over the last few years. Michael Reed's book *The Buckinghamshire Landscape* published in 1979 provided a most useful overview but thirty years later, as this book makes clear, extensive archaeological fieldwork carried out in advance of development together with discoveries made by members of the public, have substantially modified our views of the county's distant past. This new book, written by specialists with particular knowledge of early Buckinghamshire, brings together the results of this recent work for the general reader.

The Buckinghamshire Archaeological Society who are the publishers, cannot match in longevity the office of Lord Lieutenant whose history dates back to the Tudor period. However, the Society is no newcomer having been founded as the 'Architectural and Archaeological Society of the County of Buckinghamshire' in 1848 by a group of worthies, mainly clergymen. In 1907 the Society bought its first premises in Church Street and established the County Museum which still flourishes today, since 1957 managed by the County Council. The Society's publications cover the entirety of the old county and its members' interests and expertise are wide-ranging, including archaeology, geology, natural history, architecture, and history. These subject areas are reflected in its principal publication, the *Records of Buckinghamshire,* which has been produced continuously since 1854.

This well-illustrated study which is being published at the same time as a major exhibition by the County Museum – *Human: half a million years of life in Buckinghamshire* – opens our eyes to the fascinating emerging picture of Buckinghamshire's early history, most of it unrecorded in any document. I congratulate all those who have contributed. In a decade or so no doubt the book will also become part of history having briefly captured a point in time; given the pace of change there is little doubt that by then a completely revised publication will be needed!

Introduction

The five chapters of this book each describe distinct periods of Buckinghamshire's early history. They originated as a series of research papers on the archaeology of the county assembled in 2007 by Sandy Kidd, Buckinghamshire County Archaeologist, as part of an English Heritage initiative. The original papers are available on a website (http://www.buckscc.gov.uk/bcc/archaeology/archaeology.page?) and have since been published by the Society as *An Archaeological Research Framework for Buckinghamshire; collected papers from the Solent-Thames research Framework,* ed D.Thorpe 2009 (Buckinghamshire Papers No 15). The Society decided that these important papers should be recast, with the addition of illustrations, for a wider audience and this book is the result. Its publication coincides with a major exhibition on the subject assembled by the County Museum Service.

Seven authors with specialist knowledge have contributed. Each has attempted to achieve county-wide coverage and to answer some of the questions that a general reader would like answered about its past. There are inevitably some biases in the available information for some areas due, for example, to there having been more development (and thus more opportunities for archaeological investigation) in and around Aylesbury and Milton Keynes than there have been in the Chilterns, much of which is protected as an Area of Outstanding Natural Beauty.

Buckinghamshire has been fortunate in that a substantial history of the county prepared by George Lipscomb, was published between 1831 and 1847 and between 1905 and 1927 the four volumes of the *Victoria County History* were published. In 1912–13 a detailed listing of the county's architecture was produced by the Royal Commission on Historical Monuments and there have been numerous other papers (particularly in *Records of Buckinghamshire*) and many books including that by Michael Reed noted in the Foreword. These have provided an excellent working foundation for the up-to-date account of the county's early history which is presented in this book.

The enormous increase in available information that has come about over the last thirty years or so, commenced with the appointment of a Field Archaeologist to the County Museum's staff and the creation of the Milton Keynes Archaeological Unit. Funding for fieldwork initially came from many sources, including the Inspectorate of Ancient Monuments (later subsumed within English Heritage), the County Council, and in particular the Milton Keynes Development Corporation, together with contributions from developers and others. During the 1980s and 1990s as awareness of the serious impact that development was having on heritage became more widely recognised, archaeology was built into the development-control process of planning and the result was a shift to developer-funded work. This in turn led to the creation of contract archaeology with archaeological organisations competing for work and 'curatorial' archaeologists, such as the County Archaeological Officer and the Archaeological Officer for Milton Keynes, advising councils on requirements and monitoring field projects. A further important recent development has been the creation of the nationally-run Portable Antiquities Scheme set up in response to the growth of metal detecting as a hobby, and recording finds made by detectorists. New information also continues to come to light through the work of local societies and from members of the public reporting their discoveries, for example to the County Museum Service which also acts as a repository for finds and archaeological site archives for much of the historic county.

Assimilating all this data into an accessible form for public use is the job of the Historic Environment Records. These records are maintained by Milton Keynes Council and Buckinghamshire County Council, and for areas of the historic county now within Slough and Windsor and Maidenhead Council by Berkshire Archaeology, and for Linslade by Central Bedfordshire Council. The information presented in this book represents therefore the results of the cumulative efforts of numerous individuals and institutions over at least a century and a half. During the last two or three decades the flow of information has certainly speeded up and as Sir Henry notes in the Foreword there may well be a need for another book within the next decade.

Michael Farley

Chapter 1

Earliest Buckinghamshire

Barbara Silva and Lucy Farr

Palaeolithic Buckinghamshire

Throughout much of the Palaeolithic (the Old Stone Age), we find tantalising evidence for the presence of the earliest human inhabitants of the British Isles as well as hints about what their lives here might have been like and what landscapes they inhabited. Few people, when considering the earliest inhabitants of Buckinghamshire, realise just how many thousands of years have passed since the first humans walked through the landscape in the county.

The first appearance of early humans in Britain in the Lower Palaeolithic is dated to about 700,000 years ago.[1] These early inhabitants included species which were distinct from modern humans (*Homo sapiens*) such as *Homo heidelbergensis* and *Homo neanderthalensis*. The Upper Palaeolithic (commencing about 40,000 years ago) dates from the appearance of modern humans (*Homo sapiens sapiens*)[2] and lasts until about 10,000 years ago. The major archaeological evidence for the presence of our early ancestors are stone tools and debris from their manufacture. Less commonly found, but equally important, are the remains of butchered animals and very rarely, wooden tools such as the Clacton spear.[3]

It is clear that climatic conditions have influenced the migratory activity of humans and animals, and their appearance in the British Isles. The last two million years have been dominated by regular global climatic oscillations, when large parts of the Earth were covered by ice sheets, punctuated by relatively short-lived, temperate interglacials, when conditions were similar to those of today. These cyclic changes have been mapped using data from cores taken through the deep sea floor, which provide a continuous record over two million years of geological time. In this 'time line', the climate changes are numbered as 'Marine Isotope Stages' (MIS), with MIS 1 representing the present interglacial – the Holocene. Warm, interglacial periods are given odd numbers and cold, glacial stages, even numbers.[4]

The geological record on land in Britain is much more patchy; Processes, such as erosion, as well as the consequences of glacial activity on the landscape means that the sedimentary record is rarely continuous. However, the 'snap

1

FIGURE 1.1
Gravel extraction on the
Taplow terrace. Sites
such as these have
provided much of the
evidence for Palaeolithic
Buckinghamshire.

shots' we do have illustrate the dramatic changes Britain has undergone. For example, we do know that during the great Anglian Glaciation (MIS Stage 12 – *c.* 480–420,000 years ago), a polar ice cap covered much of Britain including parts of Buckinghamshire, and reached the outskirts of modern day London. South of this icecap, the landscape was a barren tundra zone, dissected by vast braided rivers. At this time, sea levels were many metres lower than at present; Britain was joined to Europe by a land bridge, and was a peninsula of Europe rather than the island it is today. As climates warmed up and the ice caps melted, sea levels rose, ultimately flooding the land bridge, and Britain was an island once more.

In addition to this broad scale view of climatic change, we can uncover detail about the local environment in which early humans lived from evidence preserved in the sediments in the ground beneath our feet. When uncovered through excavation, these sediments can give us detailed information about landscape features such as former river courses and the presence of ancient glaciers. Smaller fossils (ecological artefacts or ecofacts) recovered from the sediments, such as shells and beetles, and microscopic fossils such as pollen provide information to add to the picture of Ice Age landscapes.

Bearing in mind the points above, this chapter, exploring the Stone Age story of Buckinghamshire is essentially selective, with each occupation site providing a 'snapshot in time' during the past 700,000 years. We will outline the evidence for human presence in the county from the earliest occupation during the Palaeolithic, through the Mesolithic to the onset of the Neolithic, and place this information in a regional context.

The Lower and Middle Stone Age (Palaeolithic) in Buckinghamshire

Within the Historic Environment Records for Buckinghamshire there are some 380 records that refer to Palaeolithic and Pleistocene finds in the county.[5] In common with much of the country, few of these finds are the result of formal archaeological excavation but rather represent chance finds made during construction, quarrying or fieldwalking. The majority of the stone finds, where condition is noted, are described as being 'rolled', suggesting that they are not where originally discarded and their findspots are the result of secondary deposition. However, many of the HER records do not state the condition of the artefact. There are also sites, such as Station Pit in Taplow (Fig. 1.1), where hundreds of artefacts have been uncovered with very little evidence for degradation or rolling, suggesting that they are, if not *in situ*, then they are very close to it (Fig. 1.3. Ecofacts are rarely mentioned in the HERs, and whilst it is possible that this is a fair representation of their absence, it is more likely that this is due to a lack of reporting or recognition of palaeoenvironmental finds. However, the majority of recorded Palaeolithic finds from Buckinghamshire do appear to be clustered around the major river courses.

The landscape and topography of Buckinghamshire, and their significance for Palaeolithic and Pleistocene finds

The geology and landscape of Buckinghamshire can be divided into three broad categories, the claylands, the Chilterns and the Thames floodplain (Fig. 1.3).

The northern part of the county, to just south of Stoke Hammond and Aylesbury, is characterised by an undulating clay topography, although with some limestone, sands, and glacial sediments. This is a predominantly pastoral landscape, consisting of fields bordered by hedgerows and some woodland. These are mainly underlain by heavy blue-grey Oxford and Kimmeridge clays, and the resulting topography is gently undulating. These low hills are incised by rivers, including the Ouse, Ousel and the Thame – the latter draining towards the Thames in the south west.

Moving southwards, the chalk hills of the Chilterns dominate a landscape incised by small valleys. The Chilterns rise to just over 900 feet and stretch from the Thames in Oxfordshire across Buckinghamshire and Hertfordshire to Bedfordshire. This outcrop of chalk rises gently towards the north-west, but ends abruptly in a dramatic steep scarp slope above Aylesbury Vale. The hills are dissected by a network of valleys. Many of these are currently dry and were formed by glacial melt water in the past but some support spring-fed streams drained by tributaries of the Thames as well as the Thames itself. The Chilterns are an important source of flint – a raw material much utilised by Palaeolithic and Mesolithic peoples to manufacture stone tools.

Pleistocene (Ice Age) deposits on the Chilterns are principally represented by the clay-with-flint caps on the high ground – the result of dissolution of the chalk-with-flint deposits. In the Chilterns, clay-with-flints is also sometimes referred to as 'Pebbly Clay and Sand', because of a greater component of flint

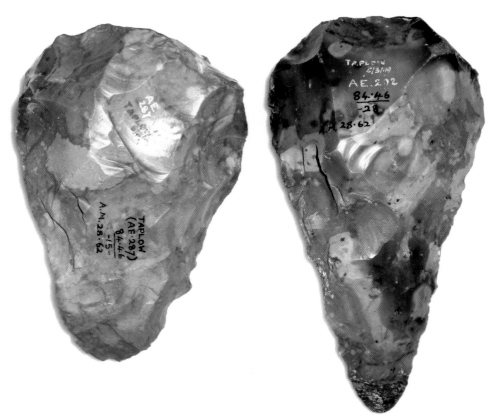

FIGURE 1.2
Two Palaeolithic
handaxes found at
Station Pit, Taplow.

pebbles and sand in some deposits, but it is notable that these deposits do not include far-travelled components[6] and therefore, by implication, formed *in situ* rather than being transported from elsewhere. In places, there are also deposits of 'brick earth' (comprised of mainly reworked earlier Tertiary geological deposits from this area[7]) and these are believed to represent infilling of chalk depressions during relatively wet interglacials.[8] When lined with clay-rich sediments, these depressions could have formed ponds and lakes[9], potentially attractive sites for early humans.[10] Within the Chilterns themselves, dry-valley gravels can sometimes be found lining the valleys as a consequence of post-glacial ice melt and draining.[11]

The south-western boundary of the Chilterns is formed by the Thames. This belt of countryside is dominated by the river and its floodplain. This southern part of Buckinghamshire is characterised by river terraces[12] – often exploited for mineral extraction – as well as by the floodplain itself.

Rivers and floodplains are thought to have been important corridors of travel for Palaeolithic peoples as they provided easy access to water and prey. The main rivers of Buckinghamshire are: 1) the Great Ouse, that flows from the north of Brackley in an easterly direction, before being joined by the Padbury and Claydon Brooks near Buckingham, and the Rivers Tove and Ouzel at Newport Pagnell, which all drain into the Fens and Wash; 2) The River Thame, a tributary of the Thames that flows from near Aylesbury towards Thame; 3) the River

FIGURE 1.3
Simplified map of
Buckinghamshire
geology.

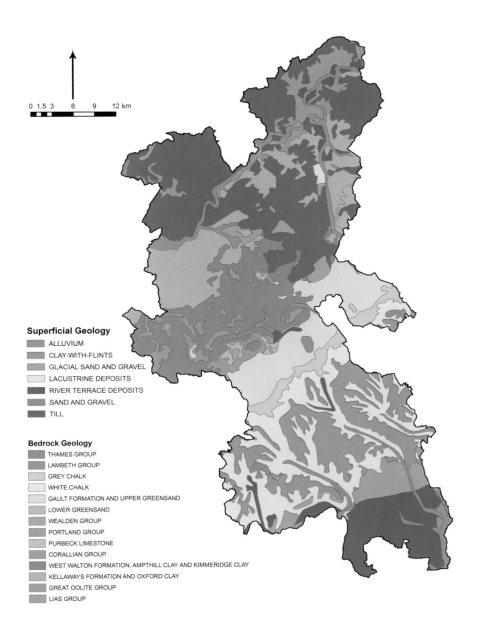

0 1.5 3   6   9   12 km

Superficial Geology
ALLUVIUM
CLAY-WITH-FLINTS
GLACIAL SAND AND GRAVEL
LACUSTRINE DEPOSITS
RIVER TERRACE DEPOSITS
SAND AND GRAVEL
TILL

Bedrock Geology
THAMES GROUP
LAMBETH GROUP
GREY CHALK
WHITE CHALK
GAULT FORMATION AND UPPER GREENSAND
LOWER GREENSAND
WEALDEN GROUP
PORTLAND GROUP
PURBECK LIMESTONE
CORALLIAN GROUP
WEST WALTON FORMATION, AMPTHILL CLAY AND KIMMERIDGE CLAY
KELLAWAYS FORMATION AND OXFORD CLAY
GREAT OOLITE GROUP
LIAS GROUP

Colne, another tributary of the Thames that marks the eastern border of the
county; and 4) the Thames itself which delineates the southern border of the old
county.

Some of the most important Pleistocene deposits in Buckinghamshire are
associated with the terraces formed on the sides of river valleys of major rivers,
such as the Great Ouse. There are four terraces associated with this river and as
they are behind the Anglian ice limits, they must postdate this major glacial
event and be younger than 430,000 yrs BP.[13] Only a little work has been
conducted to date on establishing their ages.[14] Although prolific Palaeolithic and
Pleistocene sites have been identified on the terraces of the Great Ouse, e.g. at

FIGURE 1.4
Two Palaeolithic axes
from Fenny Stratford.

Biddenham, Bedfordshire and Barrington, Cambridgeshire,[15] none have been identified in the Buckinghamshire stretch to date, although single implements have been found (Fig. 1.4).

The stratigraphy of the Thames terraces in Buckinghamshire is complex.[16] Four main terraces have been identified: the Harefield Terrace believed to be pre-Anglian in age; the Boyn Hill Terrace believed to have been deposited between ca.420,000 yrs BP (the end of MIS 12) and 340,000 yrs BP (the end of MIS 10); the Lynch Hill Terrace believed to have been deposited between 340,000 yrs BP (the end of MIS 10) and 300,000 yrs BP (early MIS 8) and; the Taplow Terrace believed to have been deposited ca. 250,000 yrs BP (the end of MIS 8) to ca.120,000 yrs BP (MIS 5d). Generally, each terrace consists of a body of sand and gravel overlain by a deposit of loess-rich material ('brick earth') or alluvium.[17] These terraces have historically been rich sources of Palaeolithic and Pleistocene finds. Around the modern river, flood deposits of alluvium and peat can also be observed.

In contrast to the Thames, only a few remnants of the river terraces associated with its tributary the Thame are still visible in Buckinghamshire. However, in the nineteenth century, Pleistocene finds were made within these sediments near Thame.

The Palaeolithic and Pleistocene record in Buckinghamshire

Pre-Anglian Glaciation (MIS 12)

As noted previously, the last twenty years have provided an increasing body of evidence for a human presence in Britain prior to the Anglian glaciation that commenced around 480,000 years ago; the event that so dramatically left its mark on our landscape. Unfortunately, we only have tantalising hints in Buckinghamshire of the presence of these earliest inhabitants. John Wymer[18] notes only one artefact – of dubious provenance – reportedly discovered in a gravel pit working the Harefield Terrace of the Thames (a supposed pre-Anglian deposit), and that is all the evidence we have to date for a pre-Anglian, early human presence in Buckinghamshire.

What kind of environments would have been experienced by these earliest visitors? The evidence from sites elsewhere such as Pakefield (Suffolk), Boxgrove (Sussex) and Waverley Wood (Worcestershire), suggests that early humans were adaptable and resourceful, capable of surviving under a range of climatic regimes. These ranged from Mediterranean-type climates (Pakefield) to conditions cooler than the present day, much like modern day Scandinavia (Waverley Wood), with hints that they may have been able to survive under even colder conditions. There is also evidence from a range of sites that suggests they were able to exploit a diverse range of landscape niches, from coastal and tidal locations (e.g. Boxgrove), to floodplains and river valleys (e.g. High Lodge).

There are few sites in the Thames catchment as a whole that preserve evidence for pre-Anglian environments. One key site is Sugworth, Oxfordshire. In the early 1970's, ancient channel deposits were exposed here during the construction of the Abingdon bypass. These four channels were the remains of ancient river deposits, which at their maximum width reached 200m.[19] One channel in particular, the 'Sugworth Lane Channel', contained fossil-rich deposits. These included plant (both microscopic pollen and larger seeds), insect and vertebrate fossils, which allowed researchers to reconstruct the contemporary landscape. This fossil evidence indicated a regional landscape that was a mosaic of mixed deciduous-coniferous woodland with alder fen carr growing alongside the river. In the floodplain, there were areas of dry and marshy ground as well as dense woodland of elm, oak, lime, yew and holly amongst other species. This dense woodland also contained some open areas. The river itself was a large, well-oxygenated freshwater river, with marshy banks in a fully-wooded landscape that in places was characterised by fast-flowing water, as well as slower areas colonised by reed beds. The river also contained a rich aquatic plant community that included various warm-loving species such as water chestnut (*Trapa natans*) suggesting that summer temperatures were as warm, if not warmer, than the present day. The river was bordered by areas of disturbed ground, possibly due to the presence and activity of large mammals coming to the river – indicated by the presence of dung beetles. The fauna that colonised the local landscape included red deer, bison and Etruscan rhino. Smaller animals included wood mice, bank vole and an extinct species of vole (*Mimomys savini*).

The Anglian glaciation (MIS 12)

The dramatic Anglian glaciation (MIS 12, 480,000–420,000 years ago) created a very different British landscape to what had existed previously. This major glacial episode reached its southernmost extent when tendrils of the ice sheet (up to 1km thick) reached the outskirts of modern day London. Major rivers were destroyed; for example, the Bytham (a river much larger than the present day

Thames that previously flowed through the Midlands into East Anglia and was a major focus for Palaeolithic activity) was overridden by the ice sheet and destroyed.[20] Prior to this glaciation, the Thames flowed not in its present course but from the Midlands, southwards across what is now the escarpment of the Cotswolds, and into the Upper Thames basin along the course of the present Evenlode Valley and eventually near the Suffolk – Essex border into the southern North Sea. With the arrival of the Anglian ice sheets, the Thames was forced south to its present course.

In front of the ice sheet, the landscape would have been a barren tundra, characterised by permafrost and severe arctic conditions – not a hospitable place to be. However, we have hints that there may have been some form of human presence, probably during relatively warmer parts of this event. At Boxgrove[21] on the south coast, there is tentative evidence that these early occupants were present even during cold, almost arctic, conditions. Similar hints are found in Oxfordshire where one gravel pit in particular, Highlands Farm, preserved more than 3000 flint artefacts. The sediments these were found in represent an ancient river channel that flowed towards the end of the Anglian glaciation. At present, we have no evidence as to *how* cold conditions were when the flint knappers were present, or the nature of the occupation; for example, whether it was seasonal during the summer or permanent.

The Hoxnian Interglacial (MIS 11)

After the ice sheets of the Anglian glaciation had receded, there is evidence to suggest that sea levels rose slowly and Britain remained connected to the continent for much of this interglacial period (MIS 11, about 400,000 years ago). As climatic conditions ameliorated, newly-available niches were colonised by fauna and flora. This fauna also included humans. An important Suffolk site, Beeches Pit,[22] revealed evidence that fire was now part of their skill set, perhaps including controlled fire exploitation and possible hearths. Whether these people possessed the skills to start fires or just utilised and controlled natural fires in the landscape is not known at present.

In Buckinghamshire, we have evidence for the landscape of this time from investigations of an infilled hollow, rich in organic sediments at Slade Oak Lane, Denham.[23] The sediments that infilled it indicate the presence of a pool, and investigation of the fossil pollen record, suggests that the pool was surrounded by dense, deciduous mixed-oak woodland dating to the second half of this interglacial. Towards the upper part of the sequence, the sedimentary and fossil evidence suggests that deteriorating climate associated with the onset of the subsequent glaciation (MIS 10), resulted in decreased vegetation cover and increased soil erosion. Unfortunately, no evidence was found for a human presence here.

The Thames terraces on the other hand, do record extensive evidence for human activity. The Boyn Hill river terrace is thought to date to this period, and has been exploited for many decades for quarrying and mineral extraction. Large numbers of finds were discovered when gravel extraction was carried out by hand prior to mechanisation of the process. Prolific collections of Palaeolithic artefacts came out of sites such as Deverill's Pit[24] and Cooper's Pit,[25] both near

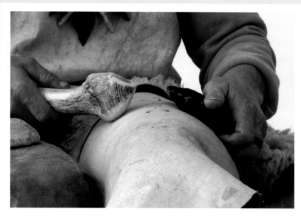

FIGURE 1.5 Making, using and identifying worked flint. Flint knapping; a core; a flake and cutting meat with a flake.

How to identify worked flint

In Buckinghamshire, flint was used as a raw material for tools from the Palaeolithic through to the Bronze Age. Newly-fractured flint has a sharp edge which can be used immediately, for example to butcher meat. It was early realised that flint could be modified to form tools, and more substantial items such as handaxes could be made by detaching flakes in sequence from a nodule. One of the best ways to control the shape of stone tools was by pre-forming a suitable block of flint (a core); several flakes could then be detached from a single core and each made into a tool e.g. a scraper or arrowhead. In the Mesolithic, small flakes were used as blade-forms known as microliths.

Several distinct marks identify worked flint. When struck by either a hard (e.g. harder stone) or soft (e.g. a piece of antler) hammer, shock waves ripple through it. Both ripples and impact point (point of percussion) can usually be seen, and also the 'bulb of percussion' – a bulge below the impact point.

Numerous flint tools have been found in Buckinghamshire by members of the public, but flakes are the commonest find and may indicate the presence of a tool-making site. Museums and Historic Environment Records will be interested to learn if you discover any.

The images show from top left: knapping a handaxe with an antler hammer; a flint core; cutting meat with a flake, and a single struck flake showing characteristic marks.

Burnham. Many of these artefacts – both handaxes and flakes – are now in the County Museum, Aylesbury, whilst others are in the Pitt Rivers Museum and the British Museum. An important point to note about these finds is that the artefacts recovered were almost all rolled. This suggests that they had been moved some distance from where they had been originally deposited – most probably on the ancient floodplain, and subsequently washed in and re-worked into river gravels. These flint tools are likely to represent a significant human presence on the Thames floodplain beside the river during MIS 11.[26] This interglacial came to an end with the onset of arctic conditions associated with MIS 10, a succeeding glaciation that lasted around 100,000 years. There is some debate amongst scientists as to how cold this event was, and at present there is no agreement as to where the MIS10 glaciers reached in Britain.

The Purfleet Interglacial (MIS 9)

The next interglacial, MIS 9, dating to about 320,000 years ago, is named the Purfleet Interglacial after the detailed record preserved in disused chalk quaries in Purfleet.[27] These quarries preserve a record of human activity within warm woodlands, in a climate similar to today, as well as during the transition to MIS 8, the next glaciation. The Thames during this interglacial was a large river, bordered by marshy areas and mixed woodlands. The floodplains were also occupied by a diverse fauna that included humans.[28]

These ancient peoples reached Buckinghamshire and left their characteristic stone tools on the then floodplain, and these tools were incorporated into the next Thames terrace in the staircase – the Lynch Hill Terrace. This terrace is reputed to contain the richest archaeological archive in the Middle Thames, although it is possible that this statement is rather a reflection of the extent of mineral extraction here.[29] The finds from this terrace are generally of a very similar nature to the Boyn Hill Terrace artefacts; most are handaxes which would probably have been used for butchering kills. A series of quarries in the Burnham area produced rich finds of handaxes and flakes. Over half the Burnham artefacts are reported as being sharp,[30] suggesting they have only moved a small distance from where they were discarded. Similarly rich sites have been found in Bakers Farm, Eton,[31] and Lavender's Pit in nearby Iver,[32] where several hundred artefacts have been found.[33]

The Aveley Interglacial (MIS 7) and the Last Interglacial, the Ipswichian (MIS 5)

At Stoke Goldington in north Buckinghamshire, excavations of one of the terraces of the Great Ouse revealed sediments associated with an ancient floodplain that existed around 200,000 years ago (MIS 7). Chris Green and colleagues investigated these sediments in 1996 and explored their fossil content.[34] One of the most fossil-rich deposits was once a pond on the floodplain that had become infilled over time. As it had infilled, the sediments had incorporated a range of fossil evidence. The plant fossils indicated that the regional landscape was open with few trees but with temperate vegetation present. Small aquatic fossils – ostracods – suggested that the water body was either a temperate pool or slug-

FIGURE 1.6
Lower jaw from lion (Panthera Leo) from the Lower Channel at Marsworth.

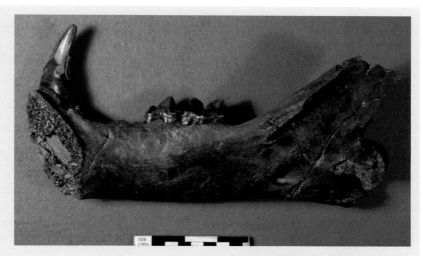

FIGURE 1.7
A mammoth tusk in situ, almost completely excavated and ready for lifting and (below) a mammoth molar from the Lower Channel at Marsworth. .

Mammoths at Marsworth

The evolution of European mammoths was rapid and associated with changing environments during the Pleistocene. The major species to appear were *Mammuthus meridionalis*, which existed between 2.6 and 0.7 million years ago, followed by *M. trogontherii* [600-200 thousand years ago] and *M. primigenius,* the more familiar woolly mammoth [200-10kya] (Lister and Sher, 2001). As these species evolved, the shape of their head, jaw and teeth changed. In particular the number of enamel plates on the chewing surfaces of molars doubled over time. This appears to mark a shift from woodland browsing to grazing in open grassy habitats.

The discoveries at Marsworth are significant as this is the only site where a late form of *M. trogontherii* and the succeeding woolly mammoth have been found in the same deposits, dating to190-150kya (layer 2, Lower Channel). Their coexistence suggests that the indigenous *M. trogontherii* was being replaced by *M. primigenius* coming in from elsewhere (Lister and Sher 2005), rather than one species evolving from the other in western Europe. North-east Siberia is the most likely origin of the woolly mammoth, where it had evolved 200kya earlier.

gish stream. The insect fossils indicated that the pool was bordered by meadow lands, and the presence of dung beetles and corpse beetles indicates the presence of large vertebrates in the area. Few vertebrate fossils were recovered, but did include elephant, mammoth and horse, as well as smaller animals such as the northern vole. This site is comparable with the finds at Marsworth (see below).

Arguably, one of the most important Pleistocene sites in Buckinghamshire was uncovered at Pitstone Quarry, Marsworth (Figs 1.6, 1.7).[35] Here the remains of two small streams were discovered. These record a climatic sequence of initially temperate conditions, passing through periglacial, arctic conditions before returning to temperate conditions. The deposits also contained a rich fossil assemblage that included pollen, molluscs, beetles, ostracods and over 11,000 faunal remains. These are thought to date from two separate interglacial episodes, MIS 7 and MIS 5e, with evidence for the intervening glacial episode. The lower channel finds (dating from MIS 7 and comparable to the record previously mentioned at Stoke Goldington) preserve a fascinating story. During this interglacial episode, tufa[36] formed next to a limestone spring within an ash-dominated woodland, (inferred from tufa fragments that bore leaf impressions of maple and ash). The area immediately around the spring would have been open, and colonised by grasses and herbs. The tufa was eventually re-deposited into a small river channel. This channel was bordered by wetlands, with evidence for disturbance, most probably from the trampling of large herbivores. During these events, the climate was as warm as the present day. The fauna included mammoth, horse, brown bear, wolf, lion and northern vole. The appearance of woolly mammoth here is particularly important, as these remains may represent the earliest occurrence of this species in the UK. The sediments then document a climatic decline into arctic, periglacial conditions, associated with MIS 6. The later, upper channel (dating to MIS 5e), contained the remains of hippopotamus, narrow-nosed rhinoceros and giant deer. These species represent a temperate assemblage that would have inhabited a mosaic of habitats including woodlands and grasslands. The presence of hippopotamus, along with other large herbivores, may also have helped maintain large areas of open ground around the channel.[37] Unfortunately, we have no evidence for human presence or activity at either of these channels.

However, the Taplow Terrace of the Thames, appears to preserve evidence for three glacial and two temperate episodes dating from ca. 250,000 yrs BP (end of MIS 8) to ca.120,000 yrs BP (MIS 5d?),[38] and has revealed tentative evidence for human presence in Buckinghamshire. Stone tools have been recovered from five quarries: Dean's Pit[39] and Marlow Brickyard[40] in Marlow; Well End Pit, also known as Fern House Gravel Pit, Well End, Little Marlow[41] Station Pit,[42] Burnham, and Wexham,[43] Langley – all sites discussed in Wymer[44] and Bridgland.[45] Unfortunately, the majority of the finds are rolled suggesting they have been reworked to some extent.

Several sites have also provided faunal remains. At Well End Pit, mammalian finds included mammoth and straight-tusked elephant teeth. The latter being a temperate species, may well date to an earlier interglacial such as MIS 7, and its remains subsequently re-worked into cold-climate gravels.[46] At Station Pit,

FIGURE 1.8 The palaeoenvironmental evidence discovered at Marsworth suggests that the landscape may have looked like this during MIS 7, about 200,000 years ago.

faunal remains included mammoth, woolly rhino and a musk ox skull,[47] an assemblage normally associated with cool conditions. More research is required to unravel and clarify the complex array of sediments preserved in these deposits.

Upper Palaeolithic

The Upper Palaeolithic, or Late Stone Age, began around 40,000 years ago and is characterised by the appearance of modern humans (our direct ancestors) in Europe. Very little is known about the Upper Palaeolithic in Buckinghamshire. At Denham,[48] a localised flint scatter of characteristic Upper Palaeolithic tools were recorded but little is known about the nature of the occupation throughout the rest of the county. The scatter included a flint core from which a number of blades and flakes had been removed (Fig. 1.9). One of these refitted onto the core suggesting that this 'knapping debris' was *in situ* and had been buried by peat exactly where the Upper Palaeolithic hunter had left them. Nearby a wild boar tusk and bone were found, suggesting that butchering had taken place here. The overlying peat was radiocarbon dated to *ca.* 9000 years ago, giving us a minimum age for this scatter.

At Three Ways Wharf,[49] just across the river from Buckinghamshire, evidence is preserved of human activity during the sub-arctic conditions of the Younger Dryas (a 1000 year long 'cold snap' around 12,000 years ago, just before the onset of the Holocene – our present interglacial). Southern England at this time would have been a tundra landscape, colonised by an arctic fauna that included horse, reindeer, arctic hare and arctic fox. There would also have been human hunters making the tools they needed to hunt their prey, and one of the places they stopped was Three Ways Wharf, where the remnants of their tool making was preserved.

The evidence from both of these sites offers some insights into the presence and nature of humans in, and around Buckinghamshire during this time period, but much more research is required to establish and fully understand the Upper Palaeolithic record.

Mesolithic Buckinghamshire

Introduction

The Mesolithic period was a time of transition and change. Over approximately 5000 years, the British landscape transformed from a glacial environment with powerful, fast-flowing rivers and tundra vegetation (probably similar to that of modern day Siberia), through to a warm climate with a landscape covered in deciduous woodland (containing oak, elm, lime and ash) and inhabited by wood-land animals (including deer, wild boar and badger). Hunter-gatherer popula-tions inhabiting Britain during the Mesolithic lived a nomadic or semi-nomadic lifestyle which adapted over time to embrace and exploit these environmental changes. By the end of the period at *c.* 4000 BC, evidence for a fully sedentary lifestyle can be seen in the archaeological record in southern England, and at the start of Neolithic we see the emergence of monument building and farming

FIGURE 1.9
Upper Palaeolithic
long-blade fragments
and a core and from the
Late Glacial site
excavated at Denham by
archaeologists from
Wessex Archaeology.

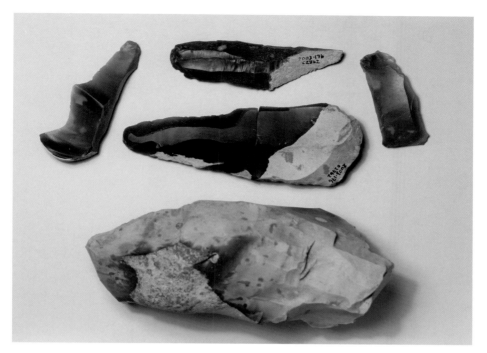

activity described in the next chapter.

The Mesolithic begins at the start of the post-glacial period, approximately 9550 years BC. However, climate warming around this time is a chronologically blurred environmental event that does not adhere to a crisp timescale. Towards the end of the glacial period, the Windermere interstadial[50] at *c.* 13,000–11,000 BC provided a temporary warm episode, before a reversal to a short-lived millennia of glacial conditions known as the Younger Dryas, and this can make it difficult to know exactly where to separate the Upper Palaeolithic and very Early Mesolithic. Artefactual evidence from the types of flint tools found in Britain suggests a process of continual change and adaptation to environmental change, without clear-cut chronologically defined distinction.[51]

The Mesolithic period in Britain: Environmental Change

The final cessation of glacial conditions at *c.* 9550 BC saw the extreme retraction of ice sheets in Northern Europe and an associated rise in sea levels.[52] The rapid sea-level changes during the early Post-Glacial period caused a dramatic alteration to the north-west Europe landscape and at *c.* 7650 BC Britain became separated from mainland Europe, leading to the partial loss of the Early Mesolithic landscape in south-east Britain beneath the sea (Fig. 1.11).

These changes in sea level are likely to have had a profound affect on Mesolithic hunter-gatherers living in and around southern England. Most impor-

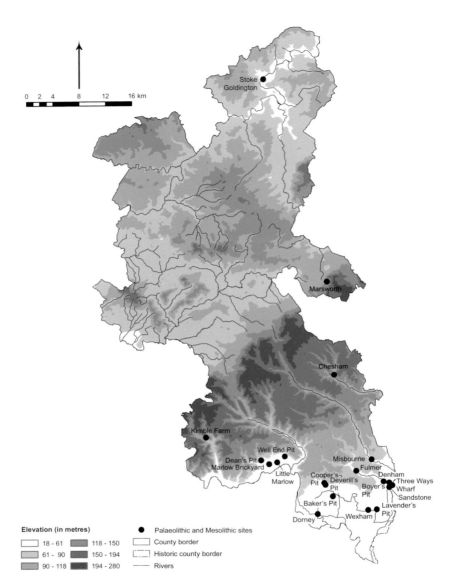

FIGURE 1.10
Buckinghamshire
Palaeolithic and
Mesolithic sites.

tantly, the nature, location and accessibility of floral and faunal resources would have continually altered, if not within an individual's lifetime, then certainly within the living memory of a couple of generations.[53] The extent to which this affected the activities of communities remains poorly investigated, mainly because the coastal Mesolithic sites in southern England remain beneath the current sea level, which makes archaeological exploration and the retrieval of finds very difficult. However, Mesolithic maritime archaeology is a growing field of interest and recent excavations at Bouldner Cliff in the Solent are beginning to shed light on Later Mesolithic activities in this area. At this site, a hearth and worked birch timbers (dated to *c.* 7000 BC) were found in association with flint artefacts.[54]

In terms of vegetation history, the Mesolithic period in Britain is characterised by a rapidly warming climate, where a glacial steppe tundra -type vegetation is replaced by a colonising assemblage of open birch and pine woodland, which was subsequently out-competed by mixed deciduous woodland from *c.* 8200 BC).[55] This change in British climatic and vegetation history can be subdivided into three main phases, known as: 1) The Pre-Boreal, *c.* 9550–8200 BC; 2) The Boreal, *c.* 8200–6900 BC; and 3) The Atlantic, *c.* 6900–4350 BC.

The start of the Pre-Boreal phase (*c.* 9550 BC) is characterised by rapid climate warming and the expansion of juniper, birch and pine, pioneer populations in southern England.[56] These species expanded in response to the ameliorating climate from 'glacial refugia'– areas beyond extreme glacial affect, where climatic and soil conditions remained accommodating enough for the continued growth of cool-temperate vegetation. These refugia might have been located in an area which is now covered by the North Sea, or further south in mainland Europe.[57]

FIGURE 1.11
Landscape transformations of the Late Pleistocene and Early Holocene (after Barker 2006).

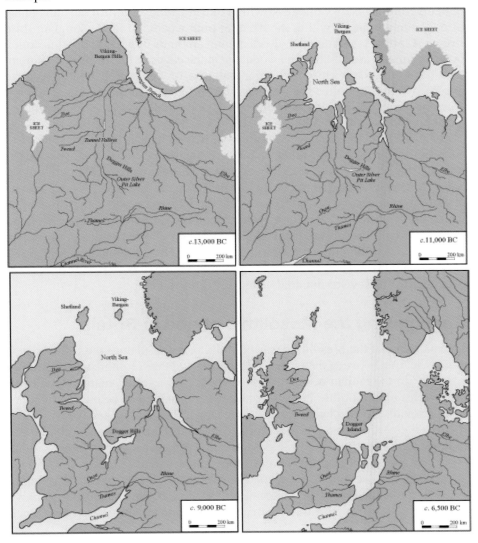

In the Thames valley, pollen records show that pine and birch woodland occurred over much of the dryland area surrounding the floodplain between about 9500–7500 BC. At Eton College Rowing Lake, Dorney in Buckinghamshire, sediments preserving pollen were found, and the results of analyses showed similar results – before c. 8200 BC.[58] Pine and birch woodland occurred here in dryland areas surrounding the Thames floodplain, with sedge and grass occupying open spaces caused by breaks in the woodland canopy. At Denham, in the Colne Valley,[59] the early post-glacial expansion of juniper is recorded in peat sediments (Borehole 4), which is quickly dominated by expanding populations of birch, and shortly afterwards, pine.

The Boreal phase of British palaeoenvironmental history is broadly characterised by the rapid expansion of pine-dominated woodland over much of central and northern England by c. 7550 BC[60] and the more rapid expansion of hazel (by c. 8200 BC). By c. 8200 BC, mixed oak and elm woodland were also becoming widely established across most of southern England and Wales.[61] The pollen remains from the Eton College Rowing Lake at Dorney confirm the emergence of oak, elm and hazel within the existing pine woodland in Buckinghamshire from c. 8250 BC. Additionally, the declining amounts of grass and sedge pollen in the sediments suggest that the woodland at the edges of the Thames floodplain was becoming very closed. Similar patterns of vegetation history can be observed from the pollen records from Little Marlow in the Thames Valley,[62] where it appears that pine-dominated woodland rapidly develops an expanding hazel population after c. 8200 BC.

By c.6900 BC the climatic conditions in Britain appear to have stabilised to conditions approximately similar to today. In fact, temperatures may have been c. 1–2°C higher than those currently experienced, and as a result the period from c. 6900–4350 BC is often referred to as the 'climatic optimum'. This phase of environmental history is characterised by the expansion and establishment of warm-loving, climax vegetation (oak, elm, lime, ash, and hazel). In wetland areas alder carr also occurs from c. 6000 BC and pollen evidence of alder carr conditions from Silvertown, Rotherhithe (c. 4500 BC) and Southwark (c. 3500 BC) indicate that this woodland spread westwards down the Thames floodplain over a period of several hundred years.[63]

Recognising the Mesolithic period in Britain

The existence of the Mesolithic was not fully recognised until the 1920's. Prior to this the time between the Upper Palaeolithic and the Neolithic was viewed as a 'hiatus' in the human occupation of Britain.[64] As a result, many of the early discoveries of Mesolithic flint in Britain were classified as belonging to either of the formally acknowledged periods, the Upper Palaeolithic and the Neolithic. Indeed, the earliest finds of Mesolithic flint from Buckinghamshire were not initially attributed to Mesolithic culture and artefacts recovered from Kimble Farm, Turville, prior to c. 1917 were simply classified as 'cone-culture'.[65]

It was Clark's seminal 1932 work *The Mesolithic Age in Britain*, that finally established the identity of the Mesolithic. This work began to synthesise archaeological findings from this time-frame, incorporating previous discoveries such as those from Kimble Farm, Turville. From this point onwards Buckinghamshire was recognised as having an extensive presence of Mesolithic archaeology. Since Clark's work in the 1930's, the division of the Mesolithic period into *at least* two broad phases has generally been accepted; The Early Mesolithic, *c.* 9500–7650 BC and the Late Mesolithic, *c.* 7650–4350 cal. BC. A Middle Mesolithic can also sometimes be recognised by the occurrence of *Horsham-type* tool types in southern England from *c.* 8000 BC – *c.* 7000 BC,[66] but this division has been observed to blur into the Early and Late Mesolithic periods.[67]

The Early and Late Mesolithic periods are separated by a combination of environmental, lifestyle and technological changes, reflected in the form of flint tools. Broadly speaking, the Early Mesolithic covers the Pre-Boreal and Boreal phases, when Britain was still attached to the European mainland, and the Late Mesolithic after the separation of Britain from the continent, when vegetation is characterised by full deciduous woodland.

The Early Mesolithic period in Britain

Early Mesolithic tool technologies[68] are characterised by a microlith culture, the tools being made from flint blades with broad width-height dimensions.[69] These flint artefacts are found in low densities in England and Wales but in greater frequency in Northern Europe, suggesting continued connections between hunter-gatherer populations in Britain and Europe during this period. Although patterns in tool form can be observed, the precise activities of human populations in Britain at this time are not well understood. We know that Mesolithic people were living a nomadic (or at least semi-nomadic) hunter-gather type lifestyle, but we do not really know how this was structured socially or economically. Fortunately, the study of modern-day hunter-gatherer societies (e.g. Eskimo, Aborigine, Native Indian and African Bushmen) provides some theories about how Mesolithic populations may have lived, moved, hunted and communicated with others within such a rapidly altering landscape. Studies of North American Indian hunter-gatherer societies show that family groups join together to form a residential group that moves around during the year to exploit various seasonal resources within their territory. A smaller, largely mobile sub-group regularly

FIGURE 1.12
Simplified model of
Early Mesolithic
settlement as suggested
by Clark (1972) at Star
Carr, Yorkshire
(after Darvill 1987).

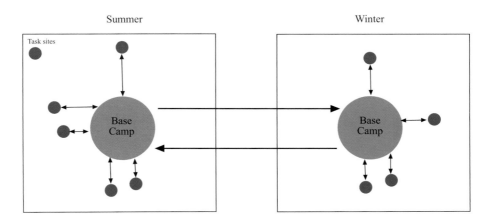

perform the hunting and gathering activities for the whole group of people.[70] It is thought that artefactual and animal bone remains found most commonly on Mesolithic archaeological sites are the remnants of *task-group* activities.

The role of ethnographic comparison in the study of Mesolithic hunter-gatherer lifestyles is, however, widely debated as it cannot be assumed that modern-day observations can be directly applied to events in the past.[71] Nevertheless, such evidence has been used alongside archaeological data, for example the types of tools and animal bones found during excavations, in an attempt to understand Mesolithic hunter-gatherer lifestyles.

This 'multidisciplinary' approach was used for the site of Star Carr in Yorkshire[72] where a combination of excavation and ethnographic data were used to model aspects of Early Mesolithic site function, including possible seasonality of site occupation and territory size. Here, Early Mesolithic hunter-gatherers are proposed to aggregate in the lowlands at base camps in the winter and disperse to upland hunting camps in the summer (Fig. 1.12). Underpinning this subsistence model was the migration of red deer, assumed from the faunal assemblage at Star Carr to be the vital food source for Early Mesolithic populations, with the deer moving from the lowlands in the winter, to grazing sources in the uplands of the Pennines in the summer months.

Early Mesolithic sites in southern England are often frequently viewed as seasonal 'hunting/task' or 'base' camps.[73] However, this view is largely based on work done in northern England where the seasonality of animal resources is likely to have been much less pronounced.

The Early Mesolithic period in Buckinghamshire

Most archaeological evidence for the Early Mesolithic period in Buckinghamshire is derived from the Colne Valley in the south-eastern part of the County. The Colne's glacial gravel and sand deposits were exploited through dredging and mineral extraction in the first half of the twentieth century and during this time the archaeologist Lacaille (amongst others) made a number of discoveries of Mesolithic date. Of most significance, were the Mesolithic flint and peat deposits discovered in two working gravel pits: Boyer's Pit, Denham, and Sandstone in Iver.[74]

The flint assemblages from both pits were classified as Early Mesolithic because they contained microliths made from broad flint blades. Both sites also contained other artefacts such as flint cores (used for the removal of flakes to make small tools, such as scrapers), and flint axes (possibly hafted and used for woodworking), see for example Fig. 1.13. At Sandstone, six scrapers and two gravers were also recovered; these may have been used for working hide or other soft materials. Both sites contained large amounts of flint material. A catalogue later produced by Wymer, recorded 1698 artefacts from Boyer's Pit and 250 from Sandstone.[75] Although both sites produced considerable amounts of lithic material, in the absence of any *in-situ* features (such as hearths) it is probably reasonable to assume that they represent one or more very brief periods of hunting or task-based activity, with a duration of maybe a day or so.

Since Lacaille's initial investigations, Early Mesolithic material has continued

FIGURE 1.13
A Mesolithic 'tranchet' axe from Iver, found during construction of the M25.

to be recovered from the surface of the Colne Valley gravel deposits. Excavations at Three Ways Wharf, Uxbridge[76] and Denham[77] have revealed scatters of flint tools, debitage (the by-product of on-site tool knapping), animal bone material and associated peat deposits which had formed over the gravel deposits in abandoned river and stream channels. The recent discoveries of flint artefacts at Denham, comprise four main flint scatters.[78] One of these, flint scatter 5, appears to be *in-situ* and consists of flint cores, burins (used to work and engrave soft materials, such as antler) and scrapers. Three microburins (by-products of microlith production) were also recovered along with unworked flint debitage, confirming the manufacture of tools here. A total of 667 pieces of worked flint were recovered. Although some of the microliths recovered from the site have length measurements very similar to Late-Glacial material, overall the assemblage is considered to be characteristic of the Early Mesolithic period.[79] A second flint find at Denham (scatter 6) had been disturbed and mixed by intrusive ploughing, bioturbation (earthworm, root penetration and animal burrowing) and possible flooding activity. However, as a collection of flint artefacts, the material was observed to contain similar components to those found in scatter 5 (flint cores, microliths and debitage), but produced slightly later in the Mesolithic period as some of the microliths were diagnostically geometric in shape.[80] Both of these scatters from Denham provide evidence for activities occurring on-site, most certainly, the manufacture of microlith tools. It is possible that other activities (such as processing animal carcasses or plant materials for food) were also occurring here, but the absence of animal bone or plant remains in direct association with the flint artefacts makes it impossible to say with any degree of confidence.Other groups of Early Mesolithic flint from Denham (flint scatters 2a and 2b) were recovered from an alluvial deposit directly underlying the topsoil. This deposit, in addition to flint artefacts, also contained some wild boar bones, including a tusk that was directly-dated using radiocarbon techniques, providing evidence that this species was present in the Colne Valley in the Early Mesolithic period at *c.* 8530–8260 BC.[81] It is likely that populations of boar would also be accompanied by red and roe deer, aurochs (an ancient form of cattle), wolves and a wide variety of bird and aquatic animal life. These animals are likely to have inhabited open pine and birch woodland, typical of the early post-glacial period.

Just across the Colne, other flint artefact and animal bone remains of Early Mesolithic date were found at Three Ways Wharf in Uxbridge. The flint assemblage from scatter C here amounts to about 7000 pieces of struck flint probably of Early Mesolithic date. The faunal remains (about 2000 fragments) were dominated by those of Red Deer.[82] Some of the flints recovered from scatter C were found to re-fit together, suggesting that the assemblage had not been subject to significant movement and was largely *in-situ*. Together, the red deer remains and the *in-situ* flint assemblage suggest that the site may be the remnants of a hunting or food processing site.

The continuing discovery of Early Mesolithic remains from the Colne Valley provides undisputed evidence of activity in Buckinghamshire from *c*. 9500–8000 BC. The combination of different types of evidence (flint, animal bone and pollen) found in the gravel, alluvium and peat deposits of the valley provide important insights into the types of activities that people were conducting and the floral and faunal environments with which they were interacting. Together, the evidence from Boyer's Pit, Sandstone, Denham and Three Ways Wharf suggest that small-scale hunting activities were taking place here within a landscape of birch and pine woodland, which later changed (by succession) to predominately oak and hazel woodland.

The extraction of gravel in the valley has opened up sedimentary sequences and exposed archaeological remains prompting continued interest in the valley's deposits since Lacaille's early work, however, there are factors which may have influenced the decisions of Early Mesolithic populations to concentrate their activities in river valleys. River systems are likely to have attracted both human and animal populations for drinking water and for the exploitation of other aquatic resources such as fish and waterfowl, but it has also been suggested[83] that the thickening pine-dominated forest of the Early Mesolithic may have limited scope for browsing resources elsewhere in the landscape, forcing the majority of animal populations (prey for hunting), into valley bottom locations.

The Late Mesolithic period in Britain

After the separation of Britain from the continental mainland, Late Mesolithic flint technologies in Britain are characterised by 'microliths' formed from blades with very narrow width-height dimensions. Unlike the tool-types of the earlier Mesolithic these tools are no longer paralleled by examples from Europe[84] which suggests that hunter-gatherer communications between Britain and the European mainland were no longer active. It is thought that the overall shift to smaller sized flint tools in the Late Mesolithic may have resulted from changes in vegetation conditions. By this time, a full deciduous woodland with a thick hazel shrub understorey is likely to have covered much of the dry land areas in southern England, and finer flint tool technologies (prepared with greater precision) may have been necessary to hunt an increasingly wide variety of the woodland animals inhabiting these areas.

Various attempts have been made to build subsistence models for the Late Mesolithic period. One example is provided by Simmons (Fig. 1.14).[85] He suggests Late Mesolithic hunter-gatherers occupied lowland sites for the majority of the year, using special-purpose coastal sites (A2–A4) together with a base camp (A1). Seasonally these groups would move to an autumn base camp (B2) where they would travel upland to specific hunting camps (B2–B8) to exploit red deer in previously de-forested areas to encourage browsing. His model was created using data from a variety of different archaeological and

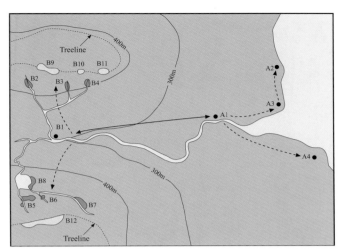

FIGURE 1.14
Late Mesolithic
resource subsistence
model (after
Simmons 1996).

environmental archaeological sources including:

(1) The study of Late Mesolithic shell middens at archaeological sites in Scotland, which has suggested the increased role of coastal resources in the Later Mesolithic.[86] (2) Analysis of the age at death of animals butchered on sites which has provided good evidence of the seasonal exploitation of resources at specialist exploitation camps.[87] (3) Pollen records from northern England recording temporary declines in tree species and increases in grassland pollen. These pollen records sometimes occur in association with increases in the amount of charcoal particles preserved in lake and peat bog sediments, suggesting that fire may have been used to clear wooded areas by Mesolithic populations.[88] (4) Evidence for a greater reliance on coastal resources provided by seasonal indications shown in the size of fish bones (otoliths) from coastal midden deposits.[89]

The integration of these variables into Late Mesolithic subsistence modelling paves the way for the onset of agriculture and a fully sedentary lifestyle at the beginning of the Neolithic period. Most importantly, evidence of woodland manipulation and the longer-duration of settlement sites evident in coastal areas, show Mesolithic lifestyles progressing in this direction.

The Late Mesolithic period in Buckinghamshire

Two main sites of Late Mesolithic date are recorded in Buckinghamshire. The first was discovered in 1969 when the Chess Valley Archaeological Society carried out a small excavation in the East Street area of Chesham, in the Chess Valley. During this work, a large quantity of struck flint was recovered underneath a covering of valley hillwash sediment. Later work at the same location recovered about 300 further pieces of struck flint including 49 microliths with narrow-blade proportions, indicating a Late Mesolithic date. Other flint artefacts recovered here included flint cores (Fig. 1.15), scrapers and an axe.[90]

The most important aspect of the Chesham site was the recovery of bone from cattle, red deer, roe deer and wild boar. Some of these bones were noted to have been split and had cut-marks indicating the *on-site* butchery of animals killed by humans. A radiocarbon date from one of the cattle bones provided a date of 5006–4504 BC, confirming a Later Mesolithic age. The animal bone assemblage from Chesham shows that Mesolithic people were hunting a variety of locally available animals.

Another Late Mesolithic site was discovered during construction work on the M25, in the Misbourne Valley, near the Misbourne railway viaduct.[91] Here a significant tufa deposit was discovered which contained a number of microliths of Late Mesolithic form (including triangular shaped 'Scalene' types). Radio-

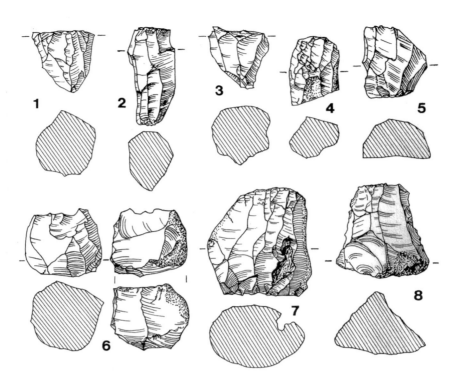

FIGURE 1.15
Mesolithic flint cores
from which flint blades
have been detached.
From Chesham.

carbon dates from the bottom of the tufaceous deposit have provided dates of
c. 5000–4000 BC, which also indicates a Late Mesolithic date for the assemblage. We know from pollen records in southern Britain that the landscape is
likely to have been characterised by deciduous woodland with oak, elm, lime,
and ash trees with hazel forming a shrub/bush understorey. Wood charcoal
recovered from the Misbourne site confirms this with oak and ash species being
identified. Many of the animals inhabiting this deciduous woodland environment were recovered as animal bones at the Misbourne site, including: cattle,
deer, wild boar, beaver, otter, badger and pine marten. In the absence of butchery
marks on the bone, it is difficult to say with absolute certainty that these animals
had been deliberately hunted, however, if we assume they were, then the
Misbourne bones indicate that Later Mesolithic people were hunting a wide
variety of woodland animals, both for food and clothing (the fur from badger and
pine marten are likely to have been particularly suitable for clothing). The animal
bone here may also suggest a degree of sedentism, with such a wide variety of
hunted animals being unlikely to represent a very small and targeted phase of
activity.

In addition to the Chesham and Misbourne sites, there appears to be widespread evidence of Late Mesolithic activity over many other parts of Buckinghamshire. Isolated flint artefacts have been found scattered over the high ground
of the Chilterns, and in Northern Buckinghamshire and significant quantities of
Late Mesolithic flint have been recovered from the Ouse Valley and its Tributaries.[92] Evidence of Later Mesolithic activity across many areas of Buckinghamshire appears to accord with observations of the Late Mesolithic in Britain
as a whole, where widespread settlement patterns are observed.[93]

FIGURE 1.16
Wet sieving samples
for carbonised
organic remains.

Mesolithic Britain: Burial and Ritual

In contrast to the succeeding Neolithic there are few Mesolithic human remains from the British Isles. Approximately seventy inhumations of Early Post-Glacial date were discovered in Aveline's Hole in the Mendip Hills more than 150 years ago, but very little is known about these and the remains were destroyed together with the excavation records during the Second World War.[94] Since that discovery only two other Mesolithic human bones have been recovered, both isolated finds from palaeochannel deposits[95] which do little to enhance our understanding of subsistence, dietary patterns and funerary practice. Considering the national paucity of Mesolithic human bone material, it is unsurprising that no finds are recorded in Buckinghamshire. However, the occurrence of several Early Mesolithic sites in the Colne region indicates the undisputed presence of Mesolithic activity in the county's river valleys and recovery of animal bone at these sites may indicate that the discovery of human bone material at similar excavations in the future is possible.

The End of the Mesolithic period

The end of the Mesolithic period is conventionally defined by the first evidence of a farming (Neolithic) culture at approximately 4000 BC. However, this is a problematic definition as many of the classic signs of the Neolithic, such as pottery are now known to exist in the Later Mesolithic.[96] Evidence from south-east England indicates that a good deal of chronological overlap may exist in material cultural, as instances of 'Mesolithic' flintwork and 'Neolithic' pottery have been found together in well-stratified archaeological contexts, such as at Brookway in Rainham, Greater London.[97] Also, any clear-cut transition in economic practice is lacking; it seems that a gradually-widening, foraging, resource-base, operated alongside a shift towards a farming economy.[98]

Attempts to clarify, and regionally define this situation are often sought through environmental records. It is generally proposed that the Mesolithic-Neolithic transition is marked by the arrival of cereal pollen and the often synchronous *Ulmus* (elm) decline at *c.* 3750 cal. BC.[99] Regional evidence from pollen records at around this time suggests some increased woodland clearance by humans, some cereal cultivation, and the accelerated spread of elm disease caused by woodland clearance.[100] The issue is further discussed in the next chapter.

Chapter 2

Prehistoric Farmers

Sandy Kidd

This chapter covers the time from the introduction of agriculture around 4000 BC through to the Roman Conquest of AD 43, both events driven by continental contact of fundamental significance to the cultural history of Britain. Great changes occurred between these seminal moments, notably the clearance of vast swathes of forest, the division of land, the adoption of metalworking, the establishment of permanent settlements and the development of a social hierarchy of chiefs and priests. This chapter encompasses the conventional archaeological periods known as the Neolithic (or Late Stone Age), Bronze Age and Iron Age. There are advantages in writing across these traditional 'age' divisions as many of the trends and transitions of prehistory do not sit neatly within this structure.

It is important to state at the outset that the concept of 'Buckinghamshire' has no meaning as a place in prehistory. This is because, unlike some other English shire counties, it is not a coherent geographical area nor, for the most part, does it have natural boundaries. Instead Buckinghamshire comprises a strip of land running across the geology of southern England from the gravels of the Thames and Colne, across the chalk of the Chiltern Hills, into the clay Vale of Aylesbury and finally into north Buckinghamshire where the Ouse valley gravels are incised through claylands. This simple four-fold division of the county has been used in this chapter, occasionally supplemented by the terms 'Icknield Belt', referring to the distinctive interface between the Chiltern scarp and Vale of Aylesbury, and 'Bernwood/Whaddon Chase', relating to the land between the Thame and Ouse valleys. It has also sometimes been necessary to look beyond the county's historical boundaries. As there are several thousand records for this period held on the county's Historic Environment Records, including several dozen major archaeological excavations, the chapter is deliberately selective in its examples and referencing.[1] (Fig. 2.1)

Only in the last century of prehistory are written sources available, so establishing reliable dates for archaeological sites and finds is fundamental to understanding the development of prehistoric societies. Dating rests upon a combination of the types of objects found and scientific dating, both linked to the analysis of sequences recorded on excavated sites. Pottery is particularly useful for dating because it is commonly found on prehistoric sites in southern England and can be divided by variations in the clay and additives used to manu-

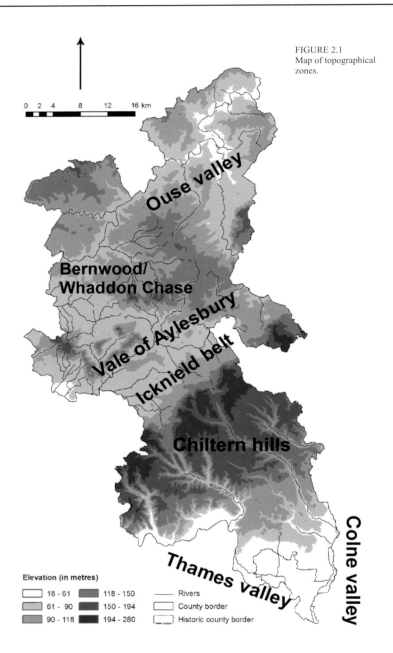

FIGURE 2.1
Map of topographical zones.

facture it (the 'fabric'), by the shapes of vessels ('form') and decoration. In the Neolithic and early Bronze Age some flint tools can be used for dating, whilst throughout the Bronze and Iron Ages changing styles of metalwork can be identified, although metal ornaments and weapons are rarely found during archaeological excavations.

Before the 1950s assigning absolute dates to prehistoric sites was little more than educated guesswork, but in the last fifty years radiocarbon dating has provided estimates for real dates of steadily increasing accuracy and precision. Today, radiocarbon dates that have been 'calibrated' for various factors can be

TABLE 1

Broad Period	Date range (approximate)	Indicator objects and styles	Exemplar Buckinghamshire sites
Earlier Neolithic	4000BC–3250 BC	Plain bowl pottery. Leaf-shaped flint arrowheads.	Dorney Lake. Whiteleaf barrow.
Later Neolithic	3250 BC–2300 BC	Peterborough & Grooved Ware pottery.	Coldharbour Farm. Few sites – mostly pits.
Earlier Bronze Age	2300 BC–1500 BC	Beaker pottery. Barbed and tanged flint arrowheads. Flat bronze axes.	Gayhurst and other Ouse valley round barrows
Later Bronze Age/Early Iron Age	1500 BC–450 BC	Deverel-Rimbury (MBA) pottery. Mostly plain angular-profiled pottery with flint-tempered fabric (LBA/EIA). Socketed axes and a wider range of bronze tools and weapons until c 600 BC.	Ivinghoe Beacon. Taplow Court. Milton Keynes hoard. Walton, Aylesbury. Dorney Lake. Bancroft.
Middle Iron Age	450 BC–100 BC	Mostly plain slack-profile pottery with sand tempered fabric. La Tène Celtic metalwork styles.	Aylesbury hillfort. Bancroft. Pennyland.
Late Iron Age	100 BC–43 AD	Wheel-turned 'Belgic' pottery. Coins, distinctive metalwork and foreign imports.	Bancroft. Bierton. Dorton burial. Whaddon Chase coin hoard.

accurate to within 200–300 years at 95% confidence. Greater accuracy, sometimes to within 50 years, is becoming achievable by using statistical techniques to link multiple radiocarbon dates from a site. Unless otherwise stated, where a date range is quoted (e.g. 2340–2035 BC) this is a calibrated radiocarbon age with a probability of about 95% that the 'real' date lies within the quoted range. The table above summarises the broad periods used in this chapter, their approximate date ranges and some of the objects and artistic styles indicative of that period.

The Arrival of Farming
(Earlier Neolithic 4000 BC–3250 BC)

Farming was developed in the Near East at the end of the last Ice Age (c 10,000 BC) reaching Greece in the seventh millennium BC from where it spread across Europe to reach Britain around 4000 BC.[2] The adoption of farming brought with it what has been described as the 'Neolithic package' of domestic animals (cattle, sheep and pig), cereal crops (wheat and barley), pottery, polished stone tools and monument building, none of which had been part of the repertoire of the preceding Mesolithic hunter-gatherers. Archaeologists still debate the extent to which the existing populations adopted agriculture by emulation or whether immigrant farmers replaced their predecessors. Certainly early farming could have supported many more people, perhaps five per square kilometre in contrast to only one per ten square kilometres, giving the agricultural lifestyle a dramatic advantage in the long run.[3] Traditional interpretations favoured population replacement[4] but in the last decade or so studies of human genetics have pointed to a majority origin for modern European populations from local Palaeolithic communities.[5] Some archaeologists now argue that the rapid and dramatic changes seen around 4000 BC can be more plausibly explained by cultural contact than by population replacement. However, whilst it is possible that native hunter-gatherers did take up farming, we can be sure that the crops and domestic animals were imported as they are not native to this country; nor is separate British invention of pottery credible as early Neolithic pottery in these islands closely resembles that found on the continent.

We therefore have to imagine the first farmers, whether native or immigrant, facing the twin challenges of hazardous crossings of the English Channel in dugout canoes or coracle-like skin-boats and of then establishing a new way of life in a landscape quite unlike the intensively managed farmland we are familiar with today.[6] Six thousand years ago southern England was swathed in deciduous forest; evidence from pollen recovered from ancient peat tells us that these 'wild woods' contained various combinations of alder, ash, elm, hazel, lime and oak. Alder carr would have grown in damp valley bottoms with tall forest trees on better-drained land. These long-disappeared wildwoods are hard to imagine today for those of us who only experience England's managed 'ancient woodlands'. Better analogies are to be found in the few surviving stands of temperate wildwood in places such as North America or New Zealand where giant forest trees up to a thousand years old stretch up to the canopy, below which lies a

FIGURE 2.2
River through
wildwood,
North Island,
New Zealand.

thick undergrowth of saplings and fallen deadwood (Fig. 2.2). Long before modern drainage there would have been extensive boggy areas, particularly on the impermeable claylands north of the Chilterns and along the River Colne where peat had formed in the valley floor. The wildwoods were not completely unchanging as a widespread north European phenomenon known as the 'elm decline' reached Britain shortly before the first signs of farming.[7] Living within the wildwood would have been red and roe deer, wolf, bear, wild boar, wild cattle (aurochs) and a huge variety of bird life. The rivers would have teemed with fish, and were also home to beaver and otter. A wide range of wild plant resources would have been available, although unfortunately apart from charred hazelnuts evidence for their use does not survive well. Travelling through such a landscape would be difficult, so it is likely early farmers would have followed natural corridors formed by rivers and distinctive features such as the Chiltern scarp, as well as using animal tracks.

Early Neolithic settlement in Buckinghamshire is often closely associated with watercourses – a pattern seen elsewhere in the Thames Valley.[8] At Dorney clusters of early Neolithic worked flint were found all along the banks of a former Thames river channel, but rarely more than 50m from it, suggesting that people lived in clearings alongside the river. Three middens (dung and rubbish heaps) containing huge amounts of material have been excavated (some 32,000 objects including 6,000 sherds of pottery from a 20% sample of the largest midden). Charred grains of emmer wheat from the middens were dated between c. 3900 BC and 3500 BC with similar dates from cattle bone and charred hazelnuts. The middens lay within a wooded environment and seem to represent around sixty episodes of activity over some 600 years, but as they are not accompanied by any buildings could represent episodic rather than permanent occupation.[9] They occupied locations previously frequented by hunter-gatherers so maybe we are seeing an indigenous population maintaining its mobile lifestyle whilst engaging in herding domestic animals and cultivating crops in small plots set in woodland clearings.

Other evidence for early farming comes from Marlow where early Neolithic pottery and flint tools were found at the brickyards in the 1920s and 30s, to which can now be added a pit containing charred hazelnut shells, cereal grains and early Neolithic pottery found in a recent trial excavation in the valley south of the town. Downstream, outside the modern county at Horton, a dramatic

FIGURE 2.3
Reconstruction of
the Neolithic house
at Horton

recent discovery has added to England's very small tally of excavated early Neolithic houses. Here Wessex Archaeology found a rectangular timber building measuring 11 × 6m with a central entrance and timber partition walls (Fig. 2.3). Three pairs of massive postholes show that the house had a post-built frame and gullies defined the lines of walls, presumed to have been of vertical planks. Finds included pottery, worked flint, splinters of animal bone and a few charred cereal grains and hazelnut shells. The form and construction technique of the house has been likened to Irish buildings of the period rather than the few recorded English examples.[10] The function of these structures is hotly debated; many archaeologists believe they were communal buildings rather than domestic dwellings.

Monuments known as 'causewayed enclosures', defined by roughly circular arrangements of sausage-shaped pits separated by short gaps, were first built between 3700 BC and 3600 BC. Excavated examples have been found to be quite variable, leading to their interpretation either as settlements or ritual sites. Current thinking favours a role as communal meeting places for social and religious activities and ceremonies, which could explain their episodic construction, the presence of 'placed' ritual deposits, domestic debris and yet lack of substantial buildings.[11] Only one possible example is known in Buckinghamshire, alongside the Thames at Dorney Reach, but two others lie in the Middle Thames Valley just outside the modern county at Eton Wick and at Yeoveney Lodge, Staines. Just outside the county, the confluence of the Rivers Colne and Thames provided a focus for early Neolithic occupation and ritual, most dramatically illustrated by the Stanwell Cursus, a 3.6km long ditched and embanked processional way probably built between c. 3600 and 3300 BC.[12] Other cursus monuments are found clustered further upstream around the confluence of the Thame and Thames at Dorchester. Until 2009 no cursus monuments had been definitely identified in Buckinghamshire. However, during the writing of this book, two parallel ditches with internal banks were discovered in a quarry at Wolverton. The ditches ran along the valley floor for at least 300m with neither terminus present within the excavation. The form of the monument is

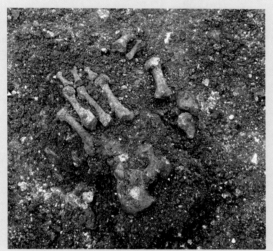

FIGURE 2.4
Topographical survey of Whiteleaf Hill.

Re-investigation of Scott's excavation of the Whiteleaf barrow. Note the
holes either side of the upper ranging pole, which held split upright posts
defining the mortuary chamber.

Human foot as discovered by Sir Lindsay Scott inside the Neolithic
barrow: the burial had been disturbed in antiquity.

The Neolithic Barrow On Whiteleaf Hill, Princes Risborough

Whiteleaf Hill is a prominent chalk ridge on the Chiltern escarpment that sits astride the
Upper Icknield Way and overlooks the Vale of Aylesbury. In the 1930s Sir Lindsay Scott
excavated a Neolithic barrow on the hilltop. The results were published in 1954 by the
eminent archaeologists Professor Gordon Childe and Isobel Smith.[38] Between 2002 and
2006 as part of a Heritage Lottery funded conservation project, the Neolithic barrow was re-
excavated by Oxford Archaeology and restored to its pre-1930s form. Two other mounds
thought to be prehistoric barrows were investigated and a curvilinear bank and ditch classified as a 'cross-ridge dyke'.[39]

Re-examination of the Neolithic barrow confirmed its oval shape and showed it to have
been a long-lived monument, beginning with the burial around 3700 BC of an adult male
in a timber mortuary- structure, defined by two large upright posts, perhaps from a single
split tree trunk. The burial it contained was not dug into the chalk bedrock so the body may
have originally lain within some form of wooden coffin before being disturbed and scattered.
Between 45 and 150 years after the burial a dark humic layer containing pottery, worked flint

and animal bone was deposited over the burial to build a low mound which was later covered by a much larger chalk mound derived from an encircling ditch, dug out using antler picks. One of these picks has been radiocarbon dated to 3365–3110 BC suggesting that the monument was used for some 500 years. Even after this act of closure the barrow was periodically revisited, attracting an urned Bronze Age cremation burial and quantities of late Iron Age and Roman pottery. The pottery, flint and animal bone from the barrow suggest ceremonial activity relating to the veneration of the ancestral spirit of the dead man. The small assemblage of bones, from red deer, pig, sheep, cattle, beaver and birds, showed use of both domestic and hunted animals.

Small-scale investigations of the other monuments on the hilltop illustrate the perils of interpreting archaeological earthworks without excavation. One mound, thought to be a barrow, was found to be the site of a post-medieval windmill whilst the other proved to be a natural knoll which had been used as a flint knapping site in the late Neolithic. A cross-ridge dyke was mapped and shown to cut off the spur with a substantial 1.7m deep ditch and bank. Unfortunately its date could not be confirmed. Snail shells in the prehistoric features were mostly from shade-demanding species indicating that the monuments were constructed within woodland.

characteristic of a cursus, whilst an early date is indicated by early Bronze Age pottery found in the upper ditch fills. At the time of writing the construction date of the Wolverton cursus has not yet been established but by analogy with other such monuments one would expect it to belong to the mid or late fourth millennium BC making it the earliest monument yet discovered in north Buckinghamshire.[13]

It is known that Neolithic groups had also established themselves in the Nene and Ouse valleys, as occupation is known at Northampton and near Bedford. However, away from the Thames in the Chilterns and north Buckinghamshire there are only hints of occupation in this pioneer agricultural phase. The only substantive site known to date to the early Neolithic is Whiteleaf Barrow which occupies a conspicuous location on the Chiltern scarp overlooking Princes Risborough. Here a single male inhumation, radiocarbon dated to 3760–3640 BC, was placed in a mortuary structure defined by a pair of split timber uprights. Between 45 and 150 years later a mound containing pottery, flint and animal bone, was raised over the burial. Later again this small mound was capped by clean chalk excavated from a surrounding ditch. The longevity of use implies the existence of a local community but as yet few other sites of this early period have been found across the Buckinghamshire Chilterns (Fig. 2.4).

Overall, the evidence would support a model of the first farmers reaching Buckinghamshire along the Thames Valley then moving up either the Thame or Wye to Whiteleaf Hill. At the same time farming was spreading up the Nene and Ouse valleys apparently establishing a foothold in the Wolverton area by the end of this period. These communities clearly embraced the 'Neolithic package' of domesticated animals, cereal growing, pottery and construction but because

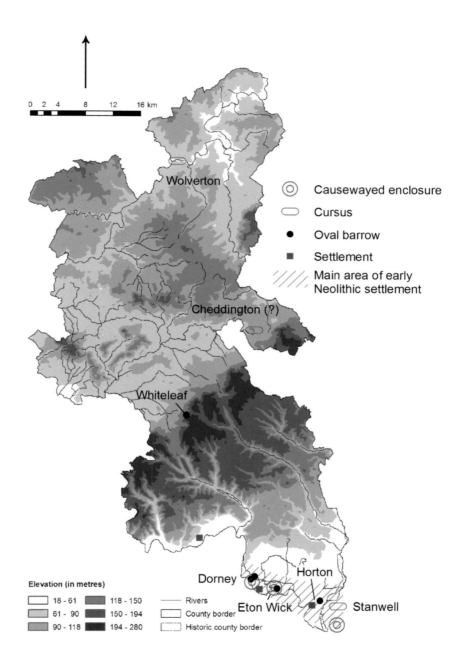

FIGURE 2.5 Map of earlier Neolithic sites and the main concentration of settlement evidence in the form of pottery, worked flint, middens and pits.

of the rarity of recognisable substantial domestic buildings and settlements it is doubtful that we should envisage settled agricultural communities (Fig. 2.5). The evidence from Dorney, and to a lesser degree Whiteleaf, could instead imply episodic activity at favoured locations, perhaps associated with feasting and other communal activities. Scatters of poorly-dated flint tools and axes found across the Chilterns may be the traces left behind by mobile communities that spent most of their time in small groups herding cattle through the woods and planting crops in temporary clearings (see on).

The Missing Millennium
(Later Neolithic 3250 BC–2300 BC)

The adoption of the 'Neolithic package' provided the potential to increase food production enabling population growth. Biological rules first expounded by Thomas Malthus in the nineteenth century, state that populations will grow exponentially until they exceed the carrying capacity of their environment, at which point famine and disease cause the population to fall back and then fluctuate. Studies of modern pre-industrial societies have found that in practice death rates and birth rates are both high and fluctuate rapidly according to natural events, such as drought and disease, to produce a relatively constant and young population.

The clearance of woodland for pasture or crops would have allowed the same area of land to produce much more food than the equivalent area used as hunting ground, thus woodland clearance could become a self-reinforcing process – with more mouths to feed more woodland would have to be cleared to avoid starvation. Depending on what assumptions one makes about initial conditions and rates of growth, it is theoretically possible that rising populations could have used up all the spare land fairly quickly, within only one to five hundred years.[14] Early farming communities would have had a number of strategies open to them to stave off crises of over-population. They could intensify their productivity through such techniques as better management of herds and flocks or intensive manuring of fields, limit population through social controls such as infanticide, or cull numbers through endemic warfare. We shall see later in the chapter that from about 1500 BC onwards, there is indeed evidence for some of these activities, which may well occur as a response to population pressure.

In addition to growing populations, there may also have been external pressures. Climate change may have been a factor as it is thought that Britain experienced a warm period known as the 'Holocene Climatic Optimum' between c. 4100 BC and 3200 BC, the effect of which would have been to extend the growing season. However, after 3200 BC the climate became gradually cooler and wetter until improving somewhat in the mid-first millennium BC. It is against this backdrop that we will now return to interpret the actual archaeological evidence.

Across Britain the Neolithic and Early Bronze Age are characterised by the construction of a diverse, and potentially baffling, array of ceremonial and burial monuments; for example the literature is littered with references to 'cursuses', 'henges', stone circles and a variety of different burial mounds and 'mortuary structures'. We will explore Buckinghamshire's rather modest contribution to this collection later in the chapter, but for the time-being my purpose is simply to point out that prior to the mid-second millennium BC much of the spare energy of prehistoric communities was directed to projects of a social and ritual/religious nature, rather than to the construction of more obviously functional features such settlements, fields or fortifications. Something fundamental changed in the mid-late second millennium as settlements and land boundaries appeared, to be followed in the first millennium BC by numerous hillforts.

FIGURE 2.6
The relationship
between woodland,
grazing and
tree-felling.

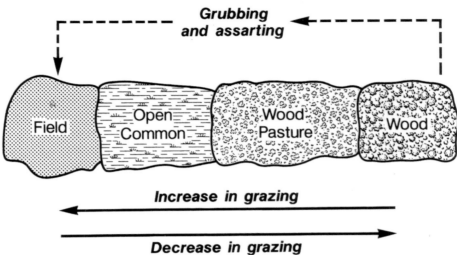

Throughout this time the ancient wildwood was gradually being cleared and converted to grassland (Fig. 2.6).

Archaeological evidence firmly attributable to the later Neolithic is remarkably sparse in Buckinghamshire, suggesting either that population was constrained at a low level, or that people lived in ways that left few recognisable traces. One characteristic of the period is a pottery called 'grooved ware' on account of its distinctive finish. In the Middle Thames Valley the scale of archaeological activity declines with relatively few pits containing this pottery. However, pollen from the river channels at Dorney Rowing Lake shows that the wooded landscape was still being opened up and there are a few human burials, 'burnt mounds' (heaps of charcoal and burnt stone) and scatters of worked flint of this date. One possibility is that the focus of activity had simply moved to the unexcavated causewayed enclosures at Dorney Reach and Eton Wick, which although probably constructed in the earlier Neolithic, could have continued in use into the third millennium BC. Further up the Thames at Marlow, a local archaeological society digging in the valley below the town has found subtle traces of small pits, gullies, stakeholes and hearths, with chemical evidence from a pit dating to about 3200 BC indicating it may have been used for tanning hides. This may be another long-lived settlement focus as it lies next to a cluster of ring ditches and other monuments known only from aerial and geophysical survey.

Unfortunately, we do not yet have sufficient evidence from pollen sequences to chart woodland clearance across Buckinghamshire, so away from the Thames we must rely upon other evidence. Direct evidence for falling trees comes in the form of so-called 'tree-throw holes', these are typically amorphous crescent-shaped hollows created when a tree is uprooted. However, it is debateable to what extent tree-throw holes represent deliberate clearance by man or are the result of natural processes such as wind-blow. Other evidence for woodland clearance comes from studies of snails shells found on archaeological sites.[15]

Finds of middle and late Neolithic pottery are not common in the Chilterns and north Buckinghamshire but do appear in tree-throw holes, and individual pits or small pit-clusters in the Vale of Aylesbury at Coldharbour Farm, Hartwell and Chilton; in the Chilterns at Chesham, and in a little cluster at Heelands, Secklow and Stacey Bushes in Milton Keynes. Coldharbour Farm shows evidence both for woodland and its clearance in the form of over a hundred tree-throw holes, one of which produced a flint axe roughout. A lone Neolithic pit contained pottery, knapped flint, charred hazelnut shells and land snails indicative of open conditions with a possible background of scrub.[16] Most of these sites are on well-drained gravel or limestone soils but those at Chilton and in Milton Keynes, which seem to have been associated with similar clearance episodes, lie on impermeable clay. It used to be thought that early farmers would have avoided clay soils because they would have been difficult to cultivate with the simple ard ploughs of the time; these discoveries show that such an interpretation is over-simplistic. Perhaps they were the homes of herdsmen for whom agriculture was a secondary concern, or perhaps horticulture was practiced in gardens without the need for extensive ploughing.

We must now turn to the vexed question of scatters of worked flint found on the surface of ploughed fields across Buckinghamshire. During the Neolithic and Early Bronze Age a wide variety of tools were manufactured from flint, an exceptionally hard glassy rock that forms naturally in chalk. Flint is readily available from the chalk of south Buckinghamshire and has been spread across most of the rest of the county by glacial action. Most struck flints are simple flakes, the by-products of flint-knapping, but the finished products are also found – typically axes, arrowheads, borers, knives and scrapers, and also the remnant cores from which these items were detached. Most flint tools were probably made from flint found on the ground surface or by shallow digging, but it is has also been suggested that mines were dug in the Chilterns in the manner of those found at Grimes Graves in Norfolk.[17] Very occasionally other types of stone tool are found, such as fine polished stone axes traded from specialised quarries such as Langdale in the Lake District. A survey conducted in the early 1990s recorded almost three hundred so-called 'lithic scatters' from Buckinghamshire with a Neolithic or Bronze Age component.[18] Their distribution shows concentrations along the Thames, across the Chilterns, along the Thame Valley and the Icknield Belt and, more sporadically, in northeast Buckinghamshire in and around Milton Keynes. There are many difficulties with interpreting such patterns. Discovery can be as a result of casual finds, systematic fieldwalking survey or recovery during archaeological excavation. Blank areas may simply reflect lack of field-work or areas of undisturbed woodland or grassland where worked flints cannot be found so easily. Several concentrations correlate with fieldwalking surveys, such as those organised by the County Museum around Aylesbury and the Chess Valley Archaeological Society in the Chess and Misbourne valleys. Another problem is that most worked flint cannot be dated with any precision and almost all of these scatters have been disturbed and spread around by hundreds or even thousands of years of subsequent cultivation. If this were not bad enough, where flint scatters have been investigated by excavation, normally few if any below-ground features are found. Despite all these limitations, flint scatters show that

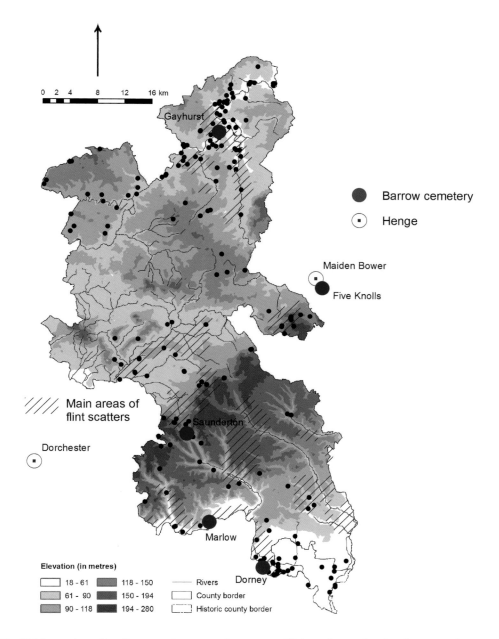

FIGURE 2.7
Map of later Neolithic
and early Bronze Age
sites and concentrations
of worked-flint finds.
Although most of the ring
ditches are thought to
mark prehistoric burial
mounds, some are
probably more recent
monuments.

Neolithic and earlier Bronze Age people were utilising the entire landscape of
Buckinghamshire and were not restricted to the river valleys and Chiltern scarp
where most burial mounds are found (see on). The fact that many more flint
axes and other finds come from the Chilterns than from further north might be
a genuine indication that the Chilterns was a more densely populated area subject
to greater woodland clearance, although it could also reflect that this is where
the best flint is to be found. What form this land utilisation took is uncertain, but
the small numbers of worked flints found in most fields can surely only indicate
transient use.

Finally, we cannot complete a discussion of Neolithic Buckinghamshire without mention of the Icknield Way, an enigmatic feature of the Chiltern landscape that has been central to the debate about prehistoric trackways in southern England.[19] Supposedly, the Icknield Way was a Neolithic route that ran along the chalk escarpment from Wessex to East Anglia but recent re-assessment has cast doubt on this traditional interpretation. Excavation at Aston Clinton where the new bypass crossed the 'Lower Icknield Way', recorded by that name on nineteenth century maps showed it could be no earlier than middle Saxon, and may in fact be a post-medieval creation. Whilst it could be contended that a prehistoric routeway might have been more a loosely defined 'zone of movement', such a nebulous concept is difficult to test and it would have cut across the emerging pattern of later prehistoric territories defined by regularly-spaced hillforts, trackways and cross-ridge dykes which run *perpendicular* to the Chiltern scarp. In the absence of centralised authority, movement along such a routeway would surely have involved numerous awkward local negotiations. The idea of a prehistoric ridgway now seems questionable.

Thus the later Neolithic period in Buckinghamshire represents something of an enigma as the population does not seem to have grown as fast as Malthusian population growth model predicts. Also, there is as yet no unequivocal evidence from the county for the construction of the sorts of ceremonial or burial monuments seen elsewhere in Southern England, nor are discrete settlements visible. Instead we see a sparse pattern of activity dispersed across the landscape accompanied by the beginnings of woodland clearance (Fig. 2.7). It may be that what we have is a semi-nomadic or transhumant cattle-rearing society where woodland clearance occurred as a result of deliberate tree-felling to create small clearings that were maintained and expanded by the steady destruction of saplings by browsing animals. Over many centuries such pressure could break up dense wildwood into sparse scrubby woodland, and eventually into open grassland. Perhaps the social gathering places of the time have yet to be discovered or maybe they lay outside the county, at places such as the great henge at Dorchester-on-Thames or the enigmatic Neolithic enclosure at Maiden Bower in the Bedfordshire Chilterns (Fig. 2.11).

Barrows and Beakers
(Earlier Bronze Age 2300 BC–1500 BC)

The last few centuries of the third millennium BC saw the introduction into Britain of metalworking in copper, gold and then bronze which is associated with the 'Beaker culture', principally recognised as a distinctive style of burial involving decorated pottery drinking-vessels and an emphasis on archery equipment, that is found across much of Atlantic Europe. It is sometimes suggested that the arrival of this 'package' represents a shift towards a more aggressive, competitive male-dominated society.

A handful of Beaker burials have been excavated in Buckinghamshire. A typical example was found at Bierton where a crouched inhumation burial was found interred with an 'all over combed' beaker, a barbed and tanged arrowhead

and flint strike-a-light (Fig. 2.8). The grave was encircled by a ditch and was presumably originally covered by an earthen mound. More unusual was a round barrow excavated at Ravenstone where two graves lay within a circular ditch built in four discrete segments separated by narrow causeways. The graves lay one on top of the other with the first being an empty coffin over which a second burial, the crouched inhumation of a woman, had been added. The woman was accompanied by a long-necked beaker, a bronze awl, a conical shale 'button' and several worked flints. The 'button' is believed to have been part of a leather bag. Together with other finds, an antler-spatula, flint 'fabricator' and a charred wooden board, the group is indicative of leather-working. The curious empty coffin was interpreted as a cenotaph (Fig. 2.12).

Locally the earlier Bronze Age sees a significant increase in evidence due to the widespread construction round barrows. In their simplest form these burial mounds comprise a single central burial pit surrounded by a circular ditch, the upcast from which was used to raise a mound. The encircling 'ring' ditches can often be seen on aerial photographs even when the mound has been ploughed flat. They vary considerably in diameter from an unusually small 6.5m at the Chessvale Bowls Club, Chesham, to 22m in the final phase of Gayhurst barrow 2; most are between 10m and 20m diameter. Some of the burials are inhumations but the majority are cremations placed either in pottery vessels or unaccompanied (although perhaps originally in a cloth or leather bag). Barrows commonly attracted later secondary burials in the mound or satellite burials around them – perhaps of family members or retainers. Round barrows are not evenly distributed across the county – they were built mainly along the valley floors of the Thames and Ouse and along the Chiltern Icknield Belt where they are found both on the ridgeline and on lower ground. Sometimes barrows occur in clusters

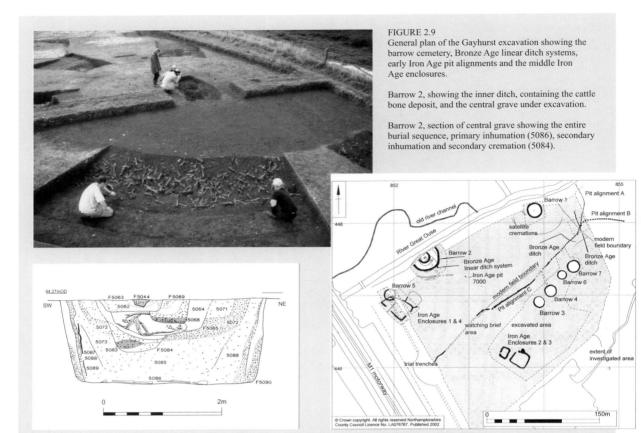

FIGURE 2.9
General plan of the Gayhurst excavation showing the barrow cemetery, Bronze Age linear ditch systems, early Iron Age pit alignments and the middle Iron Age enclosures.

Barrow 2, showing the inner ditch, containing the cattle bone deposit, and the central grave under excavation.

Barrow 2, section of central grave showing the entire burial sequence, primary inhumation (5086), secondary inhumation and secondary cremation (5084).

Investigating a Barrow Cemetery at Gayhurst

A small early Bronze Age cemetery containing seven round barrows was excavated by Northamptonshire Archaeology in advance of gravel extraction at Gayhurst Quarry near Newport Pagnell.

Six of the barrows had been ploughed flat by the medieval period. However, the largest, a double-ditched barrow 34m in diameter, which lay at the centre of the cemetery, still survived as a low earthwork and was relatively well-preserved. The six smaller ring ditches produced meagre results. However, at the centre of the largest barrow there was a massive grave pit, 3.5m long and 1.45m deep, dug into an earlier natural tree-throw hole and followed by a sequence of five successive burials. An extended inhumation of an adult man within an oak-lined chamber, accompanied only by the foreleg of a small pig, was followed by an unurned cremation, then a crouched inhumation burial within a small chamber accompanied by two flint knives and a red-deer antler, then a second unurned cremation and, finally, a cremation within a collared urn. Radiocarbon dating places the sequence of burials between *c.* 2100 and *c.* 1900 BC, while the six satellite barrows date to 1800 to 1500 BC.

What made this barrow remarkable was a deposit of cattle bones, perhaps the remains of 300 animals. The bone was found spilling down the inner edge of the inner ditch mixed with clean gravel, suggesting that it had been dragged down from the surface of the gravel-capped mound. It appears to have been buried and hidden before the outer ditch was dug and the mound enlarged with a second gravel deposit. The splitting and surface erosion of the bones showed that they had been exposed to the elements on the surface of the central mound for some time before this. A preference for limb bones indicates that the animals had been slaughtered elsewhere, and a lack of butchery marks suggests that the carcasses had been exposed to decay naturally, maybe forming a symbolic feast for the dead.

The overall scale of the bone deposit provides as vivid an indicator of the wealth of the community that could afford to make this exceptional statement as the deposition of any number of artefacts. It illustrates the central importance of both cattle and ritual sacrifice to early Bronze Age communities and bears comparison with another exceptional cattle bone deposit at a nearly contemporary barrow at Irthlingborough, Northamptonshire.

Information: Northamptonshire Archaeology.[40]

– barrow cemeteries – as for example at Gayhurst (see on). Occasionally early Bronze Age barrows occur away from these typical locations, as shown by discovery of the Bierton beaker barrow.

Excavation of ring ditches on the valley floors of the Ouse and Ouzel at Milton Keynes have provided the best evidence for this period in Buckinghamshire. Four were excavated in the early 1970s and recently a further group of seven were investigated at Gayhurst Quarry (Fig. 2.9). Writing in the 1970s Stephen Green concluded that the construction of these burial mounds was well within the capacity of small local populations but that perhaps only one in fifty of the local community received such a burial. But who was buried in them? The Warren Farm ring ditch is typical in encircling a grave pit containing the cremated remains of a young woman of between 15 and 20 years of age with a newborn baby, and later the crouched inhumation of another young woman. Most barrow burials in Buckinghamshire contain young adults under the age of 30; child burials are also common but older adults less so. This reminds us that, numerically at least, the young dominated these communities. The Gayhurst cemetery is of particular interest as it begins with the burial of a young man of sufficient importance to merit the ritual sacrifice of some three hundred cattle. His barrow is the earliest yet excavated in the Milton Keynes area and became the focus of a cemetery that lasted some six hundred years with the construction of lesser satellite barrows, the elaboration of the original mound and insertion of secondary burials. The first burial at Gayhurst is unique in the extraordinary cattle sacrifice, although one other similar and roughly contemporary barrow associated with cattle sacrifice has been excavated at Irthlingborough in the Nene valley. By this time Irthlingborough was an ancient centre with a history of monument building stretching back to the early Neolithic, in contrast to Milton Keynes where, as we have seen, there are only sparse traces of earlier settlement. It is tempting to speculate that the young man buried at Gayhurst was the revered 'founder' of a new community – a leader who brought his people from the Nene valley, literally, to pastures new.

As with the later Neolithic, substantial permanent settlements of the earlier Bronze Age are noticeably lacking and even isolated pits are rare. One of the very few traces of built structures is a curving gully next to the Bierton round barrow, which could have been an eaves-drip gully around a roundhouse. Many of the poorly-dated flint scatters mentioned in the previous section overlap with the early Bronze Age, indicating that much of the landscape was at least visited if not intensively exploited. Furthermore, environmental evidence suggests the process of woodland clearance was now well advanced. Pollen from an infilled stream-channel near Marlow, dated between *c.* 2350 BC and *c.* 650 BC, was dominated by grasses but with significant oak, lime and hazel and also evidence for arable cultivation in the form of cereal pollen with weeds of cultivated and disturbed ground. The whole showing a mixed arable/pastoral landuse with surviving stands of woodland. Land snails found in dry-valley deposits at Pitstone and those associated with the Milton Keynes barrows both tell a similar story indicating the presence of open grassland. Stephen Green suggested that settlements lay close to some of the barrows he excavated in Milton Keynes – the ring ditch at Warren Farm contained domestic pottery, flint implements and animal bone, whilst the Ravenstone beaker barrow was built on top of an earlier four-post structure.

Only a handful of metal objects of early Bronze Age date have been found in Buckinghamshire – for example, copper-alloy awls from Milton Keynes barrows, bronze axe-heads from Hazlemere, Ivinghoe Aston and the Thames at Bourne End, a rapier and dagger from the Thames at Bourne End and another dagger from Great Missenden. Neither copper, gold nor tin occur in Buckinghamshire so metal would have been a rare, mysterious and precious commodity. Metal objects could have been obtained either from itinerant craftsmen or, in the absence of a market economy, by barter or gift-exchange between the leading members of society.

In summary, the earlier Bronze Age comes across as a period of social change played out against a backdrop of daily life little changed from the previous millennium. A more competitive and socially differentiated society may be indicated by the selection of certain members of society for specialised burial, whilst the colonisation of new lands could reflect the breakdown of social mechanisms that had previously contained pent-up potential for population growth.

Dividing Land and People
(Later Bronze Age/Early Iron Age 1500 BC–450 BC)

Around the middle of the second millennium BC fundamental changes commenced across Southern England in the relationship between communities and land, resulting in the construction of recognisable settlements, fields, drove-ways and major land boundaries alongside an end to the construction of the cere-monial monuments of earlier times (Fig. 2.10). The first signs of this transition in Buckinghamshire come from the Thames Valley where regularly-organised ditched field systems were laid out at Dorney around 1500 BC, with comparable evidence from Denham in the Colne Valley. North of the Chilterns traces of later Bronze Age ditches from near Aylesbury (Weedon Hill) and Newport Pagnell (Gayhurst Quarry) may reflect the same process but on a smaller scale. Early field systems such as the one at Dorney with its paddocks, drove roads and

FIGURE 2.10 Map of
later Bronze Age and
early Iron Age sites. Only
the main excavated
settlements are shown.
Grim's Ditch and the
co-axial landscapes may
have originated at this
time but neither is
securely dated. Hillforts
with finds of this period
are distinguished from
those for which there is
no dating evidence.
Hillforts producing
middle/late Iron Age finds
are shown on Fig. 2.18.

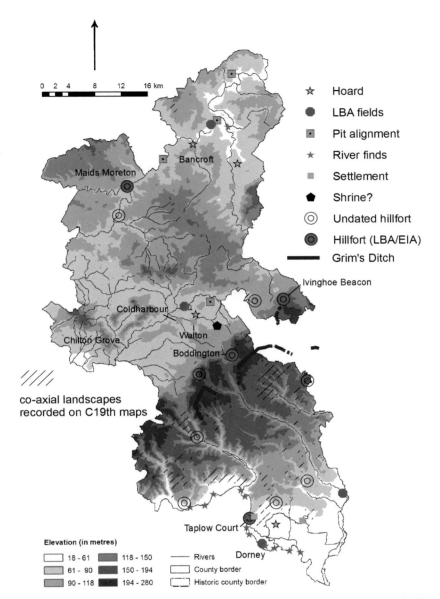

waterholes, seem to be designed for managing large herds of cattle and sheep
rather than for cultivation of crops. For the first time the landscape would have
resembled something familiar to us today as the shallow ditches only make sense
if their purpose was to provide material for drained banks on which hedges could
be planted.

In the Chilterns we can still find landscapes divided into slices by long lanes
that provided the spines for hedged fields, and the frame for the creation of long
thin medieval strip-parishes.[20] Whether these surviving Chiltern 'co-axial fields'
really have prehistoric roots is uncertain but archaeological investigation
conducted along the Aston Clinton Bypass has provided a tantalising hint. Excavation here revealed a trackway running from the Vale towards the Chiltern
scarp that had been worn down and filled with a dark soil, presumably as a

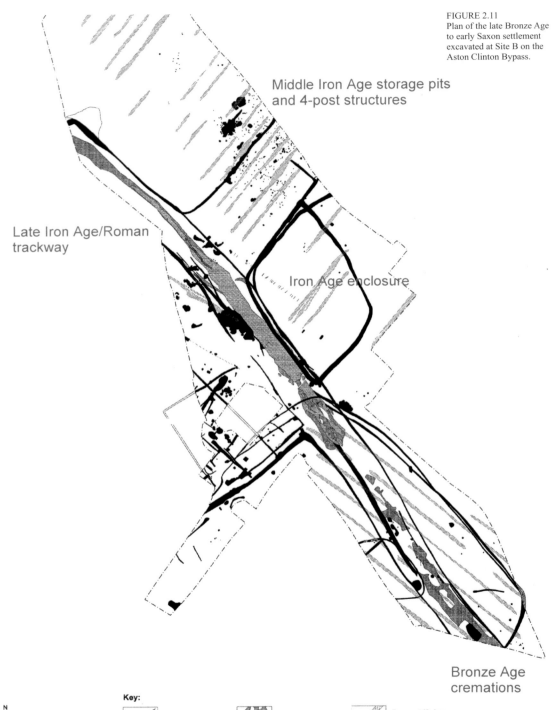

FIGURE 2.11
Plan of the late Bronze Age
to early Saxon settlement
excavated at Site B on the
Aston Clinton Bypass.

Middle Iron Age storage pits
and 4-post structures

Late Iron Age/Roman
trackway

Iron Age enclosure

Bronze Age
cremations

N

0   50m

Key:

Limit of Excavation

Archaeological
Features

 Gravel Track/Holloway

 Silt Deposits over
Gravel

 Furrows & Modern
Features

FIGURE 2.12
Grim's Ditch
at Bradenham.

Grim's Ditch – A Prehistoric Boundary

By far the most impressive prehistoric land boundary in the Chilterns is the series of linear earthworks collectively known as Grim's Ditch that run between Bradenham and Berkhamsted, with a separate and rather different outlier on Pitstone Hill. The main sections comprise an outer (northern) bank and inner (southern) ditch forming two discontinuous arcs on the high ground between the Saunderton and Wendover gaps with a third arc on Pitstone Hill. A few trial trenches have been cut – at Hastoe it was estimated that the ditch was originally V-shaped 3.5m wide and 2m deep with a bank of similar dimensions and possibly a timber palisade along the southern lip of the ditch. The ditch near Pitstone Hill had been dug in segments suggestive of gang working. A few fragments of Iron Age pottery have been recovered from the investigations but the date of construction, function and length of use of the monument are not yet properly understood. Grim's Ditch has sometimes been interpreted as a tribal boundary but functionally the western and central arcs can probably best be understood as having been constructed in open grassland to contain herds driven up the minor dry tributary valleys running north from the Wye and Chess respectively. It is tempting to see the central arc as defining the northern boundary of the territory controlled from Cholesbury hillfort.

consequence of prolonged animal traffic. Alongside the trackway were ditched enclosures probably for stock, and also human cremation burials dating back to the late Bronze Age and early Iron Age (Fig. 2.11).[21]

Land boundaries in the form of earthen banks and ditches are another distinctive feature of the Chiltern landscape; by far the most substantial is Grim's Ditch (Fig. 2.12). Smaller earthworks known as cross-ridge dykes occur along the Chiltern scarp; a good example can be found on Whiteleaf Hill. Unfortunately

FIGURE 2.13
Pit alignment
under excavation at
Calverton Quarry.

neither the date nor the function of these earthworks is fully understood, although they seem to belong to the first millennium BC and it has been suggested that they mark the boundaries of communities based at local hillforts.

North of the Chilterns, land-division began not with long earthen dykes but with enigmatic features called 'pit alignments'. As their name suggests these are more-or-less regular rows of pits set 1-2m apart, each pit being typically sub-rectangular 2m x 1.5m x1m deep. They can run for several hundred metres. Only half a dozen or so are known in Buckinghamshire, many fewer than in Midland counties such as Northamptonshire[22], and with the exception of one at Hulcott near Aylesbury they are all in the Ouse and Ouzel valleys (Fig. 2.13). Most pit alignments seem to have been constructed between 800 and 500 BC within fairly open landscapes, although an alignment of circular pits at Fenny Lock has been dated to the middle/late Iron Age. Quite why early boundaries were constructed as pit alignments remains unresolved – there is no evidence for upright posts forming a stock fence so presumably they would have been perceptible to people but permeable to their domestic herds. However, their distribution does suggest that a cultural difference was emerging at this time with communities based along the Ouse and Ousel valleys dividing land much later than those who were creating fields in the south, and using a tradition based in the East Midlands. If we interpret pit alignments as 'permeable' boundary markers, in contrast to the firm boundaries implied by dykes and hedges, then we could be looking at fundamental differences in underlying belief-systems and relationships within communities, or between communities and land.

Recognisable settlements appear surprisingly late in the archaeological record, the earliest date to around or just before 1000 BC at Walton (Aylesbury), Ivinghoe Beacon and Taplow Court and rather later (800–450 BC) at Bancroft

FIGURE 2.14
Reconstruction
drawing of the large
roundhouse excavated
at Bancroft, Milton
Keynes. The building
was defined by three
concentric rings of
postholes.

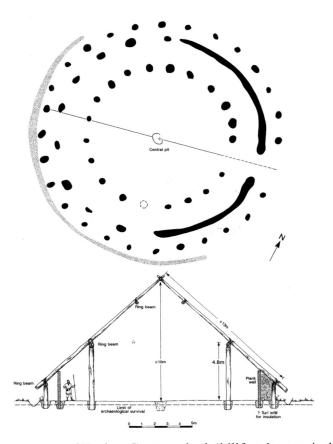

in the north. Ivinghoe Beacon and Taplow Court are both 'hillforts' strategically located on prominent spurs of land overlooking the Vale of Aylesbury and Thames valley respectively. In both cases only a small proportion of the site has been investigated but it appears that occupation began with an open or lightly-defended settlement enclosed by a timber palisade, which was later replaced by large ditches and much more substantial ramparts of earth and timber construction. Although evidence from other Buckinghamshire hillforts is even more limited it does seem likely that most were built in the early Iron Age (800–450 BC), quite possibly in places which had already been focal points of local communities for hundreds of years. The undefended settlement at Walton[23] may be typical of such early settlements – it was made up of a cluster of least five post-built roundhouses associated with pottery, animal bone (mainly cattle, sheep and pig), weaving equipment (loomweights, needles and a spindlewhorl) and a few ornaments (bronze pin and shale armlet). At Bancroft a large, and structurally complex, roundhouse stood alone except for an adjacent four-post structure and hollow (Fig. 2.14). It almost certainly had a specialised function, indicated not only by its size and complexity but by the presence of unusual pottery and numerous bones of piglets; presumably this reflects some combination of communal, ceremonial or high-status feasting activity. Other sites have produced less substantial, or less understandable, evidence for occupation,

FIGURE 2.15
Bronze Age gold torcs
and pot from Milton
Keynes.

The Milton Keynes Hoard

Five solid-gold torcs (neck rings) and bracelets were found by metal detectorists in Milton Keynes, and acquired by the British Museum. They date from the late Bronze Age, around 1150–800 BC, and make up one of the largest hoards of late Bronze Age gold ever found in Britain.

One of the most unusual things about them is that they were found together in a pot indicating that they were deliberately placed and buried, but whether it was simply to hide them, or as an offering to a god or spirit, is impossible to tell.

That these torcs were actually worn, and were not made just to be an offering, is proved by the considerable wear on their decoration. Here though lies a mystery, for the objects do not show the tell-tale stress fractures that would result from repeated opening and closing that would have been necessary to put them on. Once fitted with a torc, was the wearer saddled with this weighty ornament for the rest of their life?

Information: British Museum.[45]

mainly in the form of clusters of pits and pottery in some respects reminiscent of earlier periods. Examples include sites found along the Aston Clinton Bypass; on a Thames Water pipeline near Taplow Court, on the Stoke Hammond Bypass, at Stone Nurses' Home and at Fenny Lock. Overall, the settlement evidence for the later Bronze Age and early Iron Age is still limited but some hilltop sites were occupied, although their defences may not have been their earliest features. Settlement occurred elsewhere on open sites often in locations occupied in later periods but many sites lack coherent building plans – perhaps these were once like Walton, but unlike Walton, which had been preserved beneath a medieval village, the shallower features have been lost to the plough.

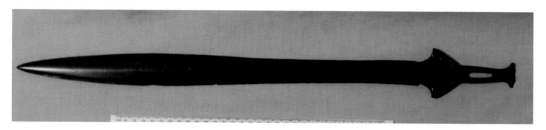

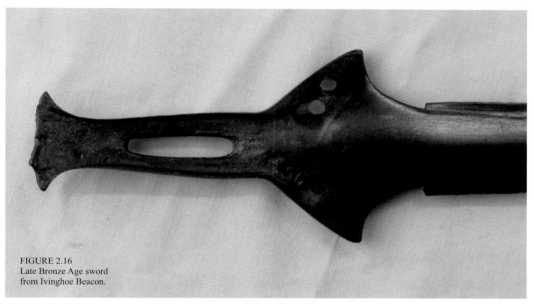

FIGURE 2.16
Late Bronze Age sword
from Ivinghoe Beacon.

Bronze objects become more common during the later Bronze Age being found on settlement sites, buried as 'hoards' in pits, deposited in the river Thames and as apparently isolated finds. A wider range of weapons, tools and personal items were being made – swords, spearheads, axes, sickles, bracelets, razors, rings and pins have all been found in Buckinghamshire. There are also a few gold objects – a couple of gold bracelets, several rings and the incredible 'Milton Keynes Hoard' (Fig. 2.15). Whilst some isolated finds or finds from settlements could be casual losses, others are clearly deliberate deposits. For example, a complete bronze sword from the settlement and later hillfort on Ivinghoe Beacon is unlikely to have been simply 'lost' (Fig. 2.16). Buried hoards of broken-up bronze objects found at Aylesbury and New Bradwell, Ivinghoe, and a hoard of palstaves from Slough could be explained in functional terms as scrap metal collected for re-use and buried for safe-keeping – it may be no coincidence that these finds were all discovered in the vicinity of one of the few known settlements of the period. However, other finds such as the swords from the Thames or the gold torcs from the Milton Keynes Hoard seem to form part of a wider pattern of 'ritual deposition' recognised in this period (see on). A brief digression is necessary here to note the invaluable role of hobby metal-detecting in many of these discoveries – with proper reporting responsible amateurs can

FIGURE 2.17
Part of a Bronze Age
'founders hoard' said
to have been found in
Buckinghamshire.

A 'Nighthawked' Bronze Hoard

'Nighthawking' is a term applied to illegal metal-detecting, conducted either without the permission of the landowner or on protected sites or failing to report items classified as treasure under the Treasure Act 1996. The legal definition of treasure covers not just items made of precious metals but also any two or more prehistoric metal artefacts found together. It is good practice to report all significant archaeological finds to the Finds Liaison Officer based at Buckinghamshire County Museum.

In 2005 a Dutchman contacted Buckinghamshire's Finds Liaison Officer to report his acquisition of a late Bronze Age hoard of 15 artefacts. The hoard consisted of one end-winged axe, fragments from at least six socketed axes, a fragment of copper alloy, possibly from a vessel, two small pieces of copper -alloy ingot and two fragments of possible casting waste. The axes show signs of heavy wear and use and some have been intentionally fragmented, which suggests that this material may have been scrap. Collections of surplus bronze, mixed with ingots of raw material formed a metal resource for recycling interpreted as founders' hoards. It is one of only three such hoards known from Buckinghamshire.

The seller reported that the find had been made a couple of years before but could provide no further details. A police investigation failed to trace the finders. Fortunately the purchaser acted responsibly donating the finds to the County Museum, but the case illustrates the harm that could have been caused by the loss of the artefacts and also the actual loss of crucial, but now irretrievable, information about where objects were found and how they came to be buried.

Information from Ros Tyrell and Sally Worrell of the Portable Antiquities Scheme.

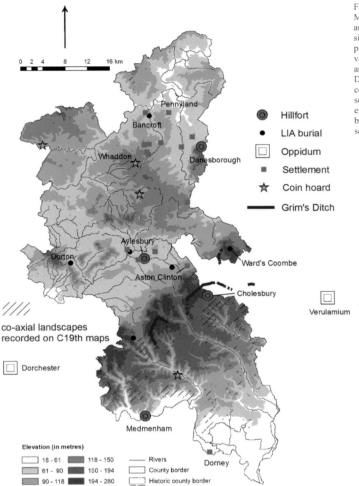

FIGURE 2.18
Map of middle and
and late Iron Age
sites. Only the
principal exca-
vated settlements
are shown. Grim's
Ditch and the
co-axial land-
scapes may have
existed at this time
but neither is
securely dated.

make important contributions to archaeological research, but sadly this does not always happen as illustrated by a recent case of internationally-traded Buckinghamshire antiquities (Fig. 2.17).

Around 1000 BC the technology for smelting iron reached Southern England but it did not become widespread until 800–600 BC, by the end of which period it largely replaced bronze for the manufacture of tools and weapons. This change will have had social consequences as the manufacture of bronze from rare copper and tin ores required widespread trading networks but iron ores are much more widely available, at least in small quantities. As yet there is no conclusive evidence for iron-smelting or smithing in Buckinghamshire in the first half of the first millennium BC. However, as the earliest iron-smelting site yet dated in Britain comes from the Thames valley near Newbury and there is increasing evidence for Iron Age and Roman iron-smelting from the Buckinghamshire Chilterns and Middle Thames valley, it would not be surprising to if this were to change with further discoveries and closer dating.

Putting all this together, what seems to be going on is that populations of people and stock reached a critical point where greater management and control was necessary. Fields and droveways would have allowed stock to be moved around more easily and excluded from over-grazed or parasite-infected land. Smaller paddocks would have enabled animals to be inspected and sorted. Dividing the land would presumably have led to closer definition of territories belonging to different communities, encouraging people to lead more settled lives and, as the intervening woodland was cleared and pressure on pasture increased, boundary disputes would bring conflict and the need for weapons and defences (Fig. 2.18).

Farms and Farmers
(Middle Iron Age 450 BC–100 BC)

Sometime towards the end of the early Iron Age the hillfort at Taplow Court was destroyed, its fired ramparts collapsing into the defensive ditch. This act marks a major disruption to development in the Middle Thames valley, which appears to decline in importance, in comparison to north of the Chilterns where settlements become much more common.

There are other signs of dislocation in the Middle Thames Valley as the Bronze Age field systems at Dorney and The Lea had apparently been abandoned by the middle Iron Age.[24] At Dorney the latest phase of the excavated timber bridges continued into the middle Iron Age, a couple of small enclosed settlements have been excavated in Slough and the hillfort at Danesfield, Medmenham, was occupied, but generally by the middle Iron Age occupation in the Buckinghamshire stretch of the Middle Thames Valley seems to become rather sparse.

In contrast, north of the Chilterns numerous domestic settlements become archaeologically visible in the second half of the first millennium BC. This phenomenon is most evident in Milton Keynes where intensive investigation over several decades has recorded a dense scatter of farmsteads along the river valleys and expanding on to the surrounding clayland plateau.[25] Similar settlements have been found around Aylesbury[26] but elsewhere patterns are less clear. North of Aylesbury in the 'Bernwood/Whaddon Chase' area, there has only been limited investigation. Monitoring of pipeline construction has picked up late Iron Age and Roman settlement but only the occasional earlier settlement, hinting that settlement of the central claylands between the Thame and the Ouse could have occurred gradually from about 400 BC to AD 100. In the Chilterns some early hillforts such as Ivinghoe Beacon were abandoned but others, such as Danesfield Camp at Medmenham and Cholesbury Camp, seem to be built now. In several places pairs of hillforts are found so close together that they could be the result of re-building on a new site – for example Danesfield Camp could be the successor to the undated Medmenham Camp which lies less than a kilometre away. Other such pairings could be suggested between the hillforts at Cheddington and Ivinghoe; Boddington Hill (Wendover) and Aylesbury and perhaps between Desborough and West Wycombe (Fig. 2.19). These Chiltern hillforts supplement the poorly-dated linear boundaries and co-axial fields

FIGURE 2.19
Artist's impression of Ivinghoe Beacon hillfort.

Aerial photograph of Cheddington hillfort, with a possible Neolithic cursus below left. Buried ditches appear as dark marks in growing crops.

Burnt timbers from the final-phase rampart at Taplow Court hillfort.

Buckinghamshire Hillforts

Defensive fortifications are rarely found in Britain before the first millennium BC but that changes around 1000 BC with the construction initially of a variety of small ringforts, palisaded enclosures and large hilltop enclosures, followed by the more numerous and substantial defended sites known as hillforts, which were built from about 600 BC. The term hillfort covers a broad range of defended places, most but not all of which were on higher ground encircled by one or more earthen and timber ramparts outside of which is a sizeable ditch. A distinction is sometimes made between hillforts with a single rampart, which are typically early and short-lived, and those with two or more ramparts that can reflect multiple building-phases on a longer-lived site.

The massive earthen ramparts and ditches make hillforts easier to recognise than most other prehistoric monuments, but sites are still being discovered where later building or ploughing has levelled the earthworks. At present seventeen hillforts can be recognised with reasonable confidence in Buckinghamshire with a further five possible candidates. Hillforts are found across most of the county but particularly along the Icknield Belt, within the Chilterns and along the Thames. The few defended sites in the Upper Ouse Valley appear anomalous as most occupy low-lying riverside locations, but understanding of this phenomenon is hampered by lack of investigation. Buckinghamshire hillforts range in size from 1 to 8.5 hectares. The smallest, a circular enclosure near Ashley Green in the Chilterns, might be an example of a late Bronze Age/early Iron Age ring-fort – a defended enclosure which seem to have housed a single high-status household. Larger hillforts must be communal structures of some kind.

Although the majority of Buckinghamshire hillforts have experienced some form of archaeological investigation only Aylesbury, Ivinghoe Beacon and Taplow Court have seen extensive excavation. Ivinghoe Beacon was investigated in the 1960s; here a substantial late Bronze Age settlement over two hectares in extent was discovered which had few recognisable structures within it but was rich in pottery, animal bone and bronze artefacts. Subsequent radiocarbon dating led to a suggestion that the ramparts were a late addition built around a pre-existing undefended settlement.[41] The discovery of the hillfort at Taplow Court in 1999 was an unexpected consequence of development. Excavation revealed a complex sequence of later Bronze Age to early Iron Age defences, beginning with a palisaded enclosure which was replaced by a V-profile defensive ditch up to 2.6m deep, and then by a U-profile ditch up to 2.8m deep enclosing a much larger area. An outer ditch, probably constructed towards the end of the hillfort's life, suggests that Taplow Court developed into an elaborate 'multivallate' hillfort.[42] The final phase timber-laced rampart was burnt and tipped into the ditch as a mass of charred timbers and fire-reddened gravel. The hillfort at Aylesbury is less well understood as it lies underneath the old town. It was built long after the previous two hillforts, between 400 and 370 BC. Dramatic signs of animal sacrifice and related feasting have been recognised pre-dating its construction.[43]

mentioned in the previous section, which probably developed throughout the first millennium BC. Non-hillfort settlements are also known along the scarp at Ellesborough and at Lodge Hill near Princes Risborough, but there is relatively little sign of non-hillfort settlement on the Chiltern dipslope – although this could simply reflect the relative lack of recent large-scale development in this protected landscape.

Most environmental evidence from excavations indicates that settlements lay within open grassland. However, this may not be the whole picture as the evidence is mainly from land molluscs that, for obvious reasons, tell only a very local story. A subtly different picture comes from pollen sequences of the first millennium BC recovered from small bogs in Whittlewood; an area of medieval forest on the boulder-clay plateau straddling the Buckinghamshire/Northamp-

FIGURE 2.20
Rough wet grassland
and scrubby
woodland near
Tingewick: a typical
landscape of Iron Age
Buckinghamshire?

tonshire border, which might be expected to have been amongst the last places to be settled in prehistory. Here a pollen sequence from Biddlesden dated to before 210 BC–220 AD shows pine-dominated woodland with beech, birch, lime and hazel being cleared by burning, presumably in the early Roman period, to create grassland and sweet chestnut woodland. Sequences from Syresham (South Northants) and Stowe show alder and willow carr set within open pine woodland and grassland in the mid-late first millennium BC. Cereal pollen was present at low levels in these samples, indicative of localised patches of cultivation. Overall the area seems to have remained sparsely occupied with a landscape perhaps resembling that of an open wooded common or heath used mainly for extensive grazing (Fig. 2.20). If so, it stands in contrast to the more structured and intensively managed landscapes emerging elsewhere in the county.

Rather undistinguished ovoid, hand-made pots dominate the material culture of the middle Iron Age settlements with other objects being very rare indeed – just the occasional fired-clay loomweight (pierced triangular objects now sometimes reinterpreted as oven-bricks) or bone weaving-comb and the odd iron item such as a sword from Pennyland and a ring-headed pin from Wavendon Gate. There are also hints of small-scale metalworking in the form of iron smithing or smelting slag and copper-alloy working crucibles from Tattenhoe.

Contact with Rome (Late Iron Age 100 BC–AD 43)

Britain's contact with the Roman world began indirectly around 100 BC with trade mediated by the Armorican tribes of Brittany coming through south coast ports such as Hengistbury Head and Poole Harbour. Buckinghamshire was too remote from these ports to be much affected but it was at this time that the first Gallo-Belgic gold coins (known as 'staters' after their Macedonian prototypes) arrived in the county. Only a handful have been found but whether they were payments for traded goods such as hides or slaves or for the services of mercenaries is not known.

Changes in settlement patterns and landscape between 100 BC and the Roman Conquest appear subtle rather than dramatic. Hillforts may already have been in decline in the middle Iron Age and all but a few seem to have been abandoned by the late Iron Age. Only Cholesbury Camp, hidden deep in the Chilterns, and Danesborough on the Greensand ridge overlooking the Ouzel valley show clear signs of occupation.[27] Changes are apparent in the layout of farmsteads with the creation of large rectilinear ditched-enclosures, interpreted as gardens, paddocks or 'closes', as seen at Bancroft and at Coldharbour Farm, Hartwell, Aylesbury. This may represent the beginning of a move towards a more mixed and diversified agriculture that was to gather pace in Roman times. In the north at least, settlements continued to increase in density and started spreading into areas that had apparently been previously less intensively occupied such as Bernwood.

During the first century BC, the arrival of coinage, apparently issued by tribal dynasties, allows tribal territories to be reconstructed from their coin distributions. Early coins attributed to the Atrebates prior to the Caesar's Gallic War, concentrate in the Middle Thames Valley. In contrast the coinage of the strongest post-Caesarian tribe, the Catuvellauni, is found mainly north of the Thames, mostly north of the Chilterns. The coins and other finds hint that in the early first-century BC, south Buckinghamshire could have been a frontier zone between the Catuvellauni and the Atrebates.[28] It has been suggested that the South Oxfordshire Grim's Ditch, which runs along the north edge of the Chilterns near Wallingford, marked the tribal boundary between the Catuvellauni and Atrebates.[29] It is tempting to speculate that the central Chiltern's Grim's Ditch could have marked, however briefly, another late Iron Age tribal frontier, but unfortunately its date of construction is not yet known. On topographical grounds the Thames is usually suggested as the border between the Atrebates and the Catuvellauni, but in reality the boundary was probably not fixed and the Chilterns could have been disputed territory. Western Buckinghamshire may also have been a frontier land, this time between the Catuvellauni and the Dobunni whose main centre lay in Gloucestershire but whose territory on the east is believed to have reached the Cherwell. To the north the coins imply that Northamptonshire was incorporated into Catuvellanian territory by the reign of Tasciovanus (25–10 BC) but the Upper Nene valley may have been a separate entity before then.[30]

This first phase of contact with the Roman world ended with Caesar's conquest of Gaul and his military expeditions to Britain in 55 and 54 BC, which focussed on the defeat of a chieftain named Cassivellaunus whose territory lay north of the Thames. Around this time a remarkable hoard of gold coins was buried in Whaddon Chase. In 1849 when the old medieval hunting forest was being cultivated for the first time, the plough hit a 'crock of gold' scattering literally hundreds of coins across the freshly-tilled earth (Fig. 2.21). The discovery initiated Buckinghamshire's only gold-rush as villagers grabbed what

FIGURE 2.21
Gold staters from
the Whaddon
Chase hoard.

they could before the landlord stepped in. Eventually three to four hundred gold coins were recovered, although by some accounts this was only a fifth of the total – even the lower figure makes this easily one of the largest such hoards ever discovered.[31] The coins are a collection of uninscribed gold 'staters' dated 55–45 BC each weighing 5.9 grams and 17–18mm in diameter. Most are of a type attributed to the tribal confederation of the British Catuvellauni/Trinovantes with a highly-abstract head of Apollo on the front and a horse accompanied by semi-abstract motifs on the reverse. About a quarter of the hoard consisted of similar coins attributed to the tribe of the Atrebates, and there were also a few from the Corieltauvi (Leicestershire/Lincolnshire), the Durotriges (Dorset) and Gaul. We may never know why such a large hoard was gathered together and how it came to be buried in such a seemingly remote location – could it have been a 'flight hoard' hidden by fugitive Britons fleeing from Caesar's troops after their capture of Cassivellaunus' woodland stronghold? Or perhaps a religious offering made at a time of unprecedented upheaval (Fig. 2.28)?

I

After Caesar's expedition, the emphasis of Roman trade, political alliances and consequent social development shifted from the south coast to the east and south-east, building on cultural links between the 'Belgic' tribes of south east England and northeast Gaul. From the second half of the first century BC until the Roman conquest, the evidence of coins and distinctive burial rites indicate that Buckinghamshire lay on the western edge of a tribal confederation of the Catuvellauni and Trinovantes which dominated a large area north of the Thames running from the coast at Colchester to the river Cherwell. The centre of Atrebatian influence seems to have shifted away from the Thames valley to the south coast. Several hundred coins of the Catuvellauni/Trinovantes have been found in Buckinghamshire, representing about three-quarters of the total pre-Roman coins found in the county.[32] This confederation was ruled by men such as Cunobelin and Tasciovanus who minted coins styling themselves as 'kings', and were recognised as such by the Romans. The main centres of the Catuvellauni/Trinovantes lay at complex proto-urban sites known as 'oppida' found in their core areas of Essex and Hertfordshire, at sites such as Camulodunum (Colchester) and Verulamium (St.Albans) that were to become important Roman towns. This was a time of rapid social and political change driven, it is thought, by a 'prestige goods' economy. What this meant was that local chiefs were able to enhance their prestige and power through diplomatic gifts and trade with Rome, obtaining privileged access to imported goods such as fine table-wares, wine and olive oil – the latter transported in distinctive Mediterranean pots called amphorae. These goods could then be used to secure the support of other chiefs in return for tribute, which could then be used to acquire more Roman imports, and so on. It is known from the Roman writer Strabo that British products in demand on the continent included cloaks, corn, hides, hunting dogs, tin and slaves. In all probability the desire to acquire exotic imports fuelled a process by which an inherently-unstable hierarchical society developed in the Catuvellaunian core area. With the prestige of chiefs depending on the ability to secure foreign imports cross-border raiding, conquest and dynastic warfare would have been necessary to provide the slaves and other surplus goods required to maintain status. Ultimately it was the dynastic crisis following the death of Cunobelin, the last Catuvellaunian paramount chief, which provided the pretext for the Emperor Claudius' invasion.

It is doubtful that daily life in Buckinghamshire changed much after Caesar's expeditions. What we do see is a gradual adoption of a new material culture. Wheel-turned pottery appears alongside handmade 'native' wares and personal adornments, particularly brooches which were previously rare, become a bit more common. Imported goods are uncommon with Gallo-Belgic pottery – a particularly recognisable ceramic – being found in only four places and early amphorae in only two. More dramatically, however, new burial rites appear, with cremated remains being placed in pots accompanied by grave goods. Small cemeteries of this period are known from Bancroft, Bledlow, Dorton, Fleet Marston and Ward's Coombe, Ivinghoe. A cluster of seventeen cremations were found at Bancroft spanning the first century AD, each accompanied by domestic pottery, animal bone and metal items. At Ward's Coombe the cremation burials lie within an earlier enclosure. A burial recovered from a pipe trench at Dorton is a western outlier of a group of rich burials more common in the eastern counties (Fig. 2.22).

None of these continental-influenced objects and burials need be earlier than the closing decades of the first century BC[33] and some are post-conquest, reminding us that in many respects the late Iron Age lifestyle continued to around AD 70/80. This material culture of central and north Buckinghamshire, perhaps lasting over a hundred years, reflects the county's incorporation into the emerging Catuvellaunian 'kingdom'. In contrast, the absence of these distinctive burials (so far at least) from the south of the county, may be significant. Some of the more important northern settlements such as Bancroft and Bierton, were to develop into Roman villas, supporting the idea of continuity but in contrast Roman villas in the Chilterns lack obvious pre-Roman antecedents. This observation reinforces the dichotomy in burial rites already noted between the land south of the Chiltern scarp, and the scarp and land to its north.

Leadership, War and Society

How were the prehistoric farming societies of Buckinghamshire organised? We can perhaps best understand them in terms of the household and wider groupings of households, to which the terms kin, lineage or tribe can be applied. The household would consist of the immediate family and its dependants (including servants and slaves), whilst kin or lineages embody associations of households through clientage, mutual obligation, performance of rituals, marriage alliances etc. In such societies groups are small in size, comprising no more than a few hundred individuals and leadership is essentially informal and consensual, based on individual prowess. At times of external strife a strong and fit man could become the local 'big man', but in times of peace skills in negotiation or religious authority may have been more valued. By the later Iron Age the term 'tribe' refers to rather larger political entities, such as the Catuvellauni, which seem to be confederations of smaller local communities under the rulership of kings. Such entities are sometimes called 'chiefdoms' or warlord societies, where leadership is authoritarian and either accepted, or contested by force.

With these thoughts in mind an attempt can be made to interpret the archaeological evidence for patterns of settlement, the production of goods and evidence of conflict and ritual practices in Buckinghamshire. Before about 2200 BC the evidence is simply too limited to say much; as intimated above it could be taken to indicate a loosely organised semi-nomadic society tied together by occasional social/ceremonial gatherings at focal points such as causewayed enclosures. The construction of barrow cemeteries between about 2200 BC and 1500 BC, marks more clearly the existence of local groups, which might equate to a 'lineage' or clan model with, for instance, the primary burial at Gayhurst being a dynamic, young, 'big man' who was successful enough to found a revered dynasty. The fact that barrows were sometimes raised over the remains of children, as at the Milton Keynes MK23 ring ditch, implies that status could be inherited.

The social tensions implied by the weaponry and hillforts of the late Bronze Age/early Iron Age would surely have favoured leaders displaying martial prowess, but the lack of a burial record denies us the sort of evidence seen earlier at Gayhurst, and there is nationally little evidence that hillforts were elite residences. The proliferation of hillforts and absence of obvious signs of higher-level social organisation, suggests that groupings remained localised, perhaps with leadership by 'big men' mediated through religious sacrifice and success or failure in endemic 'heroic' raiding. Perhaps we can interpret the few identified settlements of this period (such as Bancroft, Ivinghoe Beacon or Walton) as the homesteads of such men. Could the large Bancroft roundhouse with its unusual pots (drinking vessels?) and pig bones have been a feasting hall? Signs of insecurity and conflict can be found in the elaboration of hillfort defences, as at Taplow Court, which developed from simple wooden palisades to ditch and embanked ramparts and eventually multiple defensive ditches and entrance-works. It has been suggested that these developments were responses to the use of fire against wooden ramparts and the introduction of the sling, by which ramparts could be swept clear of defenders by missiles. The final phase of hill-fort construction may have been in the fourth century BC when the fort at Aylesbury was built. By the third century BC many of Buckinghamshire's hillforts had probably been abandoned and the others may have been in decline. The loss of hillforts is, however, more than made up for by the proliferation of undefended domestic settlements. In this new environment the individual household came to the fore and it is difficult to detect obvious signs of either wider social groups or leaders. Along the south coast and in some other parts of the country, a few large hillforts with multiple ramparts and substantial populations rose to prominence, but we cannot identify a convincing example in Buckinghamshire. There is some evidence from pottery styles and settlement patterns that the southern British tribal confederacies of the later Iron Age had already emerged in the middle Iron Age, so it may be that the dominant settlements of this period lay outside Buckinghamshire. However, at present we do not really understand what was happening at a level above the farmstead. It may be that as people settled down in better-defined self-sufficient local landholdings, the old social groups, based on semi-nomadic lifestyles faded away, leaving an atomised egalitarian society that would surely have been vulnerable to absorption into the expansionist eastern tribes of the first century BC.

Hearth and Home: daily life in later prehistory

Lacking evidence for large nucleated settlements, it is a reasonable assumption that the household was the basic unit of daily life throughout this period.

We know from the excavations along the Thames Valley that during the Neolithic the first farmers possessed domesticated cattle, sheep, pigs and dogs and cultivated wheat and barley. Cattle and sheep would have been valued for their secondary products – milk, wool and perhaps blood – as well as being kept for meat, as demonstrated by pottery vessels containing animal and milk fat residues. Hunting, gathering and fishing continued alongside agriculture although they probably made a minor contribution to the diet. Archaeological

FIGURE 2.22
Artist's impression
of Pennyland Iron
Age settlement.

A large ring gully
excavated at
Pennyland. The
gully would have
encircled an Iron
Age roundhouse.

The Pennyland Iron Age Settlement, Milton Keynes

The Milton Keynes Archaeology Unit excavated a settlement at Pennyland in advance of housing development between 1979 and 1981.[44] The site occupied a gravel spur overlooking the Ouzel Valley and illustrates many typical characteristics of farmsteads of the mid-late first millennium BC found in north Buckinghamshire. Stripping of topsoil revealed a dense concentration of archaeological features cut into the natural gravel. A ditched droveway formed the settlement's spine; on either side were arrayed five ditched enclosures, eleven ring gullies, a group of three structures defined by a square of postholes and several clusters of pits. The site was mainly used during the fifth to second centuries BC. Pennyland's earliest elements were a group of grain storage pits and ring gullies at its western side. The enclosures belonged to a later phase. The ring gullies of about 10m diameter often contained domestic refuse and are interpreted as drainage sumps around roundhouses. Small roughly-square post settings were interpreted as the footings for raised granaries. Pits were quite numerous; eighty-four being recognised. Some were clay-lined and presumably used for collecting water; other larger pits well over a metre deep, were of a type widely recognised as for storage of grain. The droveway and enclosures would have been for managing herds which, to judge by the animal bones, were made up predominantly of cattle with some sheep and smaller numbers of pigs and horses. Carbonised plant remains showed that spelt wheat, barley and small quantities of peas, oats, flax and vetch were being grown. Overall the economy seems to have been mixed agricultural and pastoral but with an emphasis on the latter for most of its life. There was little evidence for craft production, although slag and loomweights suggested domestic-scale iron-working and textile manufacture.

evidence for these activities comes principally in the form of bones of wild cattle (aurochs), wild boar, red and roe deer, pike, and charred hazelnut shells. Houses are rarely found and there are no signs of hedged or fenced fields. It may be that crops were grown in small garden plots on fertile newly-cleared land close to water-courses and that to protect them during the growing season domestic animals were herded away to browse in the surrounding woods. Islands in the Thames may have been particularly attractive for growing crops as it would have been easier to exclude both domestic and wild animals. This way of life could have continued for between two and three thousand years with a gradually increasing number of people and animals slowly expanding their clearings into the surrounding forest. The importance of cattle over other domesticated animals is evident from the beginning at Dorney, and emphasised around 2000 BC at Gayhurst, by which time large herds must have been roaming the open grasslands along the river valleys.[34] Such herds would surely have been a measure of wealth and status every bit as valued as the new exotic shiny and magical material (metal) which was making its first appearance at the time.

The first signs of a changing way of life appear after 1500 BC with fields being laid out and permanent settlements with clusters of roundhouses constructed, such as that at Pennyland, Milton Keynes (Fig. 2.22). The pace of change seems to have been gradual and piecemeal, but over a period of a thousand years the old unbounded, extensive, mobile grazing, that today we associate with remote places such as moors, mountains or deserts, gave way to more managed landscapes of fields, farms and droveways. Animal bones from excavated settlements show that cattle remained the most common animal with sheep usually of secondary importance. Pig bones usually make up less than 10% of the total, perhaps reflecting the loss of their favoured woodland. However, a few settlements, such as late Bronze Age Bancroft and Walton buck the trend, having 20–30% pig bone, possibly indicating deliberate selection for high-status feasting. Horse bones appear for the first time, initially at very low levels but increasing to between 10% and 26% on some middle/late Iron Age settlements around Milton Keynes; perhaps the Ouzel valley was used for ranching both cattle and horses. Wild animals are by now rarely represented, suggesting that hunting and fishing had become of negligible importance, and whilst cats and chickens were introduced at this time their bones are hardly ever found. Cultivation is indicated primarily by carbonised remains of spelt wheat and small quantities of barley and oats and, uniquely so far, peas and flax at Pennyland.

Settlements such as Pennyland clearly operated a mixed agricultural economy with evidence for the production, processing and storage of grain as well as the management of substantial herds. However, other settlements, typically those on heavier clay soils away from the river valleys, provide little evidence for cultivation and may have been predominantly pastoral farms. The thin scatter of spinning and weaving equipment and metalworking debris found on settlements suggests domestic self-sufficiency. In contrast to other parts of Britain there is no evidence for a regional pottery industry, or for the importation of salt in ceramic vessels (however it is possible that it was transported in perishable containers). Although life became more settled it seems likely that some aspects of earlier mobile lifestyles survived in the form of local transhumance (that is seasonal movement); for example, drove-roads linked the clayland pastures of the Vale of Aylesbury, which would have provided rich summer grazing but become boggy in winter, with the well-drained chalk downland of the Chilterns, which would have been suited to winter grazing but lacked water in dry summers.

Surprisingly little is known about the preparation and serving of food and drink in view of the quantity of pottery found; scientific analysis of food residues on and within these pots has great potential but is unfortunately not yet widely practiced. Nevertheless, a few guesses can be made from the shape of vessels. Bowls and jars are common, perhaps implying the preparation of stews and gruels, but tableware and fine drinking vessels are rarer and appear only in certain periods such as the late Bronze Age where they seem to be associated with feasting. After around 1500 BC, the impression gained from the bones and charred plants found on settlement sites is of a restricted diet focussed on meat and animal products, bread and gruel.[35] Grain was presumably also fermented to produce beer, but there is no direct evidence for this until the Roman period. The rarity of bones of wild animals, fish and wild or domestic birds in the first millennium BC is notable and implies that they were hardly ever eaten. It seems possible that this reflects a taboo on the consumption of certain creatures of the form reported by Julius Caesar, who wrote: 'Hares, fowl and geese they think it unlawful to eat, but rear them for pleasure and amusement'.

Clothes would have been made from leather or wool, possibly supplemented by linen made from flax, but these organic materials have not survived and only the occasional finds of weaving equipment and needles point to their manufacture. Personal adornments are never common but brooches, bracelets and rings appear in the Bronze Age and occur a bit more frequently at the end of the Iron Age, when the Dorton mirror illustrates a greater concern for personal appearance (Fig. 2.23).

FIGURE 2.23
The Dorton mirror after conservation.

Late Iron Age wheel-turned cup from the Dorton burial.

The Late Iron Age Mirror Burial at Dorton

Monitoring the construction of a gas pipeline in the 1970s led to the discovery of a remarkable burial. Cremated bone and a decorated bronze mirror were contained within a wooden box and accompanied in the grave-pit by pottery amphorae, flagons and a cup. The mirror was a carefully manufactured piece of Celtic art comprising a cast ring handle and a plate decorated with characteristic designs incised into the metal, probably representing stylised faces. The amphorae were storage vessels for wine and other goods imported from the Mediterranean, whilst the flagons were made in Gaul. Too little survived of the cremated bone for certainty but it is thought that this was the burial of a high-status adult woman. The Dorton burial is dated to around end of the first century BC and is the westernmost example of a 'Welwyn style' burial – a type of high status burial also found in Bedfordshire, Essex and Hertfordshire.[45]

Ritual and Religion in late prehistory

Archaeologists usually contrast the physical manifestations of ritual and religious practice found before about 1500 BC (the Neolithic and early Bronze Ages) with those found after that time (the later Bronze Age and Iron Age). Across Britain large numbers of ceremonial and burial monuments, such as barrows, causewayed enclosures, stone circles and circular earthen enclosures called 'henges', were built between 4000 BC and 1500 BC. After 1500 BC such obvious examples of religious and ritual structures become unusual, and for much of the Iron Age this is true of human burials also. In some respects Buckinghamshire offers an intriguing contrast to this national picture and challenges us to consider whether there are underlying structural similarities between religious practices throughout the four thousand years covered by this chapter. It is also important to recognise that for early societies, who held a mixture of beliefs, superstitions, taboos and conservative patterns of behaviour, boundaries between sacred and profane may well break down, and we can expect to find ritual behaviour embedded in everyday life.

Only eight possible Neolithic ceremonial or burial monuments are recorded in Buckinghamshire, and many of these identifications are doubtful. In addition to the oval barrow on Whiteleaf Hill described previously, two other possible oval barrows are recorded at Dorney, close to a cropmark that is interpreted as a causewayed enclosure. At Halton Camp at the foot of the Chiltern scarp, a rather ill-defined mound has been interpreted as a long barrow but as it produced pottery (now seemingly lost) similar to that from Boddington Iron Age hillfort this interpretation seems questionable. The newly discovered cursus at Wolverton has been mentioned above and there are hints that other such monuments may exist. Geophysical survey has led to the suggestion that a cursus or long mound underlies the later hillfort at Ivinghoe Beacon but this seems doubtful as no evidence for it was found in the 1960s excavations. However, a cropmark beside the nearby hillfort on South End Hill, Cheddington, has the appearance of the distinctive end of another cursus aligned on the Beacon, but without investigation its identification remains speculative (Fig. 2.19).

FIGURE 2.24
Reconstructed round
barrow at Dorney
Rowing Lake.

In contrast to such meagre pickings, about 150 round barrows and ring ditches are recorded. As previously noted, where excavated these monuments mostly prove to be earlier Bronze Age burial mounds dating to the period 2300 to 1500 BC, although caution is needed as a few have turned out to be medieval/post-medieval windmill mounds or natural tumps. Round barrows occur in isolation, in pairs, and in small groupings to which the term 'barrow cemetery' can be applied. The best-excavated example of a barrow cemetery is at Gayhurst Quarry near Newport Pagnell whilst others are known at Tyringham, Saunderton near Princes Risborough, and beside the Thames at Dorney (Fig. 2.24) and at Marlow. The focal point of each cemetery appears to be a complex barrow with two or more encircling ditches, and presumably multiple phases of interment as seen at Gayhurst. These cemeteries were surely focal points for local communities, but we must be careful not to exaggerate the importance of the burial mound in people's everyday lives. The known monuments imply an average build rate of only about one every five years anywhere in the county (although to allow for undiscovered sites we might want to increase this guess to one every few years). However, viewed in terms of personal experience an individual who lived to around thirty years of age could only witness the raising of one or two such mounds in their local area, making them special rather than routine events (Fig. 2.33).

For the period after *c.* 1500 BC, three possible 'shrines' can be recognised: at Aston Clinton Bypass (Site A), Prebendal Court, Aylesbury, and Wards Coombe, Ivinghoe. In each case the structural evidence is ambiguous but sufficiently unusual to raise suspicions, which are supported by the treatment of human and animal remains. At the Aston Clinton Bypass the principal structure comprised four posts set within a pennanular ditch (an almost complete ring-ditch 8.4m in diameter). Nearby pits contained a deposit of distinctive and unusual 'concertina

FIGURE 2.25
Ritual sacrifice of
sheep accompanied by
human burials, found
near St.Mary's Church,
Aylesbury.

pots' and a skull radio-carbon dated to 1430–1270 BC, thought to be already ancient when deposited. The Aylesbury 'shrine' dated to the early fourth century BC, lay within the hillfort, but may pre-date the defences. It comprised a large deposit of animal bone (mostly sheep) and nearby the remains of five humans accompanied by further sheep and a goat (Fig. 2.25). A decapitated human skull was also found in the bottom of the hillfort ditch. Wards Coombe is a 50m diameter pennanular enclosure with external bank at the head of a dry valley in what is today a secluded Chiltern wood. Trenching dated the enclosure to the early/middle Iron Age with fills containing human bone. Within it were three late Iron Age/early Roman urned cremations, and a pit with undated horse burials. Mention should also be made of the Roman-period shrine attributed to the sky-god Taranis at Wavendon Gate. The nature of this shrine, essentially a water-filled pit overlooked by a wooden wheel-icon, is entirely native in its character and quite probably simply the latest phase of a pre-Roman cult (see next chapter). What exactly each of these sites represent is open to debate: in principle they could equate to the temple or sacred grove of a god; a place for cremation or excarnation; sacrifice or execution places; the display of war trophies; the veneration of ancestors, or any combination of these.

Thus, by national standards Buckinghamshire has only a relatively short-lived and late interlude of monument building. However, other aspects of the archaeological record suggest recurring themes of ritual and religious practice: the significance of the River Thames; the making of offerings and sacrifice; and the destruction of the human body. These themes are more widely attributed to pre-Roman Celtic religion where there is ample evidence for the importance of animal and human sacrifice, the veneration of nature and river gods and the cult significance of the human head.[36]

We have already seen how early Neolithic settlement was focussed along the

FIGURE 2.26
Bronze Age ard from the Thames at Dorney.

Timber uprights of a prehistoric bridge
within a former Thames channel at Dorney.

Investigations at Dorney

The construction of Eton College's Rowing Course beside the river Thames at Dorney prompted a major series of archaeological investigations that provide a unique insight into the use of the Thames throughout prehistory. Prehistoric remains had been preserved within former river channels and beneath later alluvium washed down by floodwater. Dorney Lake has produced some of the richest evidence for early Neolithic occupation yet found in England and a remarkable series of later Bronze Age and Iron Age wooden structures.

Mesolithic people had lived alongside the river at Dorney for at least five thousand years before the changeover to farming. The earliest evidence for farming communities comes from early Neolithic middens (rubbish dumps) that built up in natural hollows and in the holes left behind by fallen trees. The largest of these middens ran for 200m and was filled with animal bone, pottery and worked flint. Middle and late Neolithic finds were also present at Dorney, including two crouched human burials and two partial animal burials. The infilled river channel contained several beaver lodges, flint tools, pottery, animal bones and also human skulls and other bones, whilst a human skeleton, cattle skeleton and other objects were deposited alongside it. Scatters of struck flint marked working-areas, including a hunting camp where arrowheads were being made around a fire. Bones indicate that cattle were the commonest animal with lesser numbers of sheep, pig and dogs. Analysis of the fats contained within the pottery confirmed use of the vessels for beef, mutton and milk. Wild species were also exploited including aurochs (native wild cattle), wild boar, red and roe deer, badger, beaver and fox; the latter three presumably for their pelts. Surprisingly, pike were the only fish consumed. Charred cereal grains were present but in small quantities, also shells from hazelnuts which would have been collected from surrounding woodland. Despite the exceptional state of preservation few recognisable structures were found, apart from clusters of pits and two circular ditches.

In the Bronze Age, burial monuments were constructed in the form of 'ring ditches', which would have encircled burial mounds. A distinctive triple-ring ditch has been preserved unexcavated on the edge of the rowing lake. In the middle Bronze Age (1600 –1200 BC) parts of the gravel terrace were divided up by ditched rectangular fields containing large waterholes. Environmental evidence indicates heavily grazed grassland nearby. Along the river, mounds and pits full of burnt flint and charcoal were found together with human bones. 'Burnt mounds' are a widely recognised and much-debated feature of Neolithic and Bronze Age Britain – they are often interpreted as saunas, perhaps with a ritual dimension akin to Native American sweat lodges.

The most remarkable discoveries were a series of timber structures interpreted as bridges or jetties, built out into the river channel. The earliest of these consisted of two parallel lines of massive upright stakes that has been radiocarbon dated to 1420–1310 BC. A similar but less substantial structure was associated with early Iron Age pottery and a wooden ard – a simple form of plough. The maple-wood ard, thought to be the oldest known in Britain, has been radiocarbon dated to 900–760 BC. Although broken, it has very little wear on its tip, and is thought to have been deposited in the river fairly new as an offering. Five further waterlogged wooden structures are interpreted as Iron Age bridges and were accompanied by near-complete pots and human bones. Human skulls and bones were also recovered from sandbanks in the river. Some of the long bones have cut-marks consistent with defleshing and disarticulation, whilst gnawing marks attest to exposure on the riverbank.

In the later middle Iron Age, a farmstead consisting of a roundhouse set within a substantial 35m square ditched enclosure was constructed.

Information from Oxford Archaeology.[37]

Thames, but it was also used for the deposition of exotic stone axes and complete pots. Ritual activities associated with water were also important during the later Bronze Age and have long been recognised in the deposition of metal artefacts and human remains in the Thames. There are Bronze Age river finds (mainly spear-heads, swords, rapiers, socketed axes and sickles) from at least ten locations along the Thames in Buckinghamshire, with a particular concentration at Taplow. Iron Age river finds are less common but include a sword, spearheads and iron bars. Excavation of a former Thames channel at Dorney Rowing Lake has shown that from the Neolithic period complete human burials were made alongside the river and human and animal skulls were placed within it. In the Bronze Age and early Iron Age a wooden ard (plough), complete pots, human and animal skulls and other bones were being placed on sandbanks within the river in an area crossed by a sequence of wooden platforms or bridges from which they could have been placed. Timber structures continued to be built in the river channel into the middle Iron Age, but whether ritual deposition also continued is as yet unclear (Fig. 2.26). Evidence for ritual deposition in other Buckinghamshire rivers is elusive, although the concentration of burial mounds along the Ouse and the finding of a Bronze Age sword in the riverbank at Newport Pagnell might hint at comparable activities. These practices are reminiscent of discoveries around the Wash at Flag Fen and from the river Witham in Lincolnshire. They could be interpreted as some form of water cult related to a sacred river as documented in Gaul where, for example, the goddess Sequana presided over a healing-shrine at the source of the Seine.

Roman writers took great glee in telling of the barbarous practices of animal and human sacrifice practiced by the Celts; and Caesar informs us that exclusion from sacrifices was the heaviest punishment that could be inflicted on a Gaul. The archaeological evidence suggests that the making of sacrifices was important throughout prehistory. Practices involving the casting of valuable objects into the Thames, the sacrifice of sheep on a hilltop in Aylesbury, or piling up the rotted carcasses of cattle on the Gayhurst barrow, must surely have marked special events and clearly involved the deliberate destruction of immense wealth. In contrast the broken pottery and bone piled over the Whiteleaf barrow, or the large roundhouse, unusual drinking vessels and relatively high incidence pig bones from Bancroft, speak more of consumption, perhaps communal feasting in a ritualised context.

Inhumation burials of complete bodies occur intermittently through prehistory but are sufficiently rare to suggest that this was not the normal burial rite at any time; indeed individuals treated in such a manner appear to be marked out as different, presumably either special or deviant. In the Bronze Age cremation seems to have been the main burial rite; sometimes the remains were placed in an urn but many were either buried loose or in a bag now long decayed. Cremated remains were placed either in the barrow cemeteries previously mentioned or in small 'flat-grave' cemeteries (such as those at Loughton and Stokenchurch) or dotted about within fields or alongside droveways (as at The Lea, Denham or Aston Clinton Bypass). No cremations can be assigned either to the preceding Neolithic or to the early/middle Iron Age when human remains seem to have been routinely destroyed or dispersed. Occasional human bones (particularly skulls) found on settlement sites and in the river Thames, may imply that bodies were left to decay in the open or placed in rivers. Towards the end of the Iron Age cremation burials re-appear, reflecting continental practice.

One possible explanation for the physical destruction of the body through cremation, excarnation or disposal into rivers is that there was an underlying belief that the destruction of the physical body was necessary to release the soul for its journey to the afterlife. According to the Roman writer Diodorus Siculus, the Celts held that the soul was immortal and would eventually return to another body. Viewed in this context the exceptional decision to bury a whole body, instead of destroying or dispersing it, could have been intended to fix the soul to the earth. Perhaps retention of a body could have been motivated by a desire to communicate with a revered ancestor after death; maybe this was why the barrows at Gayhurst and Whiteleaf were returned to for hundreds of years. At other times burial could have meant exclusion and punishment; thus a teenage boy buried on a boundary marked by a pit alignment at Olney had perhaps been cast both literally and spiritually to the margins of society.

Conclusion

At the opening of this chapter it was noted that Buckinghamshire is not a natural area within which to study prehistory and it has been shown that the north, the centre and south of the county offer rather different narratives. Farming communities first established themselves along the Thames around 4000 BC from where they seem to have moved into the Chilterns, but it is not until after 2300 BC that there are signs of widespread occupation in either the Vale of Aylesbury or the Upper Ouse Valley. The construction of round burial mounds along the river valleys and the Chiltern scarp, together with evidence for woodland clearance, suggests a significant increase in population and greater concern with staking a claim to land. One possible explanation for this is that insular cultural traditions (perhaps inherited from hunter-gatherers) which had restricted Neolithic populations to well below the land's theoretical carrying capacity, started to break down during the period of continental contact known as the Beaker period (2400–1800 BC), resulting in a more competitive society. After 1500 BC there is a gradual but fundamental change in the archaeological record across the county, apparently reflecting a shift from a mobile way of life based on cattle-herding to a settled mixed agricultural economy. The construction of an elaborate burial monument in the Ouse Valley near Newport Pagnell at the end of the third millennium BC, marks the beginning of an upsurge in activity in the northern part of the county after which the Ouse Valley shows a new vibrancy with the construction of more burial mounds followed, in the first millennium BC, by the riches of the Milton Keynes hoard, the large roundhouse at Bancroft and the gradual spread of numerous farmsteads across the landscape. Fields first appear in the Thames Valley in the later Bronze Age but their subsequent abandonment and the destruction of the Taplow hillfort mark the beginning of a period of decline. The Vale of Aylesbury and the Chilterns show some developmental characteristics of both the Thames and Ouse Valleys. Recognisable settlements appear here rather earlier than in the north and are followed in the early-mid first millennium BC by an ordered landscape of hillforts, dispersed farmsteads and a network of drove roads. After an interlude in the middle of the first millennium BC, possibly with a more egalitarian society, the arrival of renewed continental influences around 100 BC saw the peoples of Buckinghamshire absorbed into the new tribal confederacy of the Catuvellauni/Trinovantes. When the Romans arrived in AD 43 they conquered a landscape dotted with mixed and pastoral farms, inhabited by long-established settled communities with deeply embedded religious beliefs and ruled by leaders already receptive to the benefits of Roman civilisation. However, there were still places such as Bernwood or the Chiltern dipslope where, either for political or environmental reasons, settlement was seemingly less dense. How the British communities of Buckinghamshire adapted to Roman rule will be the subject of the next chapter.

Chapter 3

Roman Buckinghamshire (AD 43–410)

Bob Zeepvat & David Radford

The Iron Age Inheritance

There is sufficient evidence in Buckinghamshire to point to a general continuity of settlement from the Late Iron Age into the post-Conquest period. By the early first century AD the county formed a part of the lands held by a tribal confederation known as the *Catuvellauni*, whose territory probably extended from the river Cherwell in the west to the Cam in the east, and northwards from the Thames to the Nene valley.[1] Perhaps their most famous leader was Cunobelin, immortalised by Shakespeare as 'Cymbeline', who ruled from *c.*AD 5–40.

Of the social organisation of the *Catuvellauni,* we know very little. Classical writers such as Caesar and Tacitus suggest that the Celtic tribes were loose confederations headed by *equites* (literally, 'knights') who each held an area of the tribal territory as 'client' landowners, the land belonging to the tribe and not to individuals. On the social scale below the *equites* were freemen, and at the bottom were slaves – a commodity reported to have been exported. Membership of the latter class probably resulted from warfare, or from tribal systems of criminal punishment.

Recent research has shown that the *Catuvellauni* occupied a landscape that was for the most part intensively farmed. In the north of the county, a number of small farming settlements have been excavated in Milton Keynes. Some of these (Westbury and Caldecotte) appear to have continued in occupation beyond the mid first-century, whereas others subsequently relocated (Wavendon Gate, Hartigans and Bancroft), or declined (Furzton and Pennyland). It has been suggested that the quality of agricultural land may be a significant factor in determining which survived and prospered under Roman rule, or which declined and were abandoned.

In the Vale of Aylesbury there is good evidence for continuity of late Iron Age settlement into the Roman period on the Portland limestone soils, for example at Bierton, Walton High School and Walton Court, and further west at Long Crendon. Evidence for continuity on the heavier clays has been less forthcoming, though after the Conquest around Aylesbury soil quality appears to have been less of a consideration than factors such as access to the newly-established road network. In the southern Vale, late Iron Age pottery has been recovered from the Roman villa at Saunderton.[2]

Evidence for continuity of occupation in the Chilterns is less strong although late Iron Age pottery has been recorded at a possible villa site at Cobblers Hill, Great Missenden[3] and south of the dip slope near the Thames at the Yewden villa, Hambleden.[4] At present there is little evidence from the Burnham plateau, but late Iron Age pottery has recently been recovered at All Soul's Quarry, Wexham, suggesting that activity there had begun soon after, if not before the Conquest.[5]

There is evidence for continuing use of roundhouse-type dwellings common in the Iron Age, but also for the adoption by the native population of rectangular wooden buildings, for example at Latimer.[6] In the north of the county round-house construction continues throughout the Roman period but with the addition of a dwarf wall of stone at the base, providing a firm, dry footing. Examples vary widely in size: at Bancroft[7] there were four, ranging from 6m to 14m in diameter. This type of structure is commonest in the upper Ouse and upper Nene valleys. There also appears to be some continuity of agricultural systems, as indicated by the similarity of pre and post-Conquest animal bone assemblages, from Bierton[8] and Bancroft. A number of early Roman sites develop quickly into high status villas, for example at Bierton, Yewden and Saunderton, suggesting the rapid adoption of *Romanitas* by sections of the native elite.

None of Buckinghamshire's Iron Age hillforts seem to have had any continuing political, cultural or religious role into the Roman period, although activity appears to have continued close by, for example at West Wycombe, Cheddington and Taplow. However, it is worth noting that as yet only Cholesbury and possibly Danesborough hillforts have produced evidence of use during the later Iron Age. In the north of the county the hillfort at Danesborough, believed to have been be the local tribal centre, was probably replaced by the small town of *Magiovinium*, three kilometres to the south. Near Aylesbury a new roadside settlement was established at Fleet Marston[9] on Akeman Street.

The Roman Conquest

At the time of the Roman invasion in AD 43, Togodumnus and Caratacus, the sons of Cunobelin, ruled the *Catuvellauni*. It was the increasing power of the *Catuvellauni* that brought about the invasion. In AD 42 Verica, leader of the *Atrebates* the neighbouring tribe to the west, fearful of Catuvellaunian pressure on his territory, appealed to Rome for help. This gave the emperor Claudius a pretext for invading Britain the following year. After landing on the south coast, the invasion force advanced to the Thames, somewhere in the London area. There they awaited the arrival of Claudius before proceeding to the eastern Catuvellaunian capital at *Camulodunon* (Colchester), where he accepted the surrender of the *Catuvellauni*. Three of the four legions present then set out to subdue different parts of the country, probably pursuing Claudius's real agenda for the invasion. It seems likely that *Legio IX Gemina* (14th Legion) who were despatched to the west Midlands and north Wales, followed the route later taken by the Roman road known as Watling Street, which crosses the county from Bow Brickhill to Stony Stratford.

As there is little evidence for Roman military activity in Buckinghamshire, it is possible that this part of Catuvellanian territory was relatively easily incorporated into Roman power structures, perhaps as a result of agreement following the surrender at Colchester, and that little or no resistance was offered to the Roman advance.

Three possible 'forts' are recorded in Buckinghamshire. A double-ditched rectangular enclosure overlooking the Watling Street crossing of the Ouzel, revealed in aerial photographs, has been tentatively identified as an auxiliary fort of the Neronian period.[10] At the Yewden villa, Hambleden, an early enclosure with a V-shaped ditch could be military, and it has also been suggested that the roadside settlement at Fleet Marston originated as a conquest fort,[11] although there as yet there is no archaeological evidence for this. Some items of both first and third-century military metalwork were found at Walton Court, Aylesbury,[12] including a harness junction clip from Germany, apron or belt mounts and a spearhead. A model bronze scythe found here has parallels with military graves in the Rhineland and may point to a shrine in the vicinity. Walton could have been the site of a fort, equidistant from Alchester and another possible fort at Cow Roast, Hertfordshire. All three were fairly close to Akeman Street, which was possibly constructed shortly after the invasion as a military supply route.[13]

Communications

One of the major changes brought about by the Roman invasion was the construction of a system of roads radiating from London, which was established as the province's social, economic and political centre, a choice that affects us to this day. Like modern roads, Roman roads can be divided into major and minor categories. Many of the major roads are detailed in the *Antonine Itinerary*, a document containing directions between settlements and posting stations throughout the Roman Empire, probably compiled in the third century AD. These roads were constructed primarily as a network over which troops, supplies and communications could be swiftly moved. The only road in Buckinghamshire falling into this category is the section of Watling Street (now the A5) linking *Durocobrivis* (Dunstable) with *Magiovinium* (Dropshort Farm) and *Lactodorum* (Towcester) (Fig. 3.1). Excavations at *Magiovinium*[14] have shown that when Watling Street was constructed it cut across a grid of land boundaries associated with the earlier Neronian fort, and also a possible earlier route that crossed the Ouzel at Water Eaton, south of the Watling Street crossing.[15]

Between the major roads there was a network of minor roads, linking population centres, serving mostly non-official travel and commerce. Lesser roads that can with some certainty be identified as Roman are: Akeman Street, from *Verulamium* to Alchester; the Alchester-Towcester road, the road from Fleet Marston towards Thornborough, and the Fenny Stratford to Thornborough road. Excavations at *Magiovinium* also revealed a road running northwards from the town, suggesting a route up the east side of the Ouzel valley to the settlement at Ashfurlong, near Olney, and thence presumably on to Irchester. A road has also been suggested following the same general line as the present A40, across the county from Uxbridge to Stokenchurch.[16]

FIGURE 3.1
Aerial view of Watling
Street, running
southwards through
Stony Stratford.

Evidence suggests that the road system is mostly first century in origin (Fig. 3.2). A section excavated through Akeman Street at Billingsfield, Quarrendon, revealed a gravel surface up to 6.6m wide, with flanking ditches. Here two cremation urns of mid-first century date were inserted into pits cutting the edge of the outer ditch.[17] At the river crossing at Thornborough[18] two roads and a pre-conquest metalled trackway were sectioned. These appeared to date from the late first century, and to continue in use to the end of the fourth. However, an excavated section through one of the roads showed it to be constructed of a single layer of limestone blocks with no evidence of re-metalling or wheel ruts that might be expected from heavy use.

In addition to the above there must also have been a network of trackways linking villas and farmsteads to the road network. Examples of minor trackways have been recorded on the Aston Clinton bypass, at Berryfields, Aylesbury, and at the villa sites at Bancroft and Mantles Green, Amersham.[19]

FIGURE 3.2
Roman Buckinghamshire:
principal sites and roads.

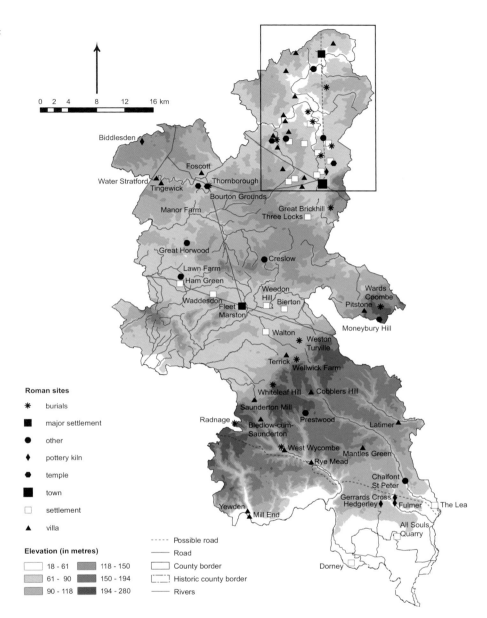

It is likely that some of the larger rivers in the county were also used for transport. Evidence for this is hard to find because of changing water levels and later works connected with mills, water management, navigation and dredging. However, the remains of a possible timber quay were noted at Thornton, and possibly of a stone quay near Hill Farm, Haversham.[20] The riverside situation of some sites such as Stanton Low (Fig. 3.3),[21] Emberton and Ashfurlong is suggestive, and the presence of a large number of 'corn drying ovens' at Yewden, close to the Thames, may indicate commercial activity utilising the river for transport.

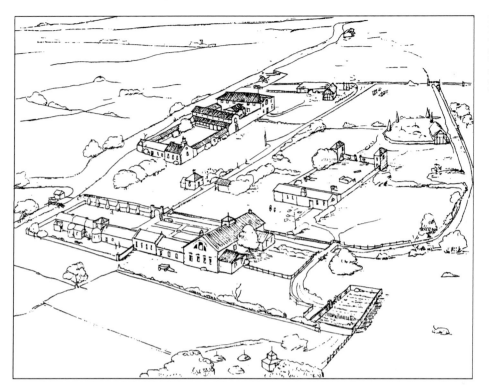

FIGURE 3.3
Reconstruction of the
extensive riverside site
at Stanton Low. This
site was destroyed by gravel
extraction in the 1950s:
only limited excavation
was possible at the time.

Towns

Historic Buckinghamshire only contains one certain small town, *Magiovinium*
at Dropshort Farm, Fenny Stratford, close to the Watling Street crossing of the
Ouzel (Fig. 3.4). From air photographs the town appears to have been
surrounded by an earth bank and ditch, and covers *c*.7.5 hectares, straddling
Watling Street. We know its Roman name because it is recorded in the afore-
mentioned *Antonine Itinerary*. As it is a scheduled monument little of it has been
examined, though evidence of stone and timber buildings within the town has
been recorded during ditching operations. It had extensive suburbs to the south-
east along Watling Street which were excavated in advance of various road
improvements,[22] revealing rows of timber buildings, probably shops, inns etc,
fronting the road.

Two large Buckinghamshire settlements may yet prove to be small towns. At
Fleet Marston, west of Aylesbury, sited at the junction of Akeman Street and the
road to Thornborough,[23] the discovery of significant quantities of first to fourth
century pottery, spreads of tile, coins, and metalwork, as well as a pewter hoard
(Fig. 3.5) and a lead coffin, points to a sizable settlement and/or perhaps a
posting station here. However, it has yet to produce any conclusive evidence for
public buildings or related villa settlement, so its status remains undetermined.
There is another large settlement at Ashfurlong, near Olney, in the Ouse valley.[24]
As at Fleet Marston, significant amounts of Roman pottery, building materials
and coins have been recovered here over time from an area covering several
hectares. Aerial photographs have revealed circular features, enclosures and

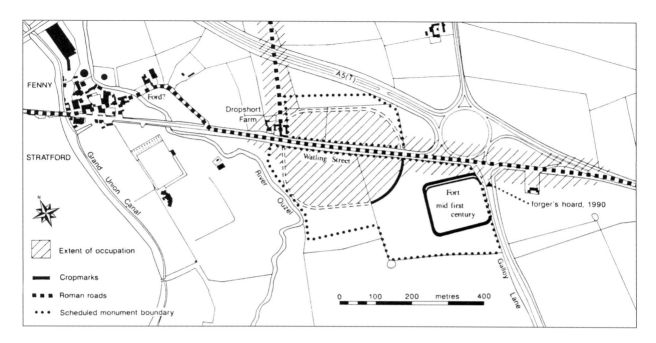

rectangular stone buildings. Ashfurlong is on the line of the road from *Magiovinium* to Irchester, close to the point where it crosses the Ouse. It could be a small town and/or a posting station, or alternatively an elaborate villa-like establishment such as that further upstream at Stanton Low. Finally, a large spread of Roman material recorded close to the Roman temple site at Thornborough located close to an important road junction could yet prove to be another nucleated roadside settlement.

FIGURE 3.4
Plan of Magiovinium. The town, located on Watling Street, appears to have had an encircling earth rampart, part of which survives. Little is known of its layout, though extensive suburbs have been excavated to the south-east, and burials have been found to the north-west, close to the river.

FIGURE 3.5
The Fleet Marston pewter hoard during excavation.

The Countryside

Until the mid-twentieth century, it was generally believed that the Romano-British countryside comprised almost idyllic parkland, with magnificent villas at intervals of a few miles. This was contrasted with a presumed pre-Roman landscape of almost continuous forest. Since that time, evidence from excavations and landscape studies has shown that during the Roman period some parts of the Buckinghamshire countryside were probably as fully populated and farmed as they were in the nineteenth century at the commencement of the Industrial Revolution; other areas seem to have been less fully exploited, and for the remainder there is at present insufficient evidence.

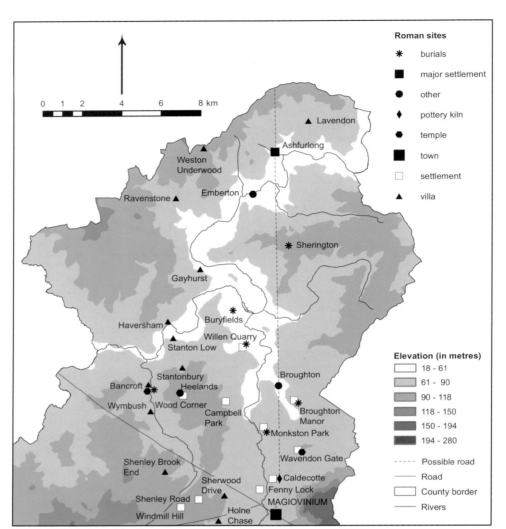

FIGURE 3.6
Principal Roman sites in
the Milton Keynes area.

In the most intensively studied area of Buckinghamshire, in and around Milton Keynes, a dense pattern of settlement, with a variety of rural settlement types of different sizes, has been recognised (Fig. 3.6).[25] These range from small completely 'native-type' farmsteads such as Wood Corner,[26] Campbell Park,[27] Woughton,[28] and Wavendon Gate,[29] to small farms with Roman-style buildings, such as Wymbush,[30] and finally substantial villas such as Bancroft, Stantonbury[31] and Stanton Low. Other villa sites in north Buckinghamshire are also known or suspected at Foscott; Gayhurst,[32] Hill Farm, Haversham,[33] Lavendon,[34] Ravenstone,[35] Shenley Brook End,[36] Sherwood Drive and Holne Chase (both in Bletchley),[37] Tingewick,[38] Water Stratford[39] and Weston Underwood.[40] There is also some evidence that a number of high-status farmsteads or villas were close to the road junction at Thornborough. Fieldwalking in the Whittlewood area, north of Buckingham, has revealed a dense pattern of settlement on the clays in the north of the county, although more work is required to confirm their character.

FIGURE 3.7
An outbuilding of the
villa at Mantles Green
Farm, Amersham under
investigation in 1983–4
before construction of
the Amersham bypass.

In contrast to the position around Milton Keynes, there is at present a noticeable absence of evidence for villas on the claylands of the Vale of Aylesbury to the south. However, where fieldwalking (systematic collection of surface finds) has been carried out, for example west of Aylesbury, a dense pattern of occupation has been noted. It is possible that these settlements on less productive clays were low to medium status farmsteads, perhaps servicing the larger settlements at Alchester and Fleet Marston. South of the central Vale, the more productive agricultural land, such as the chalk marl and Greensand of the Icknield Belt and the Portland ridge through Aylesbury, did attract villa and farm concentrations that were closely related to the road systems linking farms to their urban markets. Villas in this area include Saunderton Mill,[41] Kings Field, Terrick,[42] and Bierton. Others are known or suspected at Saunderton Lee and Pitstone.

The uplands of the Chiltern dip-slope appear to have been generally avoided in the Late Iron Age and Roman periods, occupation being confined to the chalk and alluvial soils of the valleys. Existing woodland cover and pastoral farming here may have hindered discovery and be partially responsible for the absence of evidence. However, even where fieldwalking has been carried out on the dip slope, it has proved unproductive. In contrast, in the valleys a number of villa or farm estate sites have been recorded, notably at Latimer,[43] Bury Farm[44] and Mantles Green, both near Amersham (Fig. 3.7), and the Rye , High Wycombe.[45] Others are suspected at Chalfont St Peter and West Wycombe.

South of the Chilterns on the Burnham plateau and along the Thames valley, recent large-scale excavation, for example at All Souls, Wexham, The Lea, Denham, and by the Thames on the Eton Rowing Lake at Dorney, have begun to identify farmsteads in this area but generally settlement evidence here is sparse and villa sites few and far between. A similar absence has also been noted to the north and west of London.[46] Further upstream, however, there are two notable villa sites at Yewden and Mill End[47] villas, both near Hambleden, adjacent to the Thames.

In-depth analysis of the changing fortunes of rural settlement in Buckinghamshire has to date only been attempted for the Ouse valley, with some reference to adjoining areas. In general, the pattern revealed here has been one of expansion in the late first to second centuries. Although this expansion continues into the third century on some sites, the early house at Bancroft appears to have been destroyed by fire in c.AD 170, and excavations revealed only slight evidence of activity here during most of the third century. There seems to have been an increase of prosperity in the late third to early fourth centuries, continuing until the mid-fourth, after which the picture becomes more difficult to interpret. In the south of the county, the large villa estate at Yewden was probably abandoned in late fourth century, and in the Chilterns the villa at Latimer was reduced in size by c.AD 350, though it continued to be occupied.

In the Ouse valley the character of native settlements has been examined in some detail. Excavations at Fenny Lock,[48] near Bletchley, revealed a circular buildings, field systems and paddocks that went out of use at the end of the second century. Close by, a large rectangular early Roman enclosure was succeeded by later circular enclosures, ditched field boundaries and a structure later rebuilt in stone. At Wood Corner, Milton Keynes, both continuity and evolution were also in evidence. A timber-framed rectangular structure of mid to the late second century was replaced by circular timber buildings in the late second to early third century, and in the mid to late third century a rectangular building was constructed within a substantial enclosure ditch. At Wavendon Gate, an Iron Age settlement was superseded by an early Roman ditched enclosure containing pottery kilns as well as cremation and inhumation burials.

In contrast to the Ouse valley, excavated evidence for native settlements in the Vale of Aylesbury and the Chilterns is limited. The results of fieldwalking have, for example, demonstrated evidence for the establishment of new sites in the second and third centuries close to Akeman Street at Waddesdon and Ham Green, Grendon Underwood[49] and recent investigations suggest the existence of a planned roadside settlement east of the Fleet Marston settlement at Berryfields, Aylesbury. Excavations on the route of the Aston Clinton bypass revealed a late Iron Age settlement that continued into the Roman period, with evidence for early Roman iron working. Later Roman features here included two large square pits, probably waterholes, and two square wells. Coin evidence suggested activity through to the last quarter of the fourth century here.[50] Recent excavations near Akeman Street, north and west of Aylesbury, have produced some evidence for variation in settlement function, including a malting enclosure, evidence for iron smelting and possibly viticulture (the growing of grapes). These results support the picture of a densely settled clay landscape so far lacking evidence for a 'villa' infrastructure, but suggesting that along the Akeman Street corridor there was a greater degree of specialised production, perhaps orientated around the supply of goods and materials to larger population centres, as has been previously noted.

There is little excavated evidence for native settlement within the Chilterns. However, as noted above information is now emerging about a few sites on the Thames river gravels. At Dorney,[51] a settlement which started life as a ditched enclosure in the middle to late Iron Age, continued in use into the Roman period before being finally abandoned by the end of the third century. Inside the enclosure was a rectangular building constructed on post-pads associated with a group of ovens or kilns, and tile wasters. At All Souls Farm, Wexham,[52] ephemeral wooden structures were recorded as well as enclosure ditches, large bell-shaped pits, and wells. The presence of slag suggested some form of industrial working on the edge of this farmstead. Pottery dating indicated that activity continued here throughout the Roman period. In the Colne valley at The Lea, Denham,[53] a number of burials incorporating rich grave-goods were associated with a series of rectangular enclosures, timber buildings, an oval flint-walled structure and timber-lined wells of the late second to fourth centuries.

Villas

To many people, the principal sign of Romanisation in the British countryside was the appearance of the villa. The Latin word *villa* means 'farm', implying an agricultural establishment comprising a farmhouse and outbuildings built in the Roman style, incorporating many of the trappings of Roman civilisation. This definition covers a wide variety of sites in Buckinghamshire, though none yet match the exceptional size and splendour of the palatial villas of the Cotswolds, such as Chedworth and Northleigh.

Each villa was the centre of an agricultural estate, parts of which may have been let to tenant farms. In the absence of documentary evidence, the extent of such estates can only be guessed at. In the Ouse valley near Milton Keynes, villas have been recorded at intervals of 2–3km along both sides of the river.[54] On the north bank there are villas at Deanshanger, Cosgrove, Haversham and Gayhurst, and on the south at Tingewick, Bancroft, Stantonbury and Stanton Low. In the Chilterns, a similar even spacing of villas every 2–3km along the valleys[55] has led to the suggestion that holdings of between 450–600 acres were laid out here in the second century. A similar pattern has been noted in the Nene valley in Northamptonshire,[56] also a part of Catuvellaunian territory.

The most comprehensively examined villa site in the Ouse valley area, if not in the county, is Bancroft, Milton Keynes,[57] excavated in the 1980s (Fig. 3.8). The villa was on a south-east facing slope close to Loughton Brook, a tributary of the Ouse, and was established in the late first to early second centuries. It comprised a farmhouse and adjacent farm buildings and yards, alongside a cobbled trackway following the brook. The buildings all had stone foundations, which probably supported timber-framed walls. The farmhouse had a large open interior, with two small rooms at its north-west end. On its north-east side was a small bath suite, with two heated rooms and a cold room with a tile-lined plunge bath. The walls of the bath suite were decorated with painted marine scenes showing fish, dolphins, shellfish and jellyfish on a white background (Fig. 3.9). The farm buildings comprised two large barns, a granary, and two circular buildings that possibly housed farm workers. Between the farmyard and the brook were two walled enclosures that were probably used as gardens for growing vegetables and herbs.

On the hill overlooking the villa, 250m to the north-west, a cremation cemetery was established on the site of earlier farmsteads spanning the late Bronze

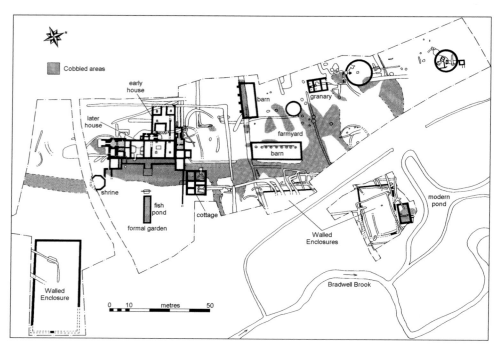

FIGURE 3.8
Top: Bancroft villa: plan of excavations, 1975–86. Bottom: model of the fourth-century phase of the villa. The house was fronted by a formal walled garden, with a large rectangular fishpond as its centrepiece.
Bottom: model reconstruction of Bancroft villa.

Age and Iron Age periods. During the second century a substantial temple/mausoleum was built close to the cremation cemetery, surrounded by an enclosure ditch (Fig. 3.10). The use of this hilltop site for burial may indicate some continuity of tenure between the occupants of the Iron Age farmstead and the early villa.

In about AD 170 the house at Bancroft burnt down, and the villa appears to have been largely abandoned. It is likely that the mausoleum also began to fall into disrepair at this time. Only slight evidence of activity on the site during the third century was found, centred on one of the circular buildings. In the late third-century a new house was built, partly overlying the site of the first house but facing south-east. Its walls appear to have been built of stone throughout; its

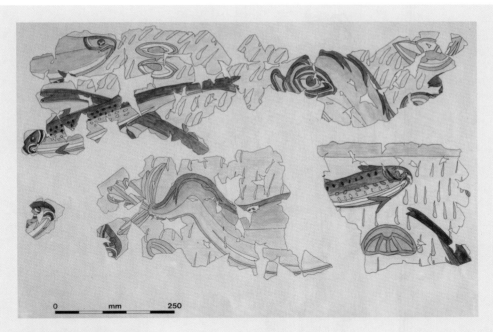

0   mm   250

Rooms in Villas

FIGURE 3.9 Wall plaster from the second-century baths at Bancroft, showing a marine scene with dolphins, fish, shellfish and jellyfish. The principal rooms in villas were usually well appointed. Underfloor heating was often provided, and walls and ceilings had painted decoration. Floors were often covered with mosaics, either of simple designs using chopped pieces of brick or limestone, or more complex patterns with combinations of different coloured stone, glass or ceramic tile. Apart from Bancroft, decorative mosaics are known from Foscott, Latimer, Rye Mead, and Yewden villas.

roof was tiled, and possibly rose to two storeys. At its south-west end was a bath suite: one of the two ground-floor living rooms was also heated. During the fourth century the house was extended, with the addition of a new, larger bath suite to the south-west, projecting rooms, a corridor and central porch to the frontage, and a second, smaller bath suite to the rear. Mosaic floors were laid in most of the rooms. At the front of the house was a formal walled garden with a large central fishpond. On the north-east side of the garden was a small house or cottage, with at least one heated room, and to the south-west was an octagonal structure, either a summerhouse or family shrine. South of this was a large walled enclosure, possibly used for growing vegetables, herbs, fruit or even viticulture. On the adjoining hilltop a small circular building, probably a shrine, was built close to the now derelict mausoleum. A small inhumation cemetery containing eight burials was established nearby in the late fourth or early fifth century (Fig. 3.11).

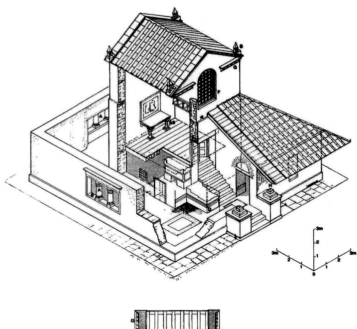

FIGURE 3.10
Reconstruction of the
second-century
temple/mausoleum at
Bancroft, based on
architectural fragments
recovered from the site.
Above the central burial
vault is a room probably
used for worship.
The corridor around the
central tower had a plain
mosaic floor.

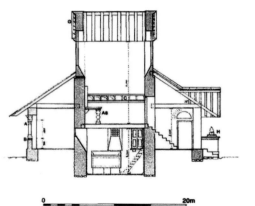

FIGURE 3.11
Left: excavating the
first-century cremation
cemetery at Bancroft.
The cremated bone is in
the largest vessel and the
smaller pots probably
contained food offerings;
beneath the cremation
vessels were bones from
joints of mutton and
pork. Right: excavating
the fourth-century
inhumation cemetery at
Bancroft. The grave cuts
were lined with
limestone rubble,
including architectural
fragments which must
have come from the
earlier temple/
mausoleum.

FIGURE 3.12
Flue tile (its decorated surface would not have been seen) and painted wall plaster from the Latimer villa.

Circumstances relating to the demise of Bancroft villa are uncertain, but the process appears to have been peaceful and prolonged. Worn and burnt patches on the mosaic floors suggest squatter occupation by people who cared little for the finer trappings of Roman life. The site now lies within one of the city parks, and the outline of the fourth-century house and the formal garden, with its central fishpond, can be visited.

In the Chess Valley the villa at Latimer[58] was subject to extensive excavation during the late 1960s. The site on the south bank of the river Chess, is now partly overlain by the buildings and yards of Latimer Park Farm, and the adjoining road. The first farmhouse on the site was a post-built timber structure, of mid to late first century date. This was replaced in the mid-second century by a stone house, comprising a range of rooms, with painted plastered walls and floors of both timber and concrete, all linked by a corridor (Fig. 3.12). There was also a small bath house. Later in the second century at least one room was given a mosaic floor. During the third century the building was extended, a larger bath suite was constructed, and additional mosaics were inserted. By the fourth century the house had become a substantial structure, similar in plan to the fourth-century house at Bancroft, with mosaic floors and painted walls in most rooms, and a large bath suite. Fronting the fourth century house at Latimer was a walled courtyard or garden, with a range of lean-to sheds in its south-east corner, and a gateway in the centre of its east side, from which a path led to the house. Part of the courtyard appears to have been used as a yard: the excavator suggested that the rest was given over to a vegetable or flower garden. A series of parallel trenches in this latter area are thought to represent vegetable beds, and a notable find from this part of the site was the iron blade of a turf cutter.

The Villa On The Rye, High Wycombe.

FIGURE 3.13 The Roman villa on the Rye, High Wycombe was first discovered in AD 1722–3. It was partly excavated in 1863–4 and again in 1932. The photo of that date shows a mosaic floor in the foreground. The results of this work were never properly published. The plan shown here was drawn during rescue excavations in 1954, just before a swimming pool was constructed on the site.

The villa was built in the late second century. The mosaic floor seen in the 1932 photograph was in its principal room which opened off a corridor at the front of the building. The villa had several additions during its life including a hypocaust. Painted wall plaster was used extensively inside. A boundary wall on the east had a gateway flanked by two small rooms. Nearby was a large bath house with a line of rooms heated by a furnace, and a cold water bath. The bath house was too large for the villa owner's family alone and might have also been used by estate workers. Some of the villa's wall plaster recovered in 1932 is shown here in a painting by Francis Colmer.

FIGURE 3.14
Reconstruction of the
Yewden villa at
Hambleden, showing the
front of the building with
its two wings and
connecting corridor.

Although the existence of more than one Roman building is suspected in the Wye valley, only one, a villa on the Rye has been investigated. Some details of this villa are given with Fig. 3.13.

Prior to the excavations at Bancroft, the most extensively investigated villa in the county was the Yewden villa, at Hambleden in the Thames Valley,[59] excavated in the early 1900s (Fig. 3.14). It lies on the north bank of the river, at the mouth of the Hamble Brook valley. The villa was established in the mid-first century. The rectangular main house was later expanded by the addition of flanking wings and corridors on both sides. It had a bath house, and tessellated pavements in some of the rooms, of which several were heated. The house stood in a walled enclosure, open to the west. Two aisled farm buildings were also identified. Within the enclosure an unusual number of corn-drying ovens (fourteen) were recorded, possibly indicating that a high level of food processing was being carried out there. Along with the discovery of a large number of *styli* (metal implements used for writing on wax tablets), this led the excavator to suggest that the villa was under government control. A number of inhumations, including ninety-seven neo-natal and infant burials, were found near the east wall of the house. Although infant burials are not uncommon on villa sites, the number recorded at Yewden is exceptional. The implications of this are unclear. Possibly a large number of female slaves were present, perhaps there were particularly harsh living conditions for the families labouring for the villa, or perhaps the owners enforced a policy of infanticide to regulate the workforce population. The villa is one of largest in the Thames valley, and must have had an interesting and usually close relationship with another villa, the unexcavated Mill End villa, which lies only 700m to the south, on the bank of the Thames.

Farming, Fishing and Land Management

Roman Buckinghamshire had a mixed farming economy, operated through a range of settlements from small farmsteads of 'native type' like Woughton and Wood Corner to small farms and larger palatial villas like Bancroft and Yewden. These settlements, with the exception of those located in the more constrained and perhaps more heavily-wooded valleys of the Chilterns, were set within a largely open farming landscape. Our evidence for this comes from the animal bone recovered during excavations and from systematic sampling of the fills of features such as pits and ditches for preserved plant material, pollen, snails and insects.

Cattle or oxen were the most commonly kept animals, followed by sheep and goats, pigs, horses and domestic fowl. Within the Chilterns there is some evidence for variations to this pattern; at Latimer, for example, there were more pigs than sheep and goats in the late third century. In terms of cereal production spelt wheat was the most common cereal variety cultivated, and free-threshing and emmer wheat and barley were also widely grown. At Wavendon Gate and Stoke Hammond,[60] evidence for flax processing was found. Evidence for fruit and vegetable cultivation was recovered from two second-century walled garden areas at Bancroft. At Latimer there were also hints of vegetable and fruit growing; a walled enclosure contained bedding trenches for vegetables, and finds included pruning saws and knives and a variety of spade irons (the metal cutting edge of a wooden spade). Bedding trenches, possibly for growing grapevines, have been identified at Waddesdon, and similar features were noted during excavations on the route of the Stoke Hammond bypass. Two pruning knives of a type used in viticulture were recovered from the large walled enclosure at Bancroft.

Evidence for grain storage is slight in Buckinghamshire. A possible granary at Bancroft has already been noted, though environmental evidence from the site pointed to short-term rather than long-term large-scale storage. A large mill-stone found near the later house indicated that some processing had taken place on site. Other evidence for grain processing in the Milton Keynes area is provided by ovens used for grain drying or malting. Though none were found at the Bancroft villa, examples have been found on native sites on the clays at Windmill Hill,[61] Shenley Road[62] and Heelands.[63] In contrast, excavations on the gravel terraces of the Ouzel valley at Fenny Lock and Caldecotte[64] – the closest known native settlements to *Magiovinium* – failed to provide evidence for large-scale food production, processing or storage. Specialised grain storage facilities are also lacking on Chiltern sites as a whole, with the exception of Gorhambury villa in Hertfordshire,[65] suggesting that grain from this area must have been fed rapidly into regional markets, principally *Verulamium*.

In the south of the county, the only significant evidence for cultivation comes from Dorney,[66] where analysis of pollen indicates an increase in cereal production and the presence of spelt wheat and corn cockle in the late first century. This is consistent with evidence from other Middle Thames sites, suggesting that large-scale cereal processing only began in this area during the Roman period. However, evidence obtained from dung beetle numbers suggests that, over time, increasing areas of land close to the Thames were given over to hay meadows, and that an increase in flooding may have reduced the area of cultivated land. A well-preserved first-century scythe blade was recovered from Dorney: perhaps this was used to harvest the crops identified in the pollen sequence.

Aerial photography on light-draining cultivated soils can often pick up evidence for Roman field systems, but is less effective in claylands and in the Chilterns generally. However, where extensive excavations have been carried out on these less photogenic soils, traces of narrow, rectilinear Roman fields have been revealed, for example at Weedon Hill, Pitstone, and Aston Clinton. At Broughton, Milton Keynes,[67] a rectilinear pattern of fields of various sizes dating from the mid-second century, was recorded on inferior agricultural land. It was typical of its class, with enclosures opening off a central trackway forming yards, closes, paddocks and arable fields for a nearby settlement.

There is little direct evidence for Roman field systems in the Chilterns, unless the small irregular fields recorded at Ashridge (Herts) prove to be of Roman date.[68] However, there are some interesting clues. One-way plough marks were found at Latimer and Gadebridge (Herts) villas, and a ploughshare recovered from *Verulamium* suggests longer narrower fields here, perhaps replacing the traditional square 'Celtic' fields in the Chiltern river valleys by the beginning of the second century (discussed in Branigan and Niblett 2003,56).

At the southern end of the county, field systems might be expected to show up on aerial photographs of the Thames gravels. However, with the exception of Hambleden and the Taplow/Dorney area,[69] they have not been recorded. This could be because there was no need for drainage ditches on the gravels. Excavations at Dorney have instead suggested a pattern of largely self-contained enclosures, where from the first century onwards a mix of arable and pastoral farming was undertaken, with little restriction on grazing the surrounding land. It may be that significant settlement shift takes place on the gravels in the late Roman period, although there is some evidence for a continuity of boundaries from the first to the third centuries at Lake End Road West, Dorney, and from the first to fourth centuries at All Souls Quarry, Wexham.

It can be assumed that the resources of the Ouse, the Thames and their tributaries would have been fully exploited for fish and fowl. However, apart from limited faunal remains direct evidence for boats or fish traps is lacking in Buckinghamshire, apart from a possible 'netting needle' recovered from Yewden that is similar to an example from Barton Court Farm, Oxfordshire.

It has been suggested that much of the scarp and dip slope of the Chilterns was under woodland during the Roman period, though at present there is insufficient evidence to confirm this. At the villa site at Mantles Green, Amersham, the evidence from charcoal was consistent with the picture of local mixed oak/alder/beech woodland being used as a source of firewood, with ash becoming more prevalent over time. The latter suggests the opening up of woodland, as ash is a more light-demanding species. In the north of the county at Bancroft and Wavendon Gate, possible coppice 'heels' were observed on preserved wood fragments cut into short, rod-like lengths, suggesting that they may have originated from coppiced or pollarded wood. The predominant species at Bancroft were willow/poplar, elder and hazel: tool marks were evident on examples of all these species. The data suggests that the larger woodland trees, such as oak, ash, elm and maple were grown away from the valley bottom, which had been largely cleared of woodland.

Ritual, Religion and Burial

Before the Conquest, it is likely that most Britons followed forms of religion based on the worship of the sun, moon and other natural forces, such deities having different names and attributes in different local tribes. One cult that was apparently more widespread at the time of the invasion was Druidism, which was concerned with the worship of Nature, placing importance in certain sacred plants and groves of trees. Druidism appears to have been a significant focus of opposition to the Romans, such that subduing the centre of the cult on Anglesey was probably one of the important objectives of the Conquest.

Roman religion also encompassed a range of deities, each with their own attributes, often related to natural forces. Rome was prepared to tolerate any religion in the Empire, as long as it allowed for the deity of the Emperor. The only exception to this was Christianity, which was persecuted until the fourth century, when Constantine I, who had previously worshipped *Sol* (the sun god), himself embraced Christianity.

Although it is likely that temples to Roman deities may have existed in *Magiovinium*, it is to the countryside we must look for the religious sites that were most important to the native population. Several possible temple/shrine sites have been identified in the county from finds and aerial photographs. The only excavated sites are the second century temple/mausoleum and adjacent circular stone shrine at Bancroft, the temple at Thornborough (Fig. 3.15),[70] the shrine at Wavendon Gate and a possible shrine at Yewden. As noted previously the Bancroft temple/mausoleum stood on the site of a former Iron Age farmstead on the hill above the later villa, suggesting some sort of ancestral connection. It had the typical concentric-square plan of a so-called Romano-Celtic temple, but was unusual in that it contained a central *cella* (burial vault). Sufficient decorated architectural stonework survived to permit a detailed reconstruction of the building. The Thornborough temple was beside a ford over the river Twin near Buckingham and close to two Roman barrows that survive today (Fig. 3.15). Its plan was similar to the Bancroft temple/mausoleum, but without the central *cella*. Built in the late third century, it remained in use until the early fifth century (Fig. 3.16 and 3.17). An excavated building close to the temple had beneath its floor a horse's head encircled with oyster shells, with a pebble placed on top, presumably some sort of ritual deposit.

FIGURE 3.15
Top: In the foreground the two large Thornborough burial mounds near the crossing of the River Twin. One mound, excavated in 1839 by the Duke of Buckingham, contained a cremation burial within a glass bottle, also other bottles, ceramic, and bronze vessels and a lamp.
Bottom: plan of Roman Thornborough.
The Roman ford was replaced by a medieval bridge which still survives to the north. The new road constructed in 1972–3 is on the site of the Roman ford.

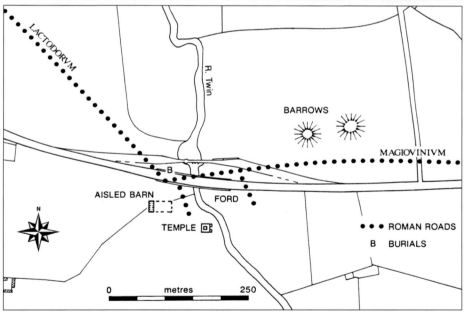

FIGURE 3.16
Reconstruction of the Romano-Celtic temple at Thornborough.

FIGURE 3.17
Two cremation burials from Thornborough. One includes both a ribbed glass bowl and glass jar, the other includes four samian dishes.

FIGURE 3.18
Wheel-shaped object, carved in oak and reconstruction, from Wavendon Gate. It is likely that this represents the solar wheel, associated with the Celtic sun god Taranis. The mortise and peg joint on its lower part suggests that it was fastened to a pole, or the end of a building.

Possible temples have been identified at Tingewick, Moneybury Hill, Pitstone,[71] Manor Farm, Bourton,[72] Creslow,[73] and at the Yewden villa. The octagonal building next to the fourth century house and garden at Bancroft has also been interpreted as a shrine. A nearby shrine may also be suggested by the discovery of several bronze bowls and two probable bronze sceptre heads at Mantles Green, Amersham (Fig. 3.18).[74] A hoard of pewter plates, cups and bowls found at Fleet Marston[75] may also have had religious significance, and could also indicate a shrine or temple in the vicinity (Fig. 3.5).

Investigation of a large pit at Wavendon Gate recovered a remarkable wooden 'solar wheel' and a hoard of at least four bronze wheel models, strongly suggesting a relationship with the cult of the Celtic thunder god *Taranis*, who can be equated with the Roman sky-god Jupiter (Fig. 3.19). A posthole was found adjacent to the pit where the wooden wheel motif was recovered, and it has been suggested that the solar wheel was affixed to a post. A late Iron Age wheel-headed pin also discovered at the site suggests that a solar cult commenced here before the Roman period.

Several other cult items have been recovered from Buckinghamshire sites; some can be assigned to the worship of particular deities, while others are more enigmatic. The most commonly represented cult is that of Mercury; for example, a Roman well at Emberton[76] contained a native carving of the god (Fig. 3.19), and a bronze Mercury figurine was discovered in nearby Olney.[77] A marble cockerel, probably part of a Mercury statuette, and a bronze cockerel brooch, were found at Bancroft (Fig. 3.19).[78] Metal detecting on the Fenny Stratford bypass near *Magiovinium* recovered a bronze figure of a ram carrying moneybags, also associated with Mercury (Fig. 3.19).[79] A number of other deities are also represented in finds from the county, most notably a bronze figurine of Isis from near the Thornborough temple, pointing to an exotic affinity here to a goddess whose popularity in Roman Britain is normally associated with urban communities.[80] A bronze furniture fitting from the villa at Rye Mead, High Wycombe, includes a bust of Minerva,[81] and a bronze finger ring showing Hercules comes from the Mantles Green villa.[82] In contrast, finds related to Christianity in the Roman period are rare; the only item recovered to date is a silver ring with a dove motif from the mausoleum site at Bancroft.

Other more enigmatic 'ritual' objects have been recovered from various sites. Groups of miniature spearheads were found in the circular shrine at Bancroft, and also at Yewden. From Yewden also came a model axe, part of a pipeclay *Dea Nutrix* (a figurine of a mother feeding a baby at each breast) and a jade scarab (Fig. 3.20).[83] Model axes and votive plaques have also been recovered from the possible shrine at Manor Farm, Bourton. Perhaps the strangest cult object is the

FIGURE 3.19
The model of a cockerel from Bancroft (carved from Carrara marble from Italy) was part of a larger group probably associated with the god Mercury. On the right a cast copper-alloy head (36mm high) from Amersham found with five copper-alloy bowls and a dish; a second head was found nearby. It may be from a 'sceptre' used in religious ceremonies or from furniture. Its features are similar to images of Jupiter but it could represent a similar local deity. Below, a copper-alloy ram figurine found by a metal detectorist near Magiovinium. Along with the cockerel and the tortoise, the ram, often carrying money bags, was associated with the god Mercury. To the right a limestone relief carving also of Mercury, possibly native work, from a Roman well at Emberton.

worn limestone carving of a sphinx found at Windmill Hill, Bletchley. This is reminiscent of the finely carved stone sphinx from Colchester, recovered from an avenue of tombs associated with wealthy soldiers based in the city. A bronze *patera* (handled dish) found near Olney is also unusual: manufactured in Campania, Italy, in the first century, it may have been used for libations in some form of religious practice.[84] A model bronze scythe from Walton Court, Aylesbury, may also have had a ritual function.

FIGURE 3.20
A carved stone model of an Egyptian scarab found adjacent to the main building of the Hambleden villa. Probably dating to c.800–400 BC, this piece may have been acquired by the villa's owner as a curio.

The significance of place is an important element in both native and Roman religious traditions. In the north of the county, the use of the site of the late Bronze Age and Iron Age farmsteads at Bancroft for burials throughout the Roman period, and the establishment there of the temple/mausoleum and subsequent shrine, is probably the most striking evidence for continued veneration of a site. At Thornborough two large Roman burial mounds[85] are close to the later temple and ford. The mounds were excavated in 1839; one contained a burial group comprising a green glass jug, a bronze lamp and bronze jugs. The burials within both mounds were presumably of high-status individuals and the rite follow a similar tradition to that seen in first to second-century Essex, also a part of Catuvellaunian territory. One might speculate on whether it was the early significance of the landscape here or of the burial mounds that led to the foundation of the nearby Thornborough temple site in the fourth century. Unexcavated mounds at Sherington[86] and Bury Fields,[87] Newport Pagnell, may contain similar high-status burials.

The use of the Chilterns scarp as a vantage point for ceremonial and burial practices is hinted at by a burial within a casket at Batt Hall, Radnage (Fig. 3.21).[88] At Whiteleaf Hill, Princes Risborough,[89] there is also evidence for re-use of the Neolithic barrow; smashed Roman pottery was placed in natural hollows and a bronze votive leaf was also found here. At Wards Coombe, Ivinghoe[90] the placing of a late first-century cremation within an early Iron Age circular enclosure on the Chiltern scarp also suggests the continued ritual resonance of this elevated landscape setting.

During the late pre-Roman Iron Age and the early Roman period the most common burial rite was cremation. One of the earliest cremation cemeteries in Buckinghamshire was adjacent to the later temple/mausoleum at Bancroft; here eighteen cremations were found with a wide range of grave goods and food offerings with dates spanning the first century AD (Fig. 3.11). A number of native occupation sites in the Milton Keynes area also have cemeteries associated with them. At Wavendon Gate a more dispersed cemetery containing twelve cremations was dated to the late first and second centuries. Other cremation cemeteries have been found at Monkston Park,[91] at Manor Farm, Broughton,[92] and at Willen Quarry.[93] Moving further afield, a small first to second-century

FIGURE 3.21
Blue and white ribbed glass bowl found in 1923 with a glass flagon at Radnage in the Chilterns. Nine samian vessels accompanied the find and the remains of a casket containing cremated bone. An unexpectedly rich second-century AD burial.

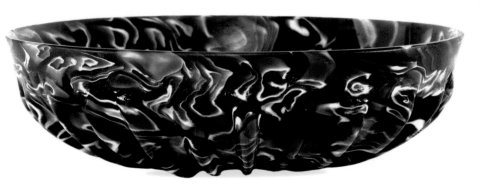

cremation cemetery was found at Thornborough; here only a portion of the cremated bone was used in the burial ceremony.[94] Two cremations at Great Brickhill and three at Billings Field, Aylesbury, may have been part of larger cemeteries.[95] Excavations along the route of the Stoke Hammond bypass revealed a small number of urned cremations, dated to the late second to early third centuries, placed in shallow pits within a Late Iron Age enclosure.

Variations in grave-goods between cemeteries provide some insight into differentials between more and less 'Romanised' settlements. Excavations on a Roman native site at Willen Quarry, south of Newport Pagnell, revealed a 'low-status' cemetery containing about thirty cremations,

FIGURE 3.22
An unusual Roman cremation rite in a cemetery at Denham. The body was burnt over or within the grave. The cremated bone can be seen and burning around the grave.

most of which had been buried with no accompanying pottery or personal items. In contrast, investigation of the Romanised farmstead at nearby Manor Farm, Broughton, revealed a higher-status cremation cemetery, characterised by the presence of a wide range of pottery vessels, including imported samian ware, and jewellery accompanying the burials.

Of particular note is a cemetery of eight cremations dated to at least *c.*AD 325, excavated at The Lea, Denham.[96] These were of a regionally rare type

FIGURE 3.23
A second century AD burial deposit accompanying a cremation burial found in 1855 at Weston Turville. Parts of four bottles, three samian dishes, other pots, two enamelled brooches and a bone needle (here placed in one of the dishes) were also found. The cremated remains seem to have been in a wooden casket.

FIGURE 3.24
Early second-century casket burial from Wellwick Farm, Wendover. Eight pottery vessels, presumably containing food offerings, along with a lamp, two glass vessels and an adze-hammer, accompanied a cremation burial. The presence of nails at the corners of the grave revealed that the burial had been contained in a box about 0.6m (2') square.

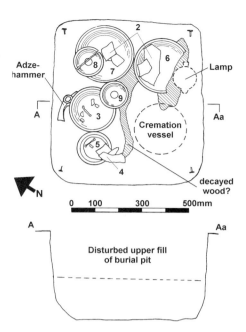

known as *Bustum* burials, the funeral pyre being constructed over a grave-shaped pit, and the burnt remains of the body, along with any offerings, fell directly into it (Fig 3.22). Finds from this site included fragments of bronze and ivory bracelets and glass, gold and jet beads.

A tradition of wooden box or casket burial is not uncommon in Buckinghamshire. At Thornborough, a samian dish and a box about 300mm square accompanied a late first-century urned cremation. In 1855, a cremation found at Weston Turville[97] dated to *c.*AD 150 was accompanied by four glass bottles, three samian dishes and other pots, two enamelled brooches a bone pin, mirror fragments and pieces of iron, and the bindings of a wooden box (Fig. 3.23).

Another cremation, dated by association to *c.*AD 135–155, was excavated at Wellwick Farm, Wendover.[98] This was probably contained within a two-handled flagon, and was accompanied by eight ceramic vessels, two glass vessels, a lamp and an adze-hammer, the latter unusual and perhaps suggesting that the deceased's profession involved woodworking. All of these objects had been placed with food offerings in a box or casket and buried in a shallow pit (Fig. 3.24). A slightly wealthier box-burial was found in the early nineteenth century on a promontory overlooking the scarp slope at Batt Farm, Radnage, as previously noted. Here the cremation was deposited within a wooden casket with iron straps and bronze rings, and was accompanied by a fine blue and white marbled-glass bowl, a flagon and nine samian dishes (Fig. 3.21).

Cremation finally fell out of favour by the late third century, when inhumation became the predominant burial rite. No large inhumation cemeteries have been excavated in the county: the biggest to date, thirteen burials of fourth-century date, was recorded at West Wycombe.[99] At Bancroft, the floor of the burial vault in the temple/mausoleum held impressions suggesting that it had once contained two coffins or sarcophagi, but no trace of the burials or their containers remained. Excavations here also revealed a single late third to early fourth-century inhumation in a wooden coffin, and a group of eight late fourth-century burials, all adjacent to the fourth-century shrine. The later graves had been roughly lined with stone which included architectural fragments from the preceding temple/mausoleum that had been demolished by this time. At *Magiovinium*, several inhumations have been recorded between the town and the crossing of the Ouzel, notably close to the river at the 'Bathing Station' site.[100] More recent excavations also revealed an inhumation cemetery to the east of the town. Finally, a small inhumation cemetery bounded by a ditch was recorded at Bledlow-cum-Saunderton.[101]

In addition to the above, a number of less common burial customs have been observed. At Gayhurst Quarry, a possible late Roman decapitation burial that had been interred in a Bronze Age barrow could relate to the Celtic cult of the head.[102] A stone cist burial has been examined near North Marston,[103] and a lead coffin from Fleet Marston indicates a burial there. Two other lead coffins have been recorded from the south of the county at Bourne End.

Crafts and Industries

As noted previously, the economy of Roman Buckinghamshire appears to have been based on an unexceptional pattern of mixed agriculture and localised small-scale industry, operated from a range of small to large villas and farmsteads. Buckinghamshire's settlements formed part of the hinterland of a number of regional towns and the road network linked them with markets at *Durocobrivae* (Dunstable), *Magiovinium*, Alchester, *Lactodorum* and Dorchester-on-Thames, and perhaps in the south of the county along the Thames river corridor to *Pontes* (Staines) and *Londinium*.

Small-scale brewing is evident on a few sites. Excavations at Bancroft revealed evidence of malting from a 'corn drier', and the crop remains were associated with an enclosure possibly used for growing them. Ovens found at Sarratt on the Bucks/Herts border could have been used to parch spelt wheat before threshing, or they could have been used in preparing barley for beer making.[104] Drying ovens have been found on several other sites, for example Yewden, Shenley Road and Windmill Hill, Bletchley, and Heelands. At Weedon Hill,[105] a possible barley maltings was identified, adjacent to a low-status farming settlement. This included a probable oven for drying malt, adjacent to a stone-lined pit that may have been used for steeping the malt until it germinated.

Although no major pottery or tile production centres are known in Buckinghamshire, there were a number of localised centres in the Ouse valley, in the Chilterns, and in the south of the county. In the Ouse valley, two small kilns at Caldecotte produced coarse wares vessels that were probably destined for the newly-established market at *Magiovinium*. It is likely that two mid first-century kilns at nearby Wavendon Gate supplied the same market. An important local Roman ware, the so-called 'soft pink grogged' pottery, has been found in significant amounts at Towcester, and on sites in Milton Keynes. Quantities of this ware have been recovered from two possible kiln sites at Stowe, near the Alchester-Towcester road, making it a strong candidate to be the source of this product.[106] Further westwards up the Ouse valley, four pottery kilns were recorded at Abbey House Farm, Biddlesden.[107] In the Chilterns, pottery production was well established during the second century in kilns at Fulmer (Fig. 3.25),[108] Hedgerley,[109] and Gerrards Cross.[110] In the south of the county, tile wasters, along with possible ovens or kilns, were noted at Dorney.[111] Elsewhere, kilns have been suggested at Stone and perhaps Taplow, but the evidence for these is inconclusive.

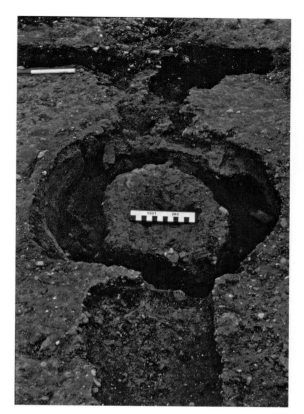

FIGURE 3.25
The base of a second-century pottery kiln at Fulmer excavated in 1967; one of a number of kilns found in the Fulmer/Hedgerley/ Gerrards Cross area, sited to make use of local sources of clay and wood.

Woodland survey in the Chilterns is increasingly detecting slag which may in time demonstrate a substantial iron smelting industry in this area, as suggested by the two tons of iron slag recovered from the settlement at Cow Roast, Hertfordshire.[112] At Common Wood, Penn,[113] late first to early third-century pottery was associated with an earthwork enclosure from which quantities of iron-smelting tap slag and fragments of furnace were recovered, although iron does not appear to have been worked on site. Trial-trench evaluation near Lawn Farm, Grendon Underwood,[114] produced large quantities of tap slag and furnace slag, and a fragment of furnace rim. The quantity of slag and the absence of hammer scale (which would indicate smithing) from this site could suggest that commercial smelting was being undertaken here.

Evidence for smithing (the working of prepared iron into implements, etc) has been recovered from *Magiovinium*, and the villas at Bancroft, Stanton Low, Mantles Green and Great Missenden.[115] A hearth and crucible fragments found at Caldecotte, Milton Keynes, suggest a small-scale bronze-working industry here, probably producing a variety of toilet instruments. At Yewden villa, slag and broken crucibles also suggest bronze smelting.

Roman Lifestyle

One of the principal features that distinguished Roman culture from that of the native British at the time of the Conquest was its materialism. Perhaps not unsurprisingly, the native population apparently embraced this aspect of Roman life quite rapidly. The commonest evidence of this materialism is provided by the wide range of pottery, locally-produced and imported, recovered from Buckinghamshire sites (Fig. 3.26), and by the widespread use of coinage.

Pieces of Roman pottery generally survive very well in the soil and are the commonest find on Roman sites. They are of great value, both for dating and for studying trading patterns. A detailed study has been made of the pottery from sites in the Milton Keynes area.[116] The general pattern of pottery supply here begins between the mid to late first and mid second centuries with reliance on locally-made coarse wares from Harrold in Bedfordshire, supplemented by pottery from kilns in the *Verulamium* region, from Oxford, and the Upper Nene valley. Foreign imports include fine wares from the Rhineland, a distinctive red pottery known as samian, imported from central Gaul, and amphorae from Seville and Cordoba in Spain, which would have originally contained olive oil, wine or fish paste. In the late second to early third centuries, existing local sources are supplemented by wares from the Lower Nene valley, the

FIGURE 3.26
Roman pottery found
in Buckinghamshire;
clockwise from top
left found at: Terrick,
Haversham, Hambleden,
Saunderton, Hambleden,
Tingewick, and
Hambleden.

Mancetter/Hartshill kilns in Warwickshire, from Much Hadham in Hertford-shire, and by so-called 'black-burnished' wares made in Dorset. In this period samian ware from east Gaul also begins to appear among the imports. In the later third century Much Hadham ware disappears from north Buckinghamshire sites, as do samian and the Spanish amphorae. From the late third century onwards, foreign imports disappear altogether and local wares from Harrold, the Nene valley, Oxfordshire and Warwickshire once again predominate. Much Hadham wares reappear, along with the products of kilns in the Alice Holt/Farnham area of Surrey and Swanpool in Lincolnshire.

There has been no systematic study of pottery found in the centre of the county, but some major excavation reports such as Bierton,[117] Mantles Green and Latimer provide clues. A substantial range of vessels was recovered at Bierton. Here, pottery from the *Verulamium* kilns predominated, and the market at *Verulamium* is likely to have been the local distribution point also for 'black-burnished' from Dorset and for Much Hadham and Colchester wares. Other important sources of supply included the Nene Valley, Oxfordshire and local 'south east Midlands' kilns. Local wares from the Chilterns kilns at Fulmer and Hedgerley were also present. The *Verulamium* area itself was a key supplier until its products declined in *c*.AD 200, and were replaced by wares such as those from the Nene Valley and Oxfordshire.

Excavations at All Souls Quarry, Wexham, have produced a useful picture of pottery supply patterns at the southern end of the county. Here, pottery from Highgate Wood and north London and handmade jars and storage vessels, probably from the Colne valley area, dominated the mid first-century assemblage. Small amounts of Silchester-type wares and Alice Holt/Surrey wares point to trading links with *Calleva* (Silchester), south of the Thames. By the end of the first century, supply was dominated by greyware products from the local Chiltern kilns at Fulmer, Hedgerley and Gerrards Cross, which developed as suppliers from *c*.AD 60. The Chiltern kilns continued to dominate the local market, supplemented by imports from *Verulamium*, London and Gaul, until the mid third century, when their products were replaced by pottery from the Alice Holt/Farnham and Oxfordshire industries.

Because of its fragility, pottery is difficult and costly to transport. The only methods of transport available would have been pack animals or carts: in both cases, pottery would presumably have been packed in straw in crates, which would have limited the amount that could be transported. Even with the Roman road system the likelihood of breakage would be high, and it is not surprising that most of the pottery found in Buckinghamshire had travelled no more than about 40 miles from its place of manufacture. This remained the position until the advent of the canal system in the late eighteenth century.

Coinage first appears in Britain in the late Iron Age in small quantities, but its use appears to have been limited, and it was only with the coming of the Romans that a true cash economy was established. During the Roman period, the issue of coinage was from licensed mints throughout the Empire, tightly controlled by the imperial court. As their first priority was payment of the army, small denomination coinage was often in short supply, and coins were produced unofficially to meet local demand, in much the same way as trade tokens were produced from the seventeenth to nineteenth centuries.

Excavated sites across the county have produced a significant number of Roman coins (Fig 3.28). Probably the largest collection comes from Bancroft, where excavations and controlled metal detecting across the villa and temple/mausoleum sites produced nearly 1,500. They range in date from late Iron Age (Catuvellaunian and Trinovantian issues and a single Durotrigan bronze stater) to late fourth-century bronzes of the emperor Theodosius. The assemblage includes two hoards, one of 75 bronze coins, the other of 16, both deposited in *c*.AD 340–350. At *Magiovinium,* interventions over many years including chance finds, metal detecting and excavations have recovered several thousand coins. These too span the whole Roman period, and also include three Republican issues, predating the Conquest. At least two hoards are recorded here: 251 fourth-century bronzes, and 296 second-century *denarii*. Excavations at other sites in north Buckinghamshire have produced more modest assemblages, for example Wavendon Gate (112) and Fenny Lock (239). Of particular interest from the *Magiovinium* area was the discovery by a detectorist of a third-century coin-manufacturing hoard; three small pots contained bronze pellets and coin blanks, accompanied by a set of iron dies for stamping coins (Fig. 3.27).[118]

An important hoard of fourth-century date found at Great Horwood in 1872, although lacking coins, may be mentioned here. A ploughed-up silver beaker contained a brooch, pin and ring together with five spoons, one of which was inscribed with the name *Veneria*, perhaps a local lady of some wealth (Fig. 3.29).[119]

FIGURE 3.27
Coin manufacturing hoard from Magiovinium, dated to the third century. The central vessel contains pellets of copper-alloy rod. These were melted and poured into circular moulds, to produce blanks, as in the right-hand jar. The blanks were then hammered out to coin size, as in the left-hand vessel, probably using the iron dies in the foreground, before having the two faces of the coin struck on them.

FIGURE 3.28
Gold solidus of Constantine I, minted in Heraclea (in modern Turkey), between AD326–330. Its reverse shows Constantine surrounded by prisoners: the inscription VICTOR OMNIVM GENTIVM translates as 'Victory over all peoples'. Roman rulers commonly used coinage as a means of transmitting propaganda. Coins of this value were rare. From the Bancroft villa.

At the south end of the county, excavations at Yewden produced over 800 coins, ranging in date from first-century Claudian coins to those of Arcadius (AD 383–408), and include a hoard of 294 Constantinian bronze issues. A hoard of 30 fourth-century coins has also been recovered here. At Chalfont St Peter, a substantial collection of 6,685 late third-century coins associated with a group of three pots was found by metal detectorists.[120] Study of the assemblage suggested that a selective process was followed during hoarding, perhaps relating to silver content. Three phases of deposition were suggested within a very close time span. Other notable finds include hoards found by detectorists at Great Missenden and Prestwood.[121] A late fourth-century hoard was found near Mantles Green, while thirty coins dated to 275–285 came from Pitstone. These hoards point to the considerable private wealth of the late Roman Chiltern elite. There has been much debate over the reason for depositing hoards; they may have been hidden because of fear of conflict, or they may be the proceeds of theft. Burying hoards may have also been a response to changes in the official monetary system.

In addition to pottery and coins, the impact of Roman lifestyle can be seen in almost all aspects of the archaeology of this period in Buckinghamshire. Evidence suggests that this new material culture was adopted across the social spectrum. At the top end it is exemplified by villas, which were equipped with the contemporary 'must have' fixtures and fittings: glazed windows, underfloor heating, bath suites, elaborately painted walls and ceilings, and mosaic pavements. There is evidence to suggest that a number of workshops grew up across Britain, supplying designs for pavements and craftsmen to lay them. For example, the pavements at Bancroft have been attributed to a workshop based in *Corinium* (Cirencester), over 70 miles from the villa (Fig. 3.30). It seems likely that similar craft workshops provided skilled tradesmen to construct heating systems and bath suites, and to decorate walls and ceilings, and even to design the houses and subsequent extensions to them.

Roman material culture also pervades sites of lesser status to villas. For example, Roman fine table wares, such as samian, are routinely found on a broad spread of settlement types in the county. Personal items such as buckles, brooches, manicure sets and hair pins, are likewise found on a range of settlement and burial sites. Excavation and chance discoveries have recorded a wealth of vessels, tools and other objects, too numerous to detail here, demonstrating the material wealth and complexity of Roman life. Examples from the north of the county include an iron-bound chest from Bancroft, a polychrome glass beaker from Holne Chase, a shale table leg from Foscott villa,[122] and an iron tumbler lock slide with an unusual bronze handle in the form of a lion from Weston Underwood.[123] Noteworthy finds from elsewhere in the county include the side of a cart or 'greedy-board' from Eton Rowing Lake,[124] a number of unusual conical fired clay objects (approximately 5cm in height) found in burial pits at The Lea, Denham,[125] and a collection of six late Roman bronze finger rings from the Amersham area, depicting human and animal figures which illustrate changing fashions in the fourth century.[126]

FIGURE 3.29
A fourth-century silver beaker and spoon found with other silver items in Great Horwood in 1872. The bowl of the spoon is inscribed Veneria Vivas – 'Veneria, long life to you'; Veneria could have been a local lady.

FIGURE 3.30
Fragments of fourth-century mosaic floors found at Bancroft villa. From their designs, it is likely that both pavements were laid by craftsmen from Corinium (Cirencester).

The end of Romanised Britain

No attempt has been made in this chapter to set the county within the history of the Roman empire as a whole; moreover, Buckinghamshire would certainly be a poor place to commence such an undertaking, since apart from the place name *Magiovinium* and a few personal names scratched on pots, there are no literary references of any kind to the area, nor do any formal monumental inscriptions survive. Nevertheless, the archaeological evidence clearly shows that a visitor to the area in the third and fourth centuries from, for example, Gaul or Germania, would undoubtedly have felt quite comfortable here, recognising many familiar aspects of Romanised life. However, during these same centuries, substantial changes were taking place within the Roman empire itself, caused by many factors, not least of which was pressure on its frontiers from peoples outside whom the Roman world considered barbarians. By the late fourth and early fifth century, much of what once was Roman Britain was in the process of becoming less a part of the empire and more an island fortress. The ultimate result was more or less complete detachment from most Roman culture during the fifth century, and the establishment of a new order. Some of these dramatic changes are reflected in the archaeological record, for example the insertion of a simple hearth into the middle of a fine mosaic floor at the Bancroft villa. The immediate 'post-Roman' period is not easy to interpret, but the limited evidence is discussed more fully in the next chapter.

Chapter 4

Saxon Buckinghamshire (AD 410–1066)

Michael Farley

The transformation from a land, whose inhabitants mainly spoke a language similar to Welsh or Gallic, to one where a few centuries later they spoke mainly English, is remarkable. This dramatic linguistic change is also reflected in the archaeology and history of the piece of land which in the tenth or early eleventh century AD become known as 'Buckinghamshire'. For the first three centuries after the Roman period there are almost no written records relating to the area of the later county and it is finds and archaeological investigation that have provided almost all of the evidence; in later centuries many more sources of information become available.

Over the last thirty years most archaeological investigation has taken place just prior to development, with the result that much more is known about the Saxon period in the Milton Keynes area for example, than in the Chilterns where development is restricted. Nevertheless there have been striking discoveries across the county as a whole (Fig. 4.1).

In the Saxon period, like the Roman period before and the succeeding medieval centuries, there were no large towns in Buckinghamshire; its character was almost entirely rural. The agricultural value and character of the landscape was, then as now, influenced by the county's varied underlying geology and soil types, so its landscape would never have looked uniform.

For convenience this chapter is broadly divided into periods, none of which would have been recognised by the inhabitants at the time although they would have been aware of some of the dramatic changes which took place within each.

Turbulent Times: AD 410 to about AD 500

For over 350 years Britain was a Roman 'colony' and as in British colonies of the Victorian period, the subjected inhabitants would have readily accepted some aspects of the invader's lifestyle but rejected others. By AD 410 (a much-discussed date marking the formal abandonment of the Roman defence of Britain), first-hand experience of the Roman lifestyle would have ensured the existence of a class of people with an interest in maintaining the status quo, some of whom would have emerged as leaders in the turbulent times which followed. Despite such leadership, within a few decades some of the sea-borne

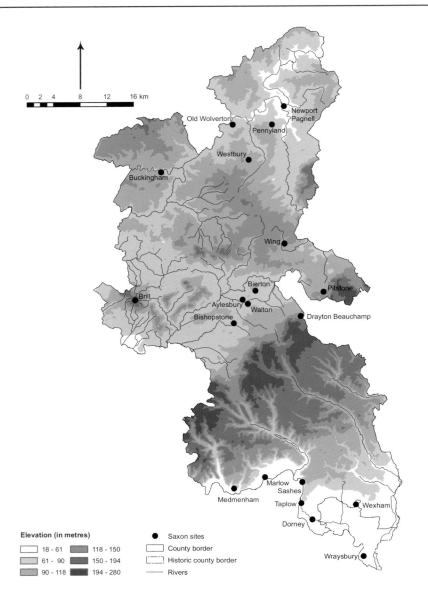

FIGURE 4.1
Location of some of the
Saxon sites discussed in
this chapter.

raiders (for convenience here called 'Saxons') who originated mainly in what is
now northern Germany and Denmark and who for at least a century had posed
a threat to Britain, had become settlers. These settlers and their warrior leaders
were in a relatively short time to replace almost all trace of Roman culture in
England with a life style not dissimilar to that which existed in these islands
before the arrival of Roman forces. There is plenty of documentary evidence
and limited archaeological evidence (although not yet from Buckinghamshire)
of strong opposition to the incomers, some of it focussed on the old Iron Age hillforts. The process of 'conquest' ultimately proved unstoppable although it was
not completed in England for several centuries.

The Germanic peoples were not literate although some of the inhabitants of
Britain certainly were, and one result of the incursion is that literacy seems to

have disappeared rapidly in much of what was later to become 'England', surviving only in ecclesiastical centres in the north and west of England, Wales, and in what eventually became Scotland. Locally, literacy may have continued for a period, for example in important urban centres such as St Albans (Verulamium) but written descriptions of events are inevitably sparse and it is not until an *Anglo-Saxon Chronicle*[1] entry of about AD 571 which refers to Aylesbury, that any Buckinghamshire place or event gets a mention (Fig. 4.2). It is another two hundred years before there is another written reference to a place or person in the county.

Following the incursions a new social structure emerged. The *Anglo-Saxon Chronicle* compiled centuries after this early period, together with other documentary evidence, describes the rise of kingdoms and the presence among the incomers of small but powerful warrior-led groups, frequently in competition, whose leaders claimed descent from earlier kings or mythological founder-figures such as Woden. Although these 'Saxons' are frequently recorded fighting 'Britons', and there was certainly a considerable degree of subjugation and slave-taking (the Old English word for Briton later could also mean 'slave'), it is likely that in practice there would have been considerable contact through intermarriage, alliances, and probably trade or barter. The only way in which this contact can be clearly demonstrated in Buckinghamshire is through a few names such as the River Thame, which is in origin Celtic,[2] or Brill which includes the element *Bre,* Celtic for hill.[3] These local names can only have been passed on by word of mouth. The extent of integration between the incomers and the local population continues to be a contentious issue but at its most local level it is obviously important; for example did fields and boundaries of the Roman period continue to be maintained, even if under different ownership?

In discussing these issues the reader should be warned that although archaeologists commonly use the term 'Saxon' for all of the finds and sites of the period, this does not imply that all 'Britons' were wiped out, or had flown. In practice a degree of contact may have led to utilisation or even manufacture of 'Saxon' material by the existing population and, for whatever reason, there has been a failure by archaeologists in southern England to isolate and identify many artefacts which can be reliably identified as specifically 'British'.[4]

The substantial transformation brought about by the incomers can be clearly seen in the abrupt disappearance of features common in the Roman period such as coinage, wheel-thrown pottery, and the use of window glass and mortar in buildings. By the beginning of the fifth century the old villas, many of which had a long history, had ceased to be repaired and the county's most significant town, Magiovinium near Bletchley, had apparently fallen into disuse, as had the only known Buckinghamshire temple at Thornborough. Many lesser settlements had either changed their character or had been abandoned. The disruptive effects of the conquest on internal trade and industry, the collapse of the monetary system and the probable interruption to supplies from across the Channel, obviously had a major effect. The impact of the new regime can be seen also in the arrival of unfamiliar kinds of structures and artefacts. Although many of these objects and structures can only be loosely dated, a few belong to the transitional period of the later fourth- later fifth century AD, such as the belt buckle plate found at

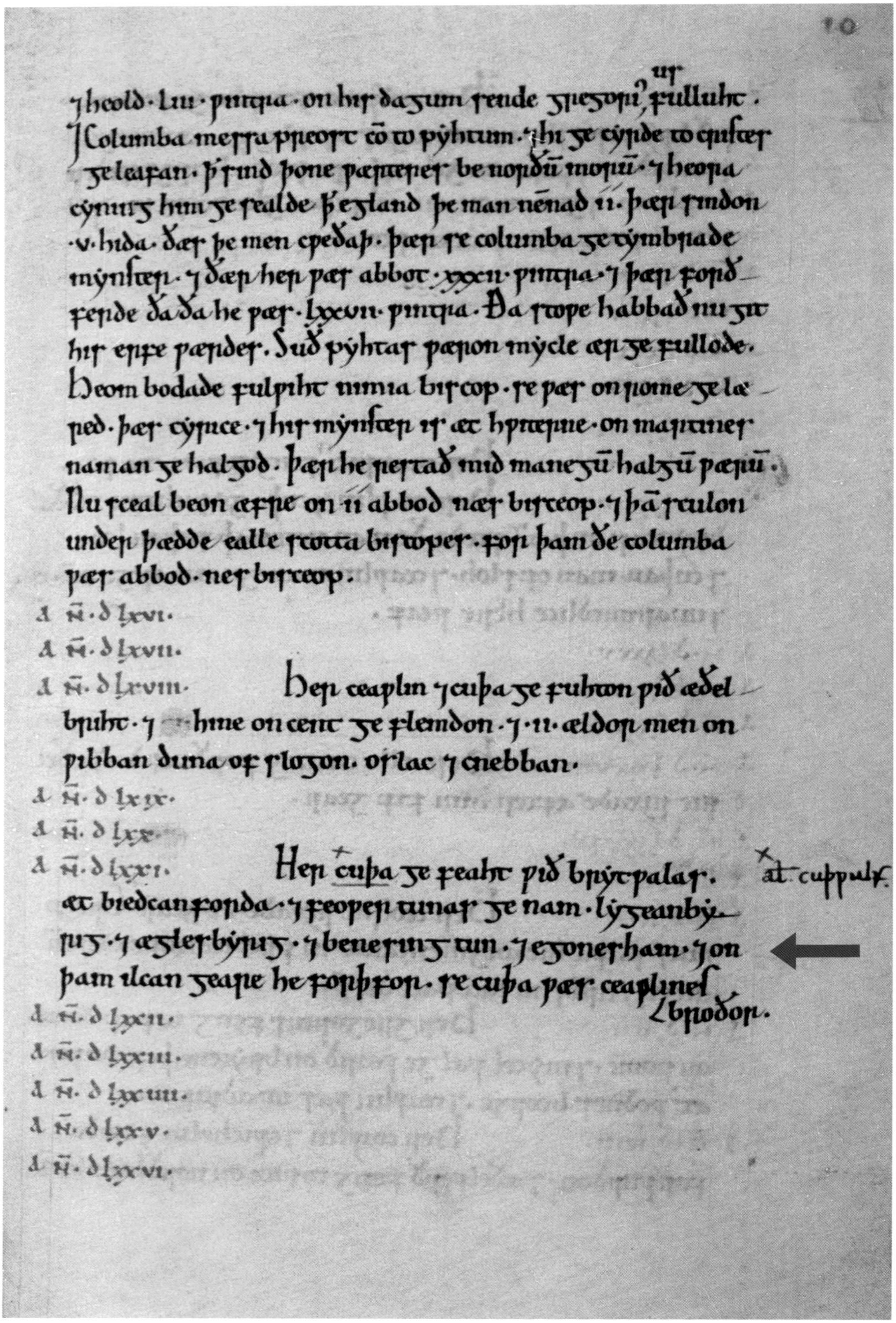

FIGURE 4.2
A page from the
Anglo-Saxon
Chronicle written in
Old English. The
arrow indicates the
reference to
Aylesbury in
AD 571.

FIGURE 4.3
Fifth century
belt-plate from
Bishopstone. Note
the small animals
around the edge;
the style is Late
Roman.

Bishopstone (Fig. 4.3) and some decorated handmade pottery from Walton near Aylesbury.[5]

There are occasional hints of some kind of continuity of site use. For instance, although coins found at the town of Magiovinium all date before AD 400, radio-carbon dates on burials just outside the town[6] allow the cemetery to have remained in use into the fifth century and elsewhere in the town there is evidence for secondary reuse of some buildings – presumably in decay – for burial. In a few counties some burials can be seen by their associations to be Christian and this leads on to the difficult question as to how far Christianity had taken hold among the British population during the later centuries of Roman rule. No arte-facts decorated with Christian symbols have yet been found in Buckinghamshire. Bede in his *Ecclesiastical History of the English People* describes Christian activity continuing at neighbouring St Albans into the mid-fifth century but it is probable, that in this outpost of the Roman Empire, Christianity was never as deeply rooted among the rural inhabitants in the late Roman period as it was in neighbouring Gaul.

Evidence for continuing activity on villa sites in Buckinghamshire into the fifth century is very limited. Sherds from Saxon-style pots, although not closely dated, have been found at the Bancroft villa Milton Keynes, and a small Saxon building was constructed close to the villa's outlying mausoleum,[7] but this is slight evidence when compared with the extensive area examined by excavation here. At Bierton early Saxon material was found very close to a villa but no structures, although the area examined was quite small.[8] At Latimer villa evidence of a late Roman or post-Roman building made from paired trunks of a split tree (crucks) has been claimed,[9] but this interpretation has not received widespread support. Close to the villa on the Rye at High Wycombe is an undated inhumation cemetery which could possibly be of this transitional phase. At the substantial villa estate at Hambleden the latest datable evidence are four coins of Arcadius (AD 383–408).[10]

The question of continuity is a little different in relation to rural settlements of lesser status than villas. There are several instances where there is at least close proximity between Roman and Saxon sites (bearing in mind the earlier caveat about distinguishing the groups ethnically). Walton, near Aylesbury is one interesting example which will be discussed later. Here there is evidence for Roman (including late Roman) activity, early Saxon occupation and a cemetery, and mid and late Saxon occupation which was succeeded by a hamlet that survives today as a distinct element of the modern Aylesbury. Although continuity of occupation is difficult to prove, this is one good candidate.[11]

A second important example is at Old Wolverton, situated between the present-day Wolverton and Stony Stratford. Several episodes of excavation, some too recent to have been fully published, are unravelling the history of this interesting place. Here there are the remains of village earthworks, probably medieval, together with a church and a motte (an earthwork castle). A short distance to the south is extensive Roman occupation, traces of early Saxon houses and a cemetery, a mid-Saxon enclosure and late Saxon occupation including buildings.[12] The whole suggests longstanding although shifting settlement in the area.

Prior to construction of the Aston Clinton bypass, excavations on the Lower Icknield Way near the Buckland/ Drayton Beauchamp parish boundary, exposed an Iron Age enclosure and land divisions flanking a trackway noted in an earlier chapter.[13] Some of these early ditches had been recut in the Roman period indicating their continuing value. Other Roman features were also present here including waterholes, and finds which indicated a nearby building. There was slight evidence for use of the site in the fifth-sixth centuries, and as at Wolverton and Walton, an early Saxon cemetery was discovered not far away, here on higher ground. A close relationship between cemeteries and settlements of early Saxon date has been noted elsewhere in Buckinghamshire and it seems that most early Saxon communities had their own nearby burial place.

At present all of the sites with firm indications of continuity (with the exception of Wraysbury, see on) are north of the Chilterns and to date what little evidence of Roman-Saxon continuity there is from the Chilterns comes from the presence of cemeteries, whose existence indicate nearby settlements. However, as noted previously, absence of evidence for early settlement in the Chilterns is most unlikely to reflect the true state of affairs.

In summary, across the county there is accumulating evidence for continuity of use of some favoured locations, although much of it remains circumstantial.[14]

There remains, however, a disparity between the sheer density of known Roman-period sites and the limited number of probable early Saxon 'successor' sites so far identified. One partial explanation for this disparity may be that geographically favoured sites are more likely to be subject to continual re-use up to the present day, and hence remain relatively inaccessible beneath existing communities, but Saxon occupation sites are also harder to detect archaeologically than are Roman ones; the first Saxon domestic building to be found in Buckinghamshire, for instance, was only discovered in 1976 whereas a number of Roman sites had been identified a hundred years previously.

Settled Saxons: c.AD 500 to AD 600

By AD 500 it is fairly likely that Buckinghamshire was to all intents and purposes a Saxon county, albeit with an assortment of its earlier inhabitants remaining, mainly occupying a subservient role and still speaking their native language. Lacking documentation it is too early to know which principal tribal grouping (e.g. Anglian, West Saxon, etc) was dominant here although there are hints of lesser 'clan' names in a few place names, such as Oving (Ufa's people) and Halling, near Stoke Mandeville (Heall's people) whose allegiances are unknown. It is in this early period that many of Buckinghamshire's present place names originated, a number indicating personal land ownership, for example Hedgerley (Hycga's clearing), Dinton (Dunna's farm), and Marsworth (Maessa's enclosure).[15]

As previously noted, some 'new' settlements may have been close to those which already existed but others would certainly have been on new sites. By AD 500 it is unlikely that there would have been any Roman-period stone structures surviving; if they did they would have been roofless. Magiovinium and the lesser town of Fleet Marston would have almost disappeared under vegetation, although because of the fertility conferred by past human occupancy, they may have been good grazing sites. The new domestic buildings which were now being erected were structurally of timber and made no use of the plentiful brick and roof tile which would have been available from the decaying towns and villas. Occasionally Roman-period objects do seem to have been acquired for curiosity value, such as a piece of red-slipped pottery from Walton which had been neatly fashioned into a whorl for use on a spindle for spinning wool.

Other aspects of the landscape would have been dramatically transformed during the hundred years since AD 410. A proportion of the land once under arable may have reverted to grass and weeds through neglect and have eventually become 'secondary' woodland. The Roman landscape of the county, as previously noted, had been quite densely occupied and even areas which were wooded during the medieval period, such as Bernwood, Whittlewood and Salcey, once contained small Roman settlements. It is possible that the initial change of use to woodland in some areas took place early in the Saxon years. A research project in the Whittlewood Forest area in the north-west of the county[16] seems to generally support this view but any change may have been patchy. For example, although a pollen diagram from the project[17] shows evidence of increasing woodland in the post-Roman period, it also shows that the land still remained substantially open. If it was no longer being cultivated from local settlements then it could still have been used for grazing from places further afield.

The Chilterns seem to present a different picture to the north of the county. During the Roman-period settlement seems to have been focussed on the more fertile valleys, leaving the hills for woodland or cultivation and although the evidence is slight, this pattern may have been maintained for a few centuries, movement into the hills for settlement mainly taking place later in the Saxon period.

Cemeteries

Before turning to the character of early Saxon settlement, it will be useful to touch on what is known of Saxon ritual, in particular that relating to burial as until a few decades ago it was only the accidental discovery of burials – many being found during the nineteenth and early twentieth centuries – that gave clear evidence for a Saxon presence in Buckinghamshire.

By AD 500 although there may still have been a few rare individuals in the county who held Christian beliefs, from a Christian viewpoint the county would have been pagan. Germanic-speaking peoples did have shrines or temples and ritual associated with them; Bede describes one in Northumbria in his *Ecclesiastical History of the English People* and there are graphic late accounts of ritual in other northern countries such as at Uppsala in Sweden.[18] However, the direct archaeological evidence for such sites in England is sparse. In Buckinghamshire one village name, Weedon, containing the word *weoh* meaning shrine in Old English, indicates the presence of one although its precise location is unknown.[19] On the whole, surprisingly little is known about the beliefs of the Saxons. The imagery on Saxon jewellery from Buckinghamshire, such as that included in the burial at Taplow which will be described later, indicates an uneasy relationship with powerful beasts, perhaps similar to those in *Beowulf* who lurked in unsavoury fens or protected buried treasure. The name 'Grims Ditch' in the Chilterns indicates that these impressive earthworks (actually Iron Age, see earlier chapter) probably of a scale unfamiliar to the settlers, were believed to be associated with the deity Odin and there is little doubt that many of the deities in later familiar from Norse mythology had their roots in this early period. An interesting piece recently found at Westbury, a striking gilt copper-alloy mount showing a head, could perhaps depict an unnamed deity (Fig. 4.4)[20] as could the face on a gilded stud from High Wycombe (Fig. 4.5).

During the early Saxon period burials were placed in discrete cemeteries and either consisted of whole bodies or cremated remains, the latter often in pots (Fig. 4.6). In Buckinghamshire the great majority of cemeteries contain inhumations and the number of known cremations can be reckoned in single figures. Some burials such as Taplow and perhaps Bledlow,[21] were placed within mounds (barrows) in prominent positions, but the majority seem to have been laid in unmarked graves. In Buckinghamshire cemeteries seem to contain numbers of burials in their tens rather than the hundreds found in some other counties such as Kent, and probably served individual communities, although it is rarely possible to be sure that the full extent of any one cemetery has been uncovered.

FIGURE 4.4
Three views of a gilded copper-alloy head from Westbury, Milton Keynes. Depiction of the human form is not common in early Saxon art so this could be a deity.

FIGURE 4.5
A small gilded copper-alloy stud from High Wycombe decorated with a face. The design is common on 'button' brooches of the period. Fifth-early sixth century AD.

FIGURE 4.6
A pot from Bledlow (left) containing a cremation, and a stamp-decorated pot from Kingsey (right) also a cremation. The latter has been partly restored.

FIGURE 4.7
Copper-alloy 'small-long' brooches from the Bishopstone cemetery.

Typically they contain cross-sections of the population – men, women and children, but rarely babies. Usually those buried were laid on their backs but a few are crouched and less commonly and, slightly disconcertingly, some were buried face down.

Unfortunately the majority of Buckinghamshire's early cemeteries, such as those at Bishopstone (Fig. 4.7), Tickford Park (near Newport Pagnell), Wooburn, Hitcham and Mentmore, were discovered before modern archaeological techniques existed and are poorly recorded; plans or photographic records rarely survive. There is also a central Buckinghamshire bias in the record, although later discoveries have redressed the old distribution pattern to some extent. Recent discoveries in the Milton Keynes area in the north of the county, for example, include finds at Westbury, Shenley Brook End,[22] Bottledump Corner[23] and Tattenhoe;[24] and in the south there is a single burial at Dorney[25] and another near the well-known burial at Taplow[26] which will be described later. For central Buckinghamshire there have been discoveries at Soulbury[27] and Drayton Beauchamp.[28] Although some of these more recent finds came to light in the course of formal archaeological investigation, other discoveries have been made by vigilant amateurs. The largest inhumation cemetery ever to be discovered in the county has recently been found during archaeological investigations in advance of development near Wolverton.[29]

When ancient bodies are discovered, whether by chance or formal investigation, in the short term their dating depends on the objects found with them. Although radiocarbon dating is nowadays in common use, the process remains expensive and takes weeks to complete. Some of the old discoveries of burials that had no recorded associated finds, or which had finds that no longer survive, may not be datable at all although they could have been of Saxons. For instance, a group of bodies discovered near Holman's Bridge, Aylesbury in AD 1818 and reburied in Hardwick churchyard and others found near Bierton about 1830,[30] were at the

FIGURE 4.8
Spears and the iron
centre of a wooden
shield from a cemetery
at Bishopstone.

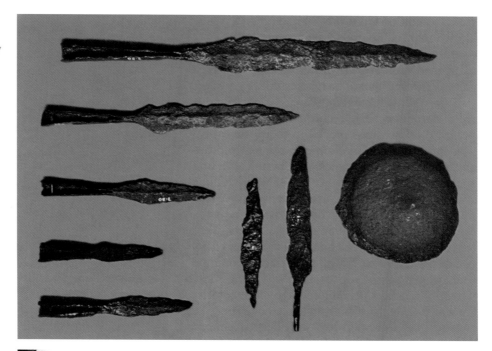

FIGURE 4.9
Front and back of a
folded sixth-century
gold 'bracteate'
pendant from
Hambleden. Although
several hundred have
been found in
Scandinavia and the
eastern Baltic there are
only a few dozen from
England. The design
on this one includes a
running animal.
Continental examples
show that the lines
above the animal
represent a head.

FIGURE 4.10
Glass 'claw-beaker' from a
cemetery at Newport Pagnell.
Small stave-built bucket
from the Newport Pagnell
cemetery. The staves have
been reconstructed.

time thought be Civil War burials, but it is now known that such burials are uncommon and they could equally be Saxon. Unfortunately the few associated items found with them no longer exist so the evidence cannot be reassessed.[31]

Some of Buckinghamshire's early Saxons were certainly buried clothed and some had personal possessions placed in their graves. An iron knife is a common object, originally probably sheathed. A few males were buried with iron spears (Fig. 4.8) and rather fewer with wooden shields of which only the iron fittings survive (the impression of wood fibres is sometimes preserved in the corrosion). A very few were buried with swords. The latter are thought to have been a mark of rank. Jewellery is quite a common find, often a pair of copper-alloy brooches, sometimes gilded, and occasionally strings of beads. A pendant found by a detectorist at Hambleden is likely to have been an accidental loss from a necklace (Fig. 4.9).

FIGURE 4.11
Enamelled copper-alloy disc from Oving. It would have come from a bronze 'hanging bowl' made in a 'British' workshop.

It can be presumed that jewellery is generally in graves that are female. Although many of these items are attractive, they are rarely as spectacular as finds from some Kentish and Oxfordshire cemeteries where brooches often incorporate garnets and other imported stones. That said, the jewellery from Buckinghamshire cemeteries, in particular beads of glass, amber etc. would have been colourful and much prized. Occasionally other personal items are also buried such as 'toilet sets' consisting of scoops, tweezers and probes, and combs of antler. Less common in Buckinghamshire are containers; there are occasional small pots, glass vessels, little stave-built buckets with copper alloy fittings (Fig. 4.10) and from Bourne End, Wooburn, a small, cylindrical, lidded metal 'threadbox'.[32] More of the latter have recently come to light at Wolverton. Most of these items could have once been part of an individuals workaday life, for example a set of balances from Wolverton, but there are occasional exotic items such as a cowrie shell with a burial at Ellesborough, clearly an import and likely to have had deeper significance. Although actual textiles are rarely preserved, the impression of fibres, and in one instance of human skin, occasionally survive on metal finds such as brooches. At Dinton fibres indicated traces of a woman's linen head-covering and use of a good quality wool, perhaps worsted, in her costume. On other brooches from Dinton, traces of textile borders, woven using small four-hole tablets (as against looms), were recorded. Although not found in any Buckinghamshire graves, enamel-decorated fittings from bronze bowls have been found at Oving (Fig. 4.11) and Brill. These are particularly interesting items as the style of decoration and use of enamel, marks them out firmly as of British/ Celtic make. As there is no evidence from the county that the skill required to make such objects survived here, they are likely to have been traded, or possibly looted, from regions to the north or west.

A few examples of cemeteries that have been examined in recent years are described below.

FIGURE 4.12
Recording a burial
during an excavation
at Dinton.

Female burial with a
pair of 'disc' brooches at
Dinton. The brooches
would have closed the
upper part of a loose
tubular garment.

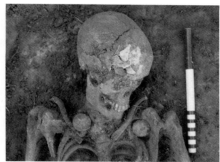

A single 'saucer' brooch
and a pair of saucer
brooches from a female
burial at Dinton.

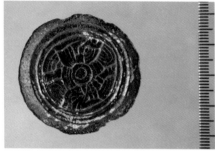

Glass beads from a
necklaces at Dinton.
Beads in another string
were mainly of amber.

Gilded great square–
headed brooch from the
cemetery at Dinton.

1. Dinton was a mixed inhumation cemetery of a minimum of twenty graves, sixteen of which had grave goods, and probably dated from the late fifth-sixth centuries.[33] The excavation in 1991 (Fig. 4.12) was near an eighteenth-century discovery which had produced a glass beaker. The burials appeared to be in two groupings, perhaps families, and the cemetery had been placed beside a field boundary. The identifiable skeletons included nine females over 25 years old and six males over 15, but no infants or juveniles. Incidentally five of those buried had quite severe dental disease.

2. At Westbury, Shenley, a small cemetery of seven inhumations of late seventh-century date was discovered in 1990.[34] Three had grave goods. The most striking burial was of a 25–35 year old female, lying face down, who had a necklace of silver rings with beads of blue glass and shell. At its centre was a looped disc-pendant with a garnet set in a shell in the middle of a simple cross design in filigree wire (Fig. 4.13) A small pair of iron shears and a knife that once had a horn handle were her other personal possessions. That two of those buried here were related is indicated by a congenital dental defect.

FIGURE 4.13
Pendant in gold silver-alloy with a central garnet set in shell. Its surface decoration is of gold wire. Seventh century from a burial at Westbury, Milton Keynes.

A princely burial at Taplow

The mound at Taplow still stands within the disused churchyard of St Nicholas beside Taplow Court. When James Rutland dug a trench through the mound in 1883 what he found made national headlines (Stevens 1884 is the earliest formal account but no proper modern study has yet been published). Initially the burial was described as Viking but we now know that it dates to the early seventh century. Accounts of the discovery are far from perfect but fortunately the objects found were deposited in the British Museum where they still remain. The mound contained the richly furnished burial of a male and as the parish name 'Taplow' can be translated as 'Taeppa's mound' we can be pretty sure of his name, although the personal name does not occur in any written record. He must have been an important ruler; if not a king then a sub-king. The extent of his territory is unknown but it obviously included a significant part of Buckinghamshire. The mound, sited close to a chalk cliff overlooking the Thames, must have been visible for some distance when it was first built. Taeppa was buried fully dressed; gold threads, probably from brocading on the edge of his jacket survived. Other textile included a fragment of tapestry, perhaps hung

FIGURE 4.14
Reconstruction of the Taplow burial chamber.
Excavation of the Taplow barrow as depicted in the *Illustrated London News* of November 17 1883.
Finds from the barrow illustrated in the *Victoria County History* published in 1905. The drawings are by Praetorius.

within a burial chamber. Items of personal attire include a fine gold buckle enhanced with garnets, probably from a sword belt, and two pairs of hooked clasps encased with decorated gold sheet. He had a substantial cache of weaponry including a sword, three spearheads and three shields. Vessels laid with him included four glasses as well as drinking horns decorated with silver gilt fittings (the horns probably from wild cattle), burrwood cups also decorated with silver gilt fittings, a bronze cauldron and buckets with yew wood staves. These items met his needs for warfare and feasting, but our man also had cultural interests as his possessions included a lyre similar to that discovered in the ship-burial at Sutton Hoo, and several composite cylindrical pieces of antler for a board game. His contacts were not confined to Buckinghamshire for among his possessions were a bronze bowl from the Mediterranean world. Interestingly, recent excavations nearby have produced a piece of an amphora also imported from the eastern Mediterranean (Anon 2006, 200). The same excavations have demonstrated another remarkable aspect of the Taplow barrow; whether deliberately or accidentally, it had been sited on the edge of a prehistoric hillfort (see Chapter 2).

3. During construction of the Aston Clinton bypass on Tring Hill in Drayton Beauchamp parish, an eighteen-grave inhumation cemetery was discovered in 2001.[35] Dating to the late sixth-seventh centuries the cemetery appeared to respect earlier boundaries as at Dinton. This dispersed cemetery included eleven burials which were supine and four crouched. The 'wealthiest' burial was of a mature female who had a pair of gilded saucer-brooches, a bead necklace and a toiletry set. The population included four infants under eleven years old, six young adults over seventeen, and five mature adults. There appear to have been more females than males among the young adult/mature population,. A number had lost teeth, some certainly through caries. Three individuals had Osteoarthritis and there was also some joint disease.

4. Only discovered in 2007, a cemetery found near Old Wolverton, previously noted, is also the most extensive to be examined in the county.[36] Over 81 burials of children, juveniles and adults have been excavated, the majority supine, some crouched, and a few prone. The cemetery dates to the seventh-eighth centuries AD. Particular features of interest include four burials arranged around a rectangular post-built structure (an unusual feature), several double burials and one which had its head tucked under its arm. Unusually for north Buckinghamshire, there are also two cremations in pots. Grave goods included a sword, balance scales, jewellery, and two or more 'workboxes' one with incised runes; the latter in the process of being interpreted is the first runic inscription to have been recorded in Buckinghamshire.

All of these cemeteries are important as they contain clues about the lifestyle of typical members of Buckinghamshire society in the first few centuries of Saxon dominance. Quite untypical, is a royal barrow burial at Taplow overlooking the Thames, excavated in 1883 by James Rutland (Fig. 4.14).[37] Prior to the discovery of the Sutton Hoo ship-burial this burial together with one found at Broomfield in Essex, was a key site for understanding the period and still remains important despite a few more recent discoveries such as a rich burial found at Prittlewell in Essex.

Sometime during the mid 700's, people ceased to be buried with accompanying grave goods, perhaps under Christian influence; unfortunate from an archaeological point of view![38]

Settlements

Until the discovery of the settlement at Walton, Aylesbury, in 1973, no early Saxon occupation site was known in the county, and examples were not common in England as a whole. Shortly afterwards discoveries were made at Wraysbury,[39] and then in Milton Keynes at Hartigan's Pit,[40] Pennyland[41] and Bancroft;[42] then at Bierton,[43] Fenny Lock,[44] Pitstone,[45] Buckland,[46] Taplow,[47] Wolverton,[48] and recently at Broughton[49] and Water Eaton[50] (also in Milton Keynes) and Wexham near Slough.[51] Despite these discoveries, evidence for buildings is still not plentiful and when they are found it is rarely possible to date them closely. A few are certainly of early Saxon date but mainly they are dateable only to the early-middle Saxon period and could have been constructed

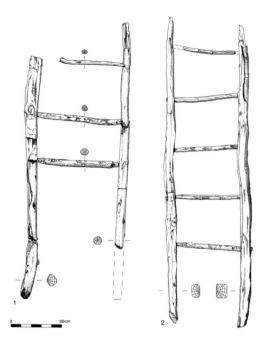

FIGURE 4.15
Ladders from two middle
Saxon wells at Westbury,
Milton Keynes.

at any time over four centuries. The dating difficulty arises from the fact that the simple types of handmade pottery that are the commonest associated find, were in use throughout most of the period. Similar pottery found elsewhere, such as on the surface of ploughed fields, may indicate the presence of other settlements. This is both good news and bad since ploughing inevitably damages buried features. By far the most extensive indicators of early-middle Saxon settlements in the county are place names containing Old English elements of the kind previously noted, but conversely, not all excavated settlements can be associated with a name.

In Buckinghamshire early-middle Saxon buildings are mainly of two kinds, those whose main rectangular structure consists of wooden wall-posts set either into individual postholes or a trench, and those built with a principal post at either end that once supported a ridge pole. The distinguishing feature of the latter structures is that they include a sunken area, normally of playing-card outline. They are called 'sunken-feature buildings' by archaeologists. Such buildings were easy to construct and seems to have been commonest in the early centuries, gradually giving way to the more complicated structures which archaeologists – in deference to Anglo-Saxon literature such as *Beowulf* usually call 'halls', although this rather grand term is not often very apt. Sunken-feature buildings are relatively easy to detect archaeologically due to the distinctive fill of their sunken area. Post-built structures are less obvious and evidence for them is more easily destroyed, for instance by ploughing. Any building which has posts set directly into the ground is likely to have had a relatively short lifespan, particularly if the principal posts are in an exposed external wall.

One of the more extensively excavated settlements of the period was at Pennyland in Milton Keynes, discovered in open fields between Great Linford and Willen.[52] Although the circumstances of investigation were difficult, thirteen sunken-featured buildings were found spread over c170 metres. On average they were about four metres long. The plans of two halls were also found, one of which appears to have succeeded a sunken-featured building. Halls were normally larger than sunken-featured buildings, being between six and ten metres long. As previously mentioned, halls become commoner as the Saxon period progresses and sunken-feature buildings rarer; eventually it appears that the latter were only used for subsidiary buildings. A distinctive feature of the plans of early Saxon settlements is an absence of obvious enclosures or boundaries. There were boundaries at Pennyland but they do not seem to have belonged to the initial stage of occupation. An interesting discovery at this site were wells. One of these was wattle lined and contained the base of a ladder made of oak and field maple with a rung of blackthorn. A ladder found at another Milton Keynes site, Hartigan's,[53] was of field maple with ash rungs. A third Milton Keynes site, Westbury, had two wells with surviving ladders; one was entirely of oak, the other had ash rungs (Fig. 4.15).[54]

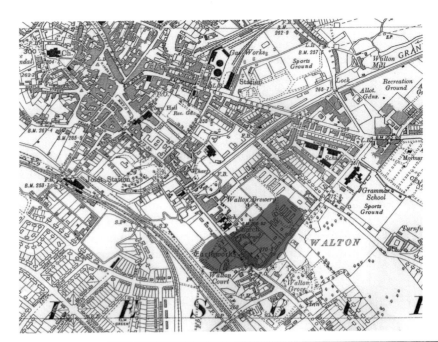

FIGURE 4.16
Approximate known
extent of the early-middle
Saxon settlement at Walton
in relation to Aylesbury
(based on OS 6" map of 1952).

The sunken base of
an early Saxon
building at Walton,
Aylesbury, exca-
vated in 1974. One
of the two principal
post holes can be
seen in the centre of
the far side.

At Walton, near Aylesbury, a series of excavations have uncovered evidence
of an extensive settlement lying beneath the later hamlet (Fig. 4.16).[55] Seven or
more sunken-featured buildings, one burnt down, were spread across a distance
of some 400m and there are at least twelve rectangular post-built structures or
'halls', of which one group of eight share a similar alignment and presumably
also date (Fig. 4.17). Many of the halls were about 10 metres long by 5 metres
wide and a few had obvious entrances in one long side, indicated by a gap or a
doorpost. One had an attached 'annexe'. The wall posts of most of the buildings were set in individual holes but the uprights of one, almost square in plan,
were set in a trench. The walling material of all these structures is likely to

FIGURE 4.17
Excavation of part of
the Saxon settlement
at Walton, Aylesbury
in 1994. The rectan-
gular slots of Structure
2, probably middle-
Saxon, can be clearly
seen. Right a plan of
the whole site (after
Ford *et al.* 2004).

have consisted of split timber. However good the above-ground joins between timbers, daub was probably used to fill gaps. In some Saxon buildings outside the county, hall interiors are often divided into two rooms. Hearths might be expected but evidence for them is rarely found, probably due to their being ploughed away; had they survived they would have been useful in distin-guishing structures used as homes from those used as outbuildings, which is otherwise rarely possible. Roofs would have been of thatch, or shingles (split timber tiles), or possibly turf.

A relatively small excavation at Pitstone in 2005, about 300 metres from the parish church, located four sunken-featured buildings.[56] Nearby an incompletely filled Roman-period ditch had been topped up with Saxon rubbish. The hollow areas of sunken-feature buildings commonly contain refuse or discarded mate-rial, and in a corner of one of the Pistone buildings were parts of ten clay loomweights used to tension the warp threads on upright looms (Fig. 4.22). There was a slot cut into the base of the building which could have supported the frame of such a loom. In its fill were three bone 'pin-beaters' thought to have been used in weaving, so it is probable that it was used as a weaving shed. A small inhumation cemetery found in the 1960s during chalk quarrying was only *c* 600m distant.[57] The proximity of the site to the church and other finds in the area[58] indicate that continuity of occupation from the Saxon period into the medieval period is a strong possibility here also. Finally, the plans of two halls have recently been recovered in the south of the county at Wexham, Slough (Fig. 4.18). These are of particular interest as radiocarbon determinations on charcoal from their postholes suggest a date in the sixth-seventh centuries AD.[59]

Only a handful of occupation sites can certainly be dated to the middle Saxon period. One of these near Lake End Road, Dorney, not far from the Thames, was investigated during construction of a flood-alleviation scheme in the

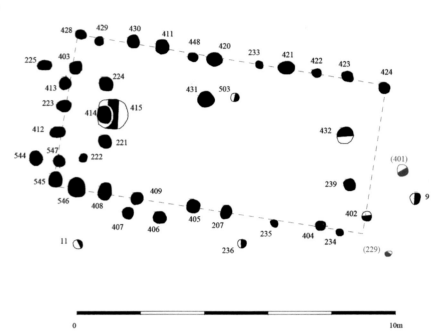

103

FIGURE 4.18
Plan of the post-holes
which once held the
timber uprights of a
'hall' at Wexham,
Slough. Radiocarbon
indicates a sixth
century date (after
Ford 2008).

0   10m

1990s.[60] A very unusual site, it consisted almost entirely of groups of large infilled pits, over 120 of them (Fig. 4.19). No accompanying buildings were recorded. The fills of the pits were not particularly distinctive but there was evidence that cess preceded the dumping of refuse in some of the fills so they could have been latrine pits. Pieces from imported German jugs (Tating ware) and North French pottery were also found. Such finds are very unusual for a rural site, and the excavators suggest it might have been a seasonal market with traders making use of the Thames.

At Wraysbury (Wigraed's burh),[61] another south Buckinghamshire parish, an excavation about 400m north of the church in 1997, located a single sunken-featured building.[62] Some years previously amateur archaeologists had dug up five middle Saxon coins and pottery just west of the church. A subsequent small-scale excavation close to the church on its north side exposed the corner of a probable post-in-trench building, as well as part of a post-built hall which had much daub (presumably from wall infilling) associated with it. In a nearby pit an unusual iron disc encased between two decorated silver sheets, of seventh-eighth century date, was found.[63] The whole suggests that although occupation around the church was early (perhaps mid-Saxon), the initial settlement focus for Wraysbury may have been a short distance north.

The cemetery near Old Wolverton in the north of the county has already been noted. Close to it is was an early 'open' settlement; the general absence of field and enclosure boundaries in the early period has previously been mentioned. Not far distant was a substantial rectangular, ditched enclosure, probably of the middle-Saxon period and so far unique in the county.[64] Its ditches had been redug on several occasions. Unfortunately it had been damaged by earlier construction

FIGURE 4.19
One of numerous
middle-Saxon pits
excavated at Dorney.
The pit has been
half-sectioned: the
labels mark different
layers of infill.

activities on the site. A radiocarbon date of AD 690–890 cal (that is calibrated for laboratory error, etc.) confirms its use in the middle Saxon period. The surviving area of the interior contained a single rectangular post-built building. Finds included a distinctive type of traded pottery called Ipswich ware, much harder than locally-made pottery. The animal bone from the site contained a larger than expected proportion of horse bones which may indicate a specialised function for the enclosure. Occupation continued into the late Saxon period after which the settlement migrated north (Fig. 4.20).[65]

A few other north Buckinghamshire Middle Saxon sites are worth noting. At Chicheley, a single ditch, either a field or settlement boundary was found in 1979 during construction of the Newport Pagnell by-pass. The ditch contained a distinctive form of pottery called 'bar-lip'.[66] The find is of interest as it seems to indicate a small settlement whose existence was to influence the layout of later fields. Work within two Milton Keynes churches, St Thomas, Simpson and Holy Trinity, Little Woolstone, surprisingly has produced pieces of the same type of pottery, suggesting, as discussed elsewhere, that there may often be evidence for early settlement within existing village cores.

A considerable number of Saxon objects have been discovered by metal detectorists across the county in recent years, often not more closely datable than to the middle-late Saxon period. Many of these are dress accessories and may represent incidental loss (Fig. 4.21) but the number of finds from one area around the Westcroft Centre, Milton Keynes may indicate a settlement here, although unfortunately the area was destroyed by development with very limited advance investigation.[67]

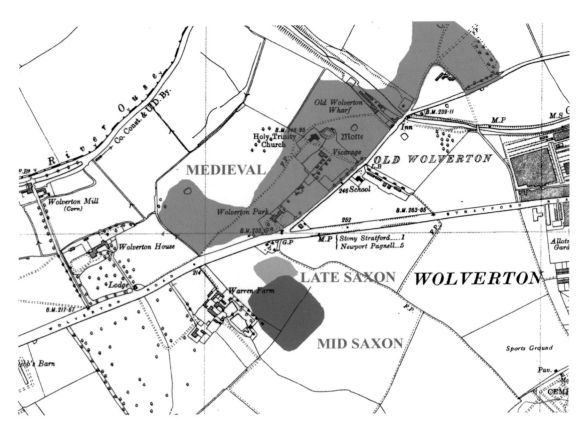

FIGURE 4.20
Simplified map of
different periods of
occupation at Old
Wolverton (based
on an OS 6" map
revised 1950).

Life in the early-middle Saxon period

Possessions

We have seen from the cemetery evidence that although the possessions of the average early-middle Saxon may have been modest, they were certainly adequate. Nearly all Buckinghamshire settlement sites produce evidence of spinning (spindle-whorls) and weaving, the latter indicated by ring-shaped clay weights which weighted the warp threads on an upright loom, and by bone thread-pickers used in manipulating threads (Fig. 4.22). A heckle with iron teeth in a wooden block for carding wool (or possibly flax), comes from the middle Saxon site at Dorney. Fabric would have been dyed using readily-available vegetable dyes such as woad and madder and garments could be bordered by tablet-woven edging. As seen from the cemetery evidence, linen was also available and there is some evidence from Dorney of flax production here. Jewellery, although not often found on settlements, is a fairly common cemetery find as has been noted previously.

Some implements were made from bone and antler, including combs (Fig. 4.23). A by-product, sawn antler is not uncommon. Pottery was handbuilt and mainly plain but occasionally stamp-decorated. It was mainly locally made and bonfire-fired, but from about AD 750 some harder-fired vessels (Ipswich ware) began to be brought in from East Anglia although whether simply as pots or as

FIGURE 4.21
Strap ends of the eight-tenth centuries. From left to right: Wendover; silver, two interlaced animals facing each other; at the narrow end are the snout and two eyes of another animal: West Wycombe; copper-alloy with niello inlay. The piece is eroded but there are eight paired Trewhiddle-style animals in the main panel: Princes Risborough; copper-alloy with a crouched animal either side of the central linear. This piece is a crude copy of more elaborate designs.

containers for traded goods is not known. Glass is a rarity on settlement sites and its presence is likely to be an indication of status; the numerous middle-Saxon pits at Dorney produced only three fragments. Apart from the small wooden stave-buckets occasionally found in some graves, and the base of an oak barrel or bucket from Westbury, there is little surviving evidence for treen (implements and containers of wood) but they must have been in common use. Woodworking on a large scale was obviously important for buildings and, for example, ploughs. Iron tools would have been invaluable for this work, axes in particular, although much initial forming can be achieved by riving (splitting) timber with wooden wedges alone. There is no direct archaeological evidence from Buckinghamshire for the use of leather, although containers of leather were probably common and some of the many bone and antler needles may have been used in stitching leather items.

The manufacture of brooches, decorative pins and small items of copper alloy was a specialist job and no doubt many would have been traded, but one would expect iron smithing to be more local as knives and other small iron objects are common site finds. Surprisingly, however, the slag produced as a by-product of this process is rarely recorded as a site find in Buckinghamshire and this is hard to understand unless there was an extensive trade in finished goods. Only at Dorney, the middle Saxon site near the Thames, has substantial evidence for smithing been found. Here some 42kgs of smithing slag and hearth material was recovered from pits spread over a distance of 200m. Small deposits of iron-smelting waste, signifying production of iron from the raw ore, have been found in north and west Buckinghamshire and the Chilterns, but these have not yet been securely dated and may be Romano-British. Whetstones for sharpening iron tools are occasionally found.

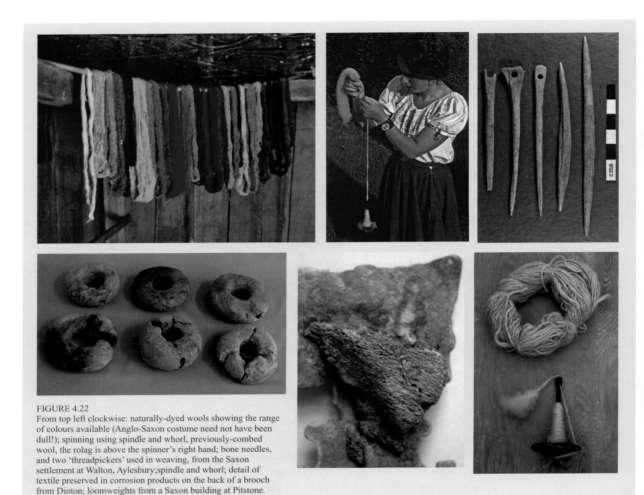

FIGURE 4.22
From top left clockwise: naturally-dyed wools showing the range of colours available (Anglo-Saxon costume need not have been dull!); spinning using spindle and whorl, previously-combed wool, the rolag is above the spinner's right hand; bone needles, and two 'threadpickers' used in weaving, from the Saxon settlement at Walton, Aylesbury; spindle and whorl; detail of textile preserved in corrosion products on the back of a brooch from Dinton; loomweights from a Saxon building at Pitstone.

Anglo-Saxon textiles

The pictures show a spindle with its whorl and a skein of wool; a spinner with a rolag of unspun wool; needles and two 'thread-pickers' – the latter thought to have been used in weaving; naturally-dyed wool; clay loomweights from a probable weaving shed at Pitstone, and mineralised textile (much enlarged) on the back of a brooch from Dinton. The latter shows how easily important information could be lost had the brooch not been cleaned by a professional conservator after its discovery. Wool was not the only fabric used in Anglo-Saxon England, linen (made from flax) was also important. There is some evidence that furs were also worn. For an important book on the subject of early Anglo-Saxon textiles see Walton Rogers (2007) in the Bibliography. In the later Saxon period English embroidery gained considerable fame. We know the name of one Buckinghamshire embroiderer, Aelfgyth of Oakley whose skills included embroidering with gold (see main text).

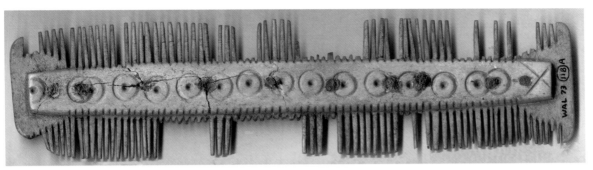

FIGURE 4.23
A bone comb from
Walton.

FIGURE 4.24
Left: a middle-Saxon
silver 'sceat' from Lacey
Green. These are the first
coins to become fairly
common in Saxon
England. Many such coins
do not show a ruler's
name, but this one has
'OF' for Offa and the
name of the moneyer
EADBERHT.

Right: a gold thrymsa
from Aston Abbotts.
These rare coins, some
copying designs on conti-
nental coins, were
produced in England
during the seventh
century.

In the early Saxon people ordinary people managed without coins. Gold coins known as 'thrymsa' were minted fairly widely in Gaul but only a limited number were minted in England during the seventh century and they would not have been used for everyday trade. The middle Saxon period saw the re-appearance of coinage in the form of the small silver coins known as *sceattas*. They are an uncommon find on excavated sites in Buckinghamshire although a number have been found elsewhere by metal detector (Fig. 4.24).

Field and Woodland

Reconstructing the extent and character of the woodland cover of early-mid Saxon Buckinghamshire is almost impossible although in theory the problem can be approached in a number of ways. These include defining 'ancient' wood-land through the character and range of species surviving today, considering the distribution of Old English names containing, for example, a *wudu* element – as in Chetwode, by considering later charters, through evidence from Domesday Book, and of course by noting species and the character of charcoal or objects recovered by archaeological investigation. Unfortunately none of these methods enable a definitive picture to be reached. One certainty, however, is that the old image of incoming Saxons hacking their way through thick forests has long been overturned by the realisation of how densely the landscape was already occupied in preceding periods. On the whole, the incomers would probably have been more than happy to utilise existing worked land rather than assailing woodland – unless population pressure dictated otherwise.

Under certain conditions pollen can survive in the ground almost unchanged for millennia and can give a very good idea of local landscape. For example the analysis of both pollen and waterlogged plant remains from one of the Penny-land wells shows that its surroundings were very open; trees contributed only 5% to the record and apart from a little hazel and gorse the dominant landscape was of grasses and herbs of cultivated and waste ground. Not surprisingly a number of semi-aquatic species were also present. At Pennyland, apart from the ladder previously mentioned, a range of timber pieces and wood chips were found. These indicated the presence of hazel, field maple, oak, ash, alder, willow, hawthorn and blackthorn. To this species list, birch and pine recovered from a well at Westbury, can be added. Evidence from well fills at Westbury also indi-cated open ground.

It might be thought that woodland would be a good source of wild game for settlements but bones, for example, from deer, are uncommon on excavated settlement sites, only 0.5% of the bone from Pennyland, 0.7% from Walton, and 1% from Pitstone. Occasionally bones of other wild species are seen; for example bones of hare, beaver, plover, redwing and crane from Walton, and from Wolverton bone from a polecat and possibly a wild boar. Dorney's numerous pits produced a good range of wild species, red deer being commonest, but also a few bones from boar, hare, badger, beaver mole and vole – plus a grass snake. Wild birds included pigeon, woodcock and one bone from a white-tailed eagle. Fish bones (commonly eel) are occasionally found, but their presence is usually only identified when deposits have been wet-sieved. At Dorney, near the river, wet-sieving surprisingly produced relatively few fish bones; eel was again common here but also pike. The great majority of bones from settlements are, however, from domesticated species.

Turning to agriculture: as previously noted there is some evidence in the middle Saxon period for the development of enclosures associated with build-ings but these are not common; nor is there much evidence for field boundaries of the kind familiar from the Roman period. This is not to say that no barriers existed but perhaps greater use was made, for instance, of unditched hedges which would leave little archaeological trace, or hurdles, one of which comes from a well at Westbury. Later in this chapter the origins of the complex agri-cultural systems associated with the development of 'open fields' common in the medieval period will be discussed and it is possible that these may have origi-nated in the middle Saxon period. At present, however, the only direct evidence for agriculture in Buckinghamshire comes from animal bone and seed remains.

Animal bone of the early and middle Saxon period varies a little in species from site to site; some sites had rather more cattle than sheep but on other sites sheep were dominant (it should be noted that it can be difficult to distinguish sheep from goat bones). The animals were smaller than modern breeds. Pig bones never represents more than 20% of the bones from any site. There are usually low numbers of domestic fowl and geese; together they usually account for about 3% of the total, except at Wolverton where the number rises to 11%. One of the Dorney pits contained a complete dog.

The process of wet-sieving (Fig. 1.16) is invaluable in recovering carbonised plant remains, particularly seeds and chaff. Sometimes impressions of both are preserved in fired clay. The small amount of evidence from Buckinghamshire suggests that the dominant cultivated cereals were free-threshing bread or rivet wheat and hulled barley. Oats and rye are less common. From Pitstone there are also peas and hazel-shell fragments, and from Walton a horse bean, and vetch as well as arable weed seeds. An important Middle Saxon deposit of seeds recently found at Taplow included rivet or bread wheat, hulled barley, oats and rye;[68] a pit at Dorney, previously noted, included many flax seeds.

Although not a common settlement find, one clear indication of grain processing is pieces of quern (rotary grinding stones). Some of these are made in a volcanic stone imported from the Rhineland and are one of the few items of cross-channel trade to reach several small settlements. Dorney produced many pieces and also fragments of quern from other sources including Surrey. One rotary quern from Walton was made from Greensand, which outcrops about ten miles distant close to the Bedfordshire border. This leads on to the question of the date at which watermills became generally available for grinding, which will be discussed later.

The influence of Christianity

As previously noted, although it cannot be proved that Christianity disappeared completely from the county during the fifth century, it seems highly likely, although of course it continued to be actively practised among the British in areas of the country beyond Saxon control. When, however, in AD 597 Augustine arrived in Kent on a mission to convert the English, he was not impressed by the British bishops he encountered who according to Bede, 'stubbornly preferred their own customs to those in universal use among Christian churches'. Augustine started at the top by winning the approval of King Ethelbert the powerful king of Kent, whose wife Bertha was a Christian Frank. We don't know into which tribal grouping Buckinghamshire fell at this time but in about AD 635, Cynegils, a converted West Saxon king, granted the former Roman town of Dorchester (on Thames) to one Bishop Birinus who from this base, as a later writer puts it, 'builds churches, sets up altars, scatters effigies, overturns heathen temples'.[69] It is possible that an initiative of Birinus may have set in motion the conversion of Buckinghamshire.

During the course of the eighth century, the political control of the county became a little clearer with the Mercians, centred on bases in Tamworth and Lichfield, becoming overkings of a large swathe of the Midlands and also controlling London, but prior to that there are a number of groups who may have had some influence in the establishment of churches. The West Saxons have already been mentioned. Others include the Chiltern dwellers (*Ciltensaete*) who have no recorded king (although the probable royal burial at Taplow must have been in their territory); possibly the Middle Angles whose western limits are

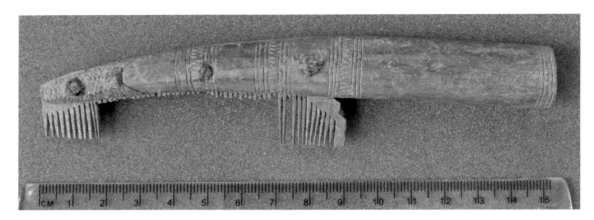

FIGURE 4.25
A middle-Saxon decorated antler comb from the Prebendal excavations, Aylesbury, possibly used at the minster.

FIGURE 4.26
One of the late-Saxon burials from George Street, Aylesbury, probably part of the minster cemetery. The town encroached over the cemetery in the medieval period and this burial was then cut by later pits.

unclear, and perhaps the Middle Saxons on the other side of the Colne in 'Middlesex'. It has also been argued that a geographically unplaced group called the Hendrica may have held some territory in the county.[70]

The first churches and their communities of priests, had large geographic areas to cover. These pioneering establishments became known as 'old minsters'. Their foundation was dependent on support and gifts of land from substantial landholders, most of whom in the early years were of royal stock. As time moved on the number of churches multiplied and some of the resources and rights of the parent churches trickled down to lesser establishments. No surviving church buildings in Buckinghamshire date to this initial phase of foundation and even their location has to be deduced from later, sources. One prime candidate for an 'old minster' is Aylesbury which remained quite a wealthy establishment in the Late Saxon period. A little archaeological work inside the present church hints at an early structure here,[71] and an investigation adjacent to the present boundary of the churchyard uncovered a middle Saxon boundary ditch which was probably the minster's boundary.[72] The same site produced an antler comb (Fig. 4.25) and a fragment from a Saxon glass vessel with a cross moulded into its base, likely to have been in use there. Further circumstantial evidence for an early church includes the discovery of numerous burials beneath the old town and some distance from the church; a few of these have been radiocarbon dated to the ninth century AD (Fig. 4.26), suggesting an extensive cemetery long ago built over.[73] Aylesbury's foundation is associated with a saintly lady, St Osyth, of Mercian royal blood.[74] Interestingly the church was sited within an Iron Age hillfort. A few other churches in Buckinghamshire such as Cholesbury and West

FIGURE 4.27
The crypt below Wing church's apse, looking towards the modern stairs. The supporting arches in the foreground are a secondary feature of the crypt.

The Saxon polygonal apse of Wing church. The modern entrance leading into the underlying crypt can just be seen. The large window is medieval.

Detail of the relief arcading on the Saxon apse of Wing church. Above the arches can be seen further triangular arcading over two blocked Saxon windows.

The Saxon Church at Wing

Wing is the most complete Saxon church in Buckinghamshire. From the outside the most obvious Saxon feature is the eastern apse or chancel. It is decorated in a manner suggestive of a ninth-century date with raised stone strips which terminate in arches. Above these are similar triangular strips over small blocked windows. Beneath the apse is a crypt, now approached from outside by steps but accessed originally from inside the church. This crypt has been modified since its construction in the eighth or ninth centuries and is thought to predate the existing apse above. Such crypts would once have held important burials or saintly relics around which a congregation could process.

Inside the church are arches opening from the nave into aisles. These openings were probably made in the later Saxon period through what were at the time the church's outer walls, however there was certainly one chamber at the east end of the nave on the north side. A blocked door from this chamber survives, leading out beside the apse. Looking east a Saxon double window can be seen above the chancel arch. This has a stone central column but the arches are formed from Roman tiles. At the other end of the nave a blocked doorway can be seen high in the north wall. This may have once opened onto a wooden gallery.

Wycombe and some in other counties are similarly sited, which leads one to wonder whether the presence of an ancient earthwork may have been regarded as particularly significant for a Christian foundation.[75]

A church at Buckingham is noted in Domesday Book. The town was flourishing in the late Saxon period and it is very likely there was a church there then, possibly founded after the town came to prominence on account of its fortification in the early tenth century. The church here has an association with an early saint, St Rumbold, a remarkably precocious child who spoke fluently before dying at three days old!

There are no early churches documented in the Chilterns and south Buckinghamshire but one pioneering church at least would be expected here, perhaps, for example at Wycombe. So far as Buckinghamshire is concerned, these shadowy early churches are more than compensated for by the existence of the fine church at Wing (Fig. 4.27). Wing is one of a handful of churches in England with both Saxon fabric and a crypt beneath its chancel, the latter providing a clue to the former presence of saintly relics or the burial of a person of rank. Much ink has been spilt on the date of Wing church; currently its foundation is considered to be late seventh or eighth century.[76] As at Aylesbury the cemetery of Wing extended far beyond its present limits. Seventy-seven burials have been excavated beyond its present boundary and there is also evidence of an outer enclosing bank and ditch.[77]

Other churches known to have existed in the late Saxon period, although their date of origin is not known, include Haddenham and North Crawley, and there is structural evidence that parts of Iver, Lavendon, Hardwick and Little Missenden are Saxon.[78] It has been argued that the now demolished St Nicholas, Taplow may also have had Saxon origins,[79] which would be particularly interesting in view of the nearby barrow, and there is archaeological evidence for a pre-twelfth century church at Great Linford.[80] A few priests are recorded in Domesday Book, for example at Wingrave. However one arrives at a total of Saxon churches for the county, it nevertheless must fall far short of the actual number which would have come into existence before the Norman conquest. In neighbouring Berkshire, for instance, fifty-seven pre-Conquest are recorded but for Buckinghamshire such useful documentation is sadly lacking.[81] However, there are over forty churches containing some Norman structural elements,[82] and a number of these could be replacements for earlier buildings.

Many of the earliest Buckinghamshire churches would have been of timber, as has been shown to be the case elsewhere and hence only be detectable by excavation. This may account for the fact that sometimes cemeteries later than the 'pagan' phase are discovered, but no church. At the village of Milton Keynes, for example, the standing medieval church lies 200 metres distant from a partially examined cemetery containing at least ninety burials dating to the ninth-tenth centuries.[83] Missing from the archaeological record at present are indications of the early quarries which must have been supplied the stone for later churches; this could be an interesting topic for local research.

The churches had great influence on the re-introduction of literacy and eventually on the production of written law-codes, king lists, grants of land and wills, and accounts of historical events; all important documents for the understanding the later period. Some of these will be mentioned in the next section.

The later Saxon period

For the first few centuries of the Saxon period we know little about constraints on individual Saxons. How free were individuals to expand their land, cut down trees, marry, keep slaves, fight their neighbours, decide what stock they would keep or what seeds to plant? Such rules as there were would have been initially defined by social custom, ties to family groups and by leaders, whether members of powerful local families, sub-kings or kings, but not by reference to written documents. As time progressed constraints became more codified for many everyday matters including the payment of taxes, to the extent that by the late ninth and early tenth centuries under the rule of Alfred and Edward the Elder, it was possible in the face of Viking incursions to fortify and arrange for the defence of a series of centres across southern England which eventually extended into the Midlands (see on). By Alfred's time firm elements of a structure of taxes, defence, landholding, government and justice as well as social class were well-established. With increasing documentation it becomes possible to identify individual landholdings, landowners and some officials in Buckinghamshire but writing a coherent history in the traditional sense remains an impossibility. For example, sometime during the tenth or eleventh century, Buckinghamshire was created as an administrative unit, but we do not know for certain when, or who decreed it, and we can only infer why Buckingham was chosen as its focus.

Villages and estates

A key document for the period is Domesday Book, assembled in AD 1086 at the behest of William the Conqueror.[84] The king's commissioners attempted to list all sources of income available to the king and his principal subjects by quizzing locals down to the level of groups of villagers. However, the surveyors also noted the previous value *'TRE'*, that is *Tempore regis Edwardi* – 'in the time of Edward the Confessor', monarch just prior to the Norman invasion. The Domesday entries therefore provide a pretty close guide to the character of late Saxon landholdings, many of which were later to become parishes. For example, the entry for Medmenham reads:

> Land of Hugh of Bolbec. In Desborough Hundred.
> Hugh holds Medemenham himself. It answers for 10 hides. Land for 10 ploughs; in lordship 4 hides; 2 ploughs there. 10 villagers with 8 smallholders have 8 ploughs. 4 slaves; from the fishery 1,000 eels; meadow for all the ploughs; woodland, 50 pigs. The total value is and was 100s; before 1066 £8. Wulfstan, a thane of King Edward's held this manor; he could sell to whom he would

It can be seen that the size of Hugh's Medmenham manor, assessed in land units of a hide (roughly 120 acres) is given, that it lay within the much larger admin-

FIGURE 4.28
The Black Hedge,
Monks Risborough:
referred to in a Saxon
charter of AD 903 it is
still recognisable as a
boundary.

istrative area of Desborough, that villagers, smallholders and slaves lived there amongst arable fields, meadow and woodland, and that the nearby Thames was a good source of eels. The previous Saxon lord had been Wulfstan, a king's thegn, a man close to the king, but he had lost his land to Hugh of Bolbec (Bolbec is near the mouth of the Seine).[85] The presence of slaves here is not untypical; at nearby Hambleden there were nine. There were eighteen of the administrative areas known as 'hundreds' within the county. Probably created in the early tenth century, they survived in one form or another into the nineteenth century. They were assemblies of landowners, officials and village representatives and met for consideration of various matters including justice. Their meetings seem initially to have been in the open air at a prominent location. One such, the hundred mound of Secklow, survived as a mound to be shown on a plan of 1641 as 'Selly Hill'[86] and is now preserved within central Milton Keynes. It lies at the junction of three parishes boundaries confirming the antiquity of their bounds. In an Upper Winchendon charter of AD 1004, a 'hundred tree', perhaps a meeting point, is noted.[87]

The great majority of what were later to become Buckinghamshire parishes are to be found in Domesday. The extent of a few had previously been recorded in charters which take the form of a perambulation around the bounds. The features described in these can sometimes, but by no means always, still be identified. For instance an extract from a charter describing the bounds of Monks Risborough in AD 903 includes the following written in Old English. The translation is that of Michael Reed.[88]

First from the gore into the black hedge from the hedge down the foul brook from the foul brook to the west of the ash tree on the river bank …

The 'Black Hedge' still survives having been identified by its botanical richness at the southern end of the present elongated parish (Fig. 4.28).[89]

Despite the well-documented existence of numerous Buckinghamshire settlements in the late Saxon period, it is disappointing that direct archaeological evidence for their character in these centuries at present far more limited than for earlier periods. The principal reason for this is that most undoubtedly lie beneath modern villages and it is only on rare occasions that such areas can be investigated. However, even longstanding villages are not static in their footprint, and as will be noted in the next chapter, some have shifted a little over time, others have shrunk, and a number, such as Quarrendon, have been abandoned completely. This village migration has allowed a number of 'abandoned' areas to be excavated in the Milton Keynes area. These include Great Linford,[90] Loughton,[91] Tattenhoe and Westbury,[92] Woughton[93] and Caldecotte.[94] Interestingly, investigation of many of these 'abandoned' areas has only infrequently produced evidence of early Saxon occupation and only sparse evidence for middle Saxon occupation. At Great Linford where evidence for early occupation was discovered it was beneath the parish church some distance from the excavated area.[95] On the whole, evidence from these 'abandoned' or migrated settlement areas seems to suggest that occupation did not commence here until the late Saxon or Norman periods.

Recovering the plans of buildings of this later period has proved difficult. At Bradwell (Bradwell Bury), investigation of a later medieval moated site under unfavourable conditions did find traces of three, post-built structures.[96] The best evidence, however, may again come from Old Wolverton, where an interim report records post-built structures within plots laid out in the late Saxon period.[97]

Away from Milton Keynes, a research project centred on Whittlewood Forest in the north-west of the county, previously noted, studied the development of settlement.[98] It used test-pitting *within* existing villages to retrieve datable pottery sherds, and fieldwalking outside the villages. The results are open to interpretation but based on relatively few finds, pottery from both the early-middle and late Saxon periods was found within the core of the villages of Akeley, Lillingstone Dayrell and Leckhampstead. The type of pottery known as St Neot's ware, in use from about AD 850 for two centuries, was the key to identifying late Saxon settlement here. Elsewhere in north Buckinghamshire this type of pottery was also found in some quantity at Weston Underwood, a village which also produced quite an amount of Roman and early-mid Saxon finds.[99] In the centre of the county the same readily-distinguishable sherds have turned up at the hamlet of Walton, Aylesbury, a location previously mentioned. Here there was a substantial tenth-eleventh century boundary close to a subsequent manorial site itself enclosed within an earthwork. The earlier boundary is parallel to Walton Street, connecting Walton with Aylesbury, suggesting that the road already existed by this date. Not far distant, St Neot's sherds have been found at Bedgrove, once a hamlet now beneath the estate. Sherds of St Neot's ware have also been found within at least a dozen existing settlements across the Vale

including Shabbington, Warmstone, Lower Winchendon, Ashendon, Ellesborough, Haddenham, Stone, Halton, Monks Risborough, Marsh, Kimble and Weston Turville.[100]

Direct archaeological record for late Saxon activity in the Chilterns is at present very sparse in comparison with the Domesday record. No finds of the distinctive St Neot's sherds have been reported, but this absence may just indicates the southern limit of its distribution, and the character of late Saxon pottery within the Chilterns has not yet been closely defined. An extensive excavation in Dorney parish at Lots Hole in what was until recently open fields did locate some settlement evidence of tenth to fifteenth century date.[101] By the twelfth century this had begun to take the form of an oval enclosure but prior to this, although late Saxon pottery was present, the hard-to-interpret structural remains consisted only of a droveway and a ditched feature with an entrance. There was evidence for buildings on the site, but these were hard to tie to a particular phase of occupation. The late Saxon settlement at Wraysbury has previously been mentioned.

Small personal dress items such as strap ends and brooches of the ninth-tenth centuries are also found quite frequently by detectorists. Some of these are highly decorated and show the continuing influence of animal ornament in the late Saxon period (Fig.4.29). Clusters of such finds may indicate settlement sites.

In compensation for the scarcity of excavated evidence for the character of late Saxon buildings in the county, a number of domestic buildings of the medieval period survive whose form which may give some clues to the character of earlier structures, although the earliest are of the thirteenth century and of relatively high status.

Agriculture

Between the eighth and tenth centuries a remarkable change occurred in a large part of the Buckinghamshire landscape and across much of central England. In

FIGURE 4.29
Left; a tenth-century copper-alloy disc brooch with coloured enamel melted within shaped cells. From Stone. Right: a ninth-century silver buckle from Amersham with traces of an inlay of niello (a black sulphide of silver). Its two animals are in a style known as the Trewhiddle style, after a discovery in Cornwall.

essence, farmed land associated with settlements was divided up into massive 'fields' which were themselves divided into 'furlongs', which in turn were sub-divided into individual ploughable strips of land. It can be seen from later documents that one individual could hold strips in a number of furlongs; the whole suggests a considerable communal sense of purpose. Contrary to earlier theories on the development of what became known as the 'open field' system (that is without hedges), it is clear that in some areas at least the process was initiated on a grand scale and preceded the establishment of some estate and parish boundaries.[102] In Buckinghamshire this idea has yet to be completely reconciled with another important aspect of the Saxon landscape, the presence of a number of parishes along the Chiltern edge, of elongated form extending from good arable land for a distance up into less easily cultivatable land and woodland on the Chiltern plateau; the probable early date of some of these has been noted in Chapter 2. That some of the Chiltern land was less desirable for cultivation than that of the Vale to the north, can be seen in the survival into recent times of quite extensive areas of commons and heath here, such as Stoke, Iver and Wycombe heaths.[103]

As there are so few excavated late Saxon sites, archaeology has little to say about what cereals were cultivated or what stock raised, nor does Domesday give many clues. The commonest animals to be mentioned in Domesday are pigs, always linked with woodland on account of their being pastured there. At Wendover for example 2,000 pigs are recorded, at Bledlow 1,000, and 800 at Tingewick. There is one direct reference to woodland in Domesday linked to Newport Pagnell, where taxes are taken from 'the men who live in the woodland'. By inference, but occasionally by direct reference, draught oxen are indicated in noting the numbers of ploughs present, but Domesday has nothing to say about what is grown, except that corn is mentioned as a due to Aylesbury church. However mills certainly had an important role in the agricultural economy and a number of these are listed. Most would have been watermills, some perhaps animal-powered mills, but none would have been windmills which were first introduced into Buckinghamshire in the late twelfth century.[104]

The king's land

Brill was a royal holding at the time of Edward the Confessor and was retained by William. Both probably used it as a base for hunting in Bernwood Forest but there is not yet any direct archaeological evidence from Brill of this period. There are earthworks close to the church and although they have not yet been reliably dated it is in this locality that evidence of late Saxon activity is likely to lie. It has been argued that Brill had once been the centre of a much larger early estate.[105] One curiosity of this important place is that its church was subsidiary to nearby Oakley at the foot of the hill. Forest was an important resource and by the medieval period complex controls over Bernwood were in place. It is likely that other wooded areas of the county were similarly controlled by powerful landowners. Later, Walter Giffard of Long Crendon, one of William's men, had a 'park there for woodland beasts', but it is not known whether it existed before the Conquest. Aylesbury was another of William's manors (see on) and it was also in royal hands in the Late Saxon period. Royal manors such as Aylesbury,

Brill and (Princes) Risborough, together with forest, produced substantial revenue and were not lightly gifted out of royal hands.

Towns and markets

There were no 'towns' in the county in the early-middle Saxon period. Later, defining the difference between a town and a large settlement is not a straightforward matter. Various criteria have been used including defence, the presence of a mint, markets or fairs or freemen (burgesses). In the late Saxon period Buckingham fulfils several of these criteria. In AD 918 the Chronicle records that King Edward went there with his levies and spent four weeks constructing fortifications, one on either side of the river. A document of similar date known as the Burghal Hidage defines the length of its fortifications.[106] As Buckingham sits on raised ground within a loop of the Ouse and was later the site of a castle (Fig. 4.30), it is clear where one of the two fortifications would have lain although there is as yet no archaeological evidence, but the location of the second fortification remains uncertain. The significance of these defences will be discussed later. The existence of a church at Buckingham has already been noted. By the later tenth century it also had twenty-six burgesses, individuals with more freedom than most in the countryside and who personally owned holdings in the town but who still owed allegiance (and taxes) to a master. For instance, six of them were men of Azor son of Toti, and another was Burghard of Shenley's man. It can be presumed that burgesses were mainly craftsmen or merchants. From about the 960s, Buckingham also became a mint town (Fig. 4.31) and continued to be so intermittently until the Conquest[107] although its output was not great. Despite all this activity, the revenue value of the town to the king was less than a quarter of that of Aylesbury.

Newport (Pagnell) was held by Ulf, a thane, and was the only other place in the county to have had burgesses, although the number is not recorded. Its revenue value – greater than Buckingham – may be accounted for by the extent of its ploughland and possession of two mills (Buckingham had one). The 'new' element in its name suggests a deliberate creation. Arnold Baines has suggested that it was founded in the 870/880s by the Danes as a combined trading and frontier post (see on).[108] It was probably also a mint town for a short period although this has not been proven due to possible confusion with another 'Newport'.[109] No church is recorded here but it is likely that its foundation would have included provision for one. There is another place in the county which includes the element 'port' meaning town or market in its name, Lamport in Stowe parish.[110] A place of little consequence later, during the Saxon period it could have been perhaps, an occasional market as has been suggested for the site mentioned previously at Dorney.

The town of Aylesbury has previously been noted. There were no burgesses here but it was still worth more than either Buckingham or Newport. The early establishment of a minster here made it an important place as did the probable existence of a king's residence. When King Edward was here he might have been attended by his priest Wulfmer, whom Domesday records held land in adjoining Hartwell. Much of the town's income would have come from a market and associated tolls. It was also intermittently a mint town commencing in the

FIGURE 4.30
Buckingham,
showing the loop of
river which probably
contained the late
Saxon burh. The
green area with trees
in the centre of the
picture is the site of
the Saxon church.
After it was demol-
ished the new
church, visible in the
photograph, was
built between AD
1777–81 on the site
of Buckingham's
medieval castle.

FIGURE 4.31
Left: silver penny of
Edward the
Confessor minted in
Aylesbury about
AD 1046–8.
Right; silver penny
of Edward the
Confessor minted at
Buckingham in about
AD 1050–53

early 990s.[111] The name 'Silver Lane'[112] although just outside the area of the former hillfort, may pinpoint the general area of the coiners' workshops (Fig 4.31). It can be assumed that the king's sheriff (shire-reeve), an important figure in collecting the king's revenue, would have been based at Buckingham, but it is worth noting that King Edward's sheriff, Godric, had a manor at Weston Turville, close to Aylesbury, which would obviously be convenient when the king stayed here and in the town was one freeman who 'always serves the King's Sheriff' so Godric seems to have had a base here perhaps in addition to Buck-ingham. Sheriff Godric provides one of the few human touches in the Bucking-hamshire Domesday which records that 'Aelfgyth, a girl', had two and a half hides of land at Oakley, half a hide of which Godric the Sheriff had assigned to her from King Edward's household revenue 'so that she might teach his [Godric's] daughter gold embroidery'. Oakley is some distance from Aylesbury but adjacent to Brill, another of King Edward's bases, so it is entirely likely that Aelfgyth had duties there also.

There is little doubt that although undocumented, other towns would have been emerging in the late Saxon period, whose history may yet be uncovered by archaeological investigations. Some possible candidates include: Olney which had a large Romano-British settlement nearby, has tantalising clues to the existence of an early church[113] and which appears in a charter of AD 979: Amersham, with a Roman villa on its outskirts and a possible early Saxon cemetery nearby, and Wycombe, another place with an adjacent villa and on an important routeway towards Oxford. A post-Conquest reference notes St Wulfstan (d. 1095) staying there[114] and it was formerly known as 'Chepping' Wycombe. 'Chepping' is Old English *cieping*, a market place. Marlow, mentioned in a will of AD 1015, certainly had a bridge over the Thames in the thirteenth century and its manor was also referred to as 'Chepping' Marlow in the early fourteenth century.[115] Chesham is mentioned as a place in a royal will of *c.*977–975. Its origins may lie near its church rather than on the present High Street which is probably a medieval replanning. Other possibilities include Winslow, early in church hands and a market town in the medieval period, and Burnham. Finally, in Princes Risborough, another king's holding, the County Archaeological Service has noted a rectangular area on the town's plan which could indicate an early enclosure within the later market town.[116]

Many of these towns, or proto-towns, would have possessed churches established by local lords.

Communications

Although it is unlikely that during the early and middle Saxon periods there would have been any mechanism for maintaining the former Roman roads which crossed the county, some lengths remained viable. Akeman Street running from St Albans towards Bicester, passed through Aylesbury but in later times there seem to have been alternative routes via Grendon Underwood or Quainton. Watling Street, named in a treaty of AD 886–890 apparently maintained its importance as a through-route, later providing a focus for the Stony and Fenny Stratford. The place name Water Stratford indicates the continuing significance of the Bicester (Alchester)-Towcester road. The status of the Icknield Way, once considered pivotal to communication between Wessex and East Anglia, has in recent years been challenged both on historical and archaeological grounds,[117] although the name is certainly ancient; *icenhylte* appears in a Late Saxon Risborough charter.[118] In the same charter a 'King's Street' is noted but it seems quite an insignificant road. The road from Aylesbury to Oxford is certainly of antiquity as was the principal road through High Wycombe. There was obviously also a network of local roads; for example, many Chiltern holloways are likely to have been in use at this period and the existence of other routes is hinted at in fieldnames and charter boundaries.[119]

Sadly we know nothing about river navigation in the county during this period. In the thirteenth century the Thames was certainly navigable as far upstream as Oxford, although with difficulty around the numerous small islands later removed or bypassed.[120] There must have been wharfs; Marlow seems one likely location, and perhaps Hedsor another. How far the Ouse was navigable past Bedford is uncertain, but there were hints of a wharf at Stanton Low during the Roman period (see previous chapter).[121]

FIGURE 4.32
Left: two views of a silver coin of Cnut. He was king of England AD 1016–1035 and for much of that period also ruler of Denmark, Norway, and Lord of Orkney and Shetland etc. Found near Radclive.

Right: decorated copper-alloy fittings from a leather stirrup-strap. The flanged lower end would have hooked into the suspension loop of the stirrup. The design shows Scandinavian influence. Eleventh century, from Wendover Dean.

Vikings

Although Buckinghamshire receives little direct mention in the *Anglo-Saxon Chronicle*, the ninth and tenth centuries were full of conflict between the English and the raiders, occasionally described as 'Danes' in the *Chronicle* but more commonly as 'the host'. Much of their initial activity was coastal but in AD 839, for example, there was 'great slaughter in London' and in AD 851 'the heathen' overwintered in Thanet and 350 ships appeared in the Thames. Canterbury was then stormed before the host moved on to Surrey. By 870 Danes 'overran the entire kingdom'. In AD 871 they are reported locally in Reading and by 873 Mercia had fallen. In AD 878 King Alfred began to reverse the position and one Danish leader, Guthrum, accepted baptism. Alfred agreed a treaty with him in about AD 886 defining the 'Danelaw' frontier which ran from Bedford 'up the Ouse to Watling Street;[122] the Ouse crossing being at Stony Stratford this would have left the area of Castlethorpe, Hanslope etc. in Danish hands. Over the next two decades the Danes were mainly in control of East Anglia and Mercia, including e.g. Northampton and Bedford just over the county border. As previously noted, Baines has suggested that Newport Pagnell may have been founded as a Danish border post during these years.[123]

Probably during Alfred's reign and certainly that of his son Edward, a number of southern English towns were fortified, including in AD 918 Buckingham as previously mentioned. Another fort, probably designed to cope with raids up the Thames and attacks on Reading, was constructed at 'Sashes', an island on

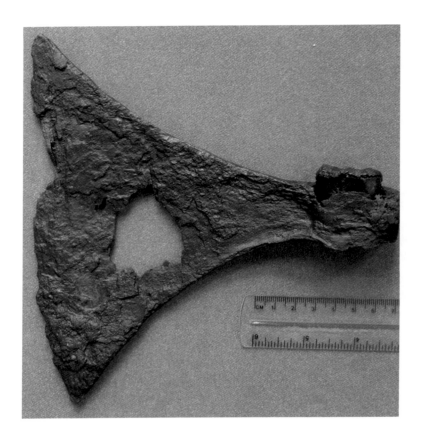

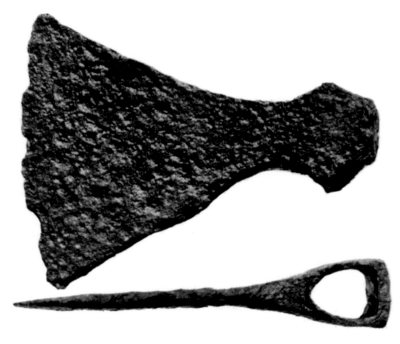

FIGURE 4.33
Top: a Viking-period axe, probably a battle axe, from Boulter's Lock, Taplow. Bottom: drawing of an axe from a Viking grave at Birka near Stockholm.

the Buckinghamshire/ Berkshire border. Although the Danish host was highly mobile on land, making considerable use of horses, boats were their favoured transport and many of their own fortifications in England were on or close to water. The impact of such raids on Thames traffic can be imagined, not least on embryo riverside trading settlements of which Marlow could be one. Despite Buckinghamshire's fortifications, in AD 921 having failed to take Towcester, the *Chronicle* records that the Danes 'sailed forth in marauding bands at night and waylaid unsuspecting folk, taking considerable spoil both in captives and cattle between Bernwood and Aylesbury'. In spite of continuing conflict there was gradual English recognition of the occupation. For example in the same year it is recorded that 'the entire Danish host in East Anglia swore union with him [Edward]' and over subsequent decades a new generation of Danes, some of whom may have known no other home became absorbed, a process probably not dissimilar to that of the earlier settlement by the Saxons. There are a few Buckinghamshire place names that include Scandinavian elements such as Skirmett but there has been no comprehensive study of these.

Recognition of one set of Norsemen did not mean that there were no more adventurers ready to try their luck and renewed incursions from the 960s led to attempts to buy off the invaders with tribute. The repercussions can be seen directly in Buckinghamshire where an estate at Risborough belonging to Archbishop Sigeric was transferred to the Bishop of Dorchester in AD 994/5 in exchange for ninety pounds of refined silver and two hundred mancuses of purest gold – no mean sum – so that the archbishop could buy off Danes threatening to destroy his church in Canterbury.[124] Locally, relationships cannot have been helped by a massacre of Danes in Oxford in AD 1002. In 1006 the Danish host again 'went where it pleased' and late in the year 'proceeded through Hampshire into Berkshire to their well-stocked food depot at Reading'. Massive tribute was paid in the ensuing years as they ranged freely, including making an incursion '… through the Chilterns, and so came to Oxford, and burned down the borough'. In 1010 still pretty well unchecked in southern England 'those who had horses rode towards the ships, and then quickly turned westward into Oxfordshire, and thence into Buckinghamshire … destroying by fire ever as they went' – one of the few direct references in the *Chronicle* to the county during these turbulent years. In AD 1017 King Edmund died and the Dane, Cnut, younger son of Swein Forkbeard, King of Denmark, who by then had 'visited' a great deal of England, became its king (Fig. 4.32).

Considering the conflict of the later ninth to early eleventh centuries, it is remarkable that so few Viking graves have been discovered in southern England, and none in Buckinghamshire.[125] A few weapons of general ninth-tenth century are recorded, for example a spearhead from Haversham[126] and others from Thornborough and Buckingham.[127] From Boulter's Lock, Taplow, there is an iron axe with copper-alloy fittings which is likely to be a Viking battle axe; a comparable example from a grave at Birka, near Stockholm[128] is also illustrated (Fig. 4.33).[129] A number of decorated copper-alloy fittings from stirrups have in recent years been found by detectorists, for example at Shenley Brook End,[130] Little Missenden, and Ivinghoe Aston.[131] Most of these are datable to the eleventh century and need have no military connection, but the design on some, such as the one illustrated here from Wendover Dean has Scandinavian elements (Fig. 4.32).[132]

On the 28th September AD 1066, four rulers subsequent to the death of King Cnut, a body of men who formerly themselves came from the north but had earlier settled on the other side of the Channel in 'Normandy' landed at Hastings, and a new chapter begins.

Chapter 5

Medieval Buckinghamshire
(AD 1066–*c*.1540)

Kim Taylor-Moore

Introduction

Domesday Book, William the Conqueror's great record of landholdings, shows that by 1086 the social and economic frameworks that underlay much of medieval England were already largely in place. The great Anglo-Saxon estates had fragmented into the more compact units of the manorial system, and smaller parishes had probably formed out of the large territories of the earlier minster churches. The Norman Conquest resulted in the almost complete replacement of the Anglo-Saxon aristocracy with one of Norman origin but the social structure remained that of a wealthy, landholding elite supported by the labours of peasants. Open-field farming, in which large, unenclosed fields were farmed communally, with individual tenants working separate strips, and probably the villages associated with it, had become the norm over large parts of the country. This included much of the northern part of Buckinghamshire, the most heavily populated part of the county, but the Chilterns and the south remained, for the most part, areas of dispersed settlement.

The county of Buckinghamshire seems to have been an entirely artificial creation with its borders reflecting no known earlier tribal or political boundaries. It had come into existence by the beginning of the eleventh century when it was defined as the area providing support to the fortifications at Buckingham. As Buckingham's strategic importance declined, the disadvantages associated with its position in the far north of the county quickly became apparent and, under Norman rule, many of the county functions were transferred to Aylesbury, which already had many urban attributes, such as a market, a mint and a minster church, and which was more centrally located. Apart from Newport Pagnell, where Domesday Book reveals the presence of burgesses (townsmen), there is no indication that any other place in the county had any claim to urban status at the end of the eleventh century.

The development of Buckinghamshire after Domesday needs to be seen against wider social and economic trends. In most of England the period of expansion and growth, which had begun in the ninth century, continued into the twelfth and thirteenth, a period characterised by the increase in the number and

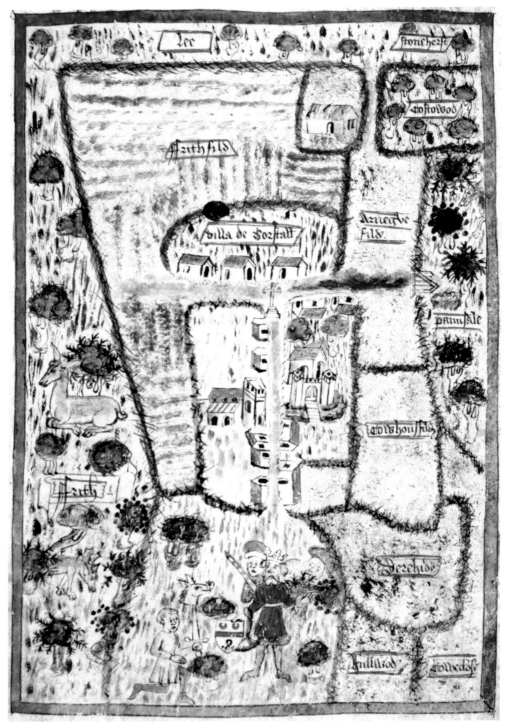

FIGURE 5.1 The earliest surviving Buckinghamshire map, a plan of the Boarstall estate dating from *c.*1440, shows the village with its surrounding fields and woodlands. The map was made to illustrate the claim of the Fitz-Nigel family to the hereditary keepership of the royal forest of Bernwood and depicts the king granting the keepership to Nigel in return for slaying a troublesome wild boar. The severed head of the boar can be seen impaled on Nigel's sword.

size of settlements, the bringing into cultivation of marginal land, particularly woodland, and the foundation of most of the towns known today. Growth was halted in the fourteenth century when the Black Death, following a series of failed harvests, famines and animal disease, led to a collapse in the population. Settlements shrank or were abandoned altogether and much of the land least suited to arable agriculture was taken out of cultivation as declining rents and the scarcity of labour saw lords increasingly turning to sheep farming as a source of profit. Some of Buckinghamshire's abandoned villages, now only visible as earthworks in the fields, date to this period. The changes were, in many ways, to the benefit of the peasants that had survived the crises as generally wages rose and the landholdings of dead neighbours could be acquired relatively cheaply. Some of the more enterprising peasants built up large landholdings and became substantial graziers or farmers themselves.

The effect, and timing, of the slump on towns was more mixed and depended largely on the extent to which they were able to take advantage of markets away from their own, declining, hinterlands by, for example, producing cloth for export, or supplying raw materials and agricultural produce to London.

Landscape and rural settlement

The earliest comprehensive maps of Buckinghamshire are those of Jefferys and Bryant which date, respectively, from the 1760s and 1820s, but, used in conjunction with earlier documents, maps and plans, they can be shown to depict a situation that had applied since at least the late medieval period. At that time the county could be divided, along the Chiltern scarp, into two broad but distinct regions. The Vale of Aylesbury and the clay lands to the north were 'champion' landscapes – that is landscapes characterised by large villages and extensive open fields. To the south lay the Chilterns, a woodland landscape with hamlets, farmsteads, irregular patches of open field (five or more per village), and much enclosed land.[1] The division was only approximate, so, for example, smaller areas of wooded and pastoral country broke up the monotony of the champion north, in Bernwood, Whaddon Chase, Whittlewood, Salcey and on the Greensand towards Woburn on the eastern edge of the county. South of the Chilterns, on the banks of the Thames, was a further small area of villages and open fields.

With the exception of a fifteenth century map of Boarstall (Fig. 5.1), there are no maps of Buckinghamshire villages before the sixteenth century. It is clear, however, that this division of the county into two landscape types goes back to the earlier medieval centuries, as deeds and surveys from the champion areas depict open fields divided into furlongs and strips in the twelfth and thirteenth centuries, whilst in the Chilterns the same types of written sources refer to multiple fields, hedged closes and newly cleared land. The Domesday survey of 1086 indicates a concentration of woodland in the Chilterns, and in the northern corners of the county, with a distinct absence in the centre. Ploughed land was most plentiful to the north of the Chilterns so, although we cannot be certain that large numbers of villages existed in the eleventh century, the features associated with them were already in existence.

FIGURE 5.2
Aerial photograph of
the nucleated village of
Ashendon. The parish
church is in the centre
of the picture.

FIGURE 5.3
Common-edge
settlement at Cholesbury.
This form of dispersed
settlement is common
in the Chilterns.

If eighteenth-century maps reflect the broad pattern of landscapes, and probably settlements, going back to *c.*1100, it is possible that they also depict the layout of the medieval settlements themselves. The maps show that many of the villages in the champion country consisted of houses grouped around a road junction, without obvious evidence of planning (Fig. 5.2). In others, however, signs of planning were more clearly visible, with lines of equally spaced houses arranged close together on either side of a street or green, as at Mursley and Maids Moreton.[2] In contrast, in the southern Chilterns there were many isolated farmsteads and interrupted rows in which houses stood side by side along roads, but separated from each other by a small field or croft. In the northern Chilterns, for example in Great Missenden and Cholesbury (Fig. 5.3), common edge settlements were present where houses were grouped around a common or green, and these also had an air of regularity, as if some authority ensured that the houses were set at roughly equal distances apart. This division was not absolute and a scatter of common edge settlements and interrupted rows was to be found in the wooded north-west and north-east of the county and some cluster type villages had grown up in the river valleys of the Chilterns and the south of the county.

Exploration of locations by excavation and by examination of old documents can tell us if the village layouts on later maps really reflect those of the medieval period. Results so far, from a relatively small sample, give a variety of indicators. In the Chilterns many of the settlements recorded in the nineteenth century were relatively new, as cottages on unoccupied and uncultivated land had proliferated after c.1600. Some Chiltern farms and hamlets, however, carry names recorded in the thirteenth century, suggesting the possibility of continuity of occupation and settlement form and an isolated farmstead, occupied in the twelfth and thirteenth centuries, has been investigated near West Wycombe.[3] In the champion area of the northern part of the county, the only nucleated village to be completely excavated, Great Linford, had building plots occupied continuously from the twelfth and thirteenth centuries into modern times, so its plan seems to have survived essentially unaltered for many centuries.[4] The complete plan of the medieval village would not, however, have been evident on eighteenth or nineteenth-century maps as it had already been partly depopulated in the seventeenth century. At Lillingstone Lovell the village was re-planned in the thirteenth century, when an ambitious lord occupied the central cross roads of an earlier clustered village with a new manor house, barn, dovecot and fish ponds. A new row of peasant houses was laid out on the eastern side of the lord's new complex.[5] In the same period, Ashendon seems to have expanded considerably, with the addition of a new street, and at Stewkley two settlements, either side of the church, each expanded in the direction of the church, resulting in one very long village.[6] The most common reason for a village to change its shape would be the abandonment of part of the settlement: for example investigations at Leckhampstead have shown that while at present it is a dispersed village with three 'ends', its layout was once even more complex, and one of the former 'ends' has shrunk to a single farm.[7]

These general patterns apart, most Buckinghamshire villages reduced in size in the later middle ages. There are 119 known examples where 'village shrinkage' has been noted on the ground. There are also eighty-three abandoned village sites (Fig. 5.4), a number which is comparable with the belt of midland counties running from Oxfordshire to Lincolnshire but the density in Buckinghamshire is very high, when it is remembered that almost all are concentrated in the champion country north of the Chiltern edge. Documents show that cultivation was in retreat by 1340, well before the Black Death. This is reflected in the early shrinkage of villages: part of Tattenhoe ceased to be inhabited by c.1300, and houses were abandoned at Ashendon and Westbury in the early fourteenth century.[8]

This slow attrition of houses in villages is apparent in documents (such as the court rolls of Akeley) and from archaeological evidence at Great Linford and settlements in Whittlewood. Also playing a part in the desertion of whole

FIGURE 5. 4
Aerial photograph of the
site of a deserted village
at Burston, near Aston
Abbotts. A sunken road
runs through with minor
tracks and the sites of
houses and enclosures
beside.

FIGURE 5. 5
Quarrendon. Quarrendon
estate is to the bottom
left; centre-right is the
site of the medieval
village with moat and
fishponds among trees.
The rectangular
earthwork centre-left
enclosed the gardens of
Sir Henry Lee during the
Tudor period. Left again
are other village
earthworks.

villages was the removal of the inhabitants by the landlord or his agents, for example at Quarrendon, where the Lee family of graziers who had become landed gentry, remodelled the manor house and imposed a large garden next to the village site (Fig. 5.5).[9] Deliberate depopulation to make way for pastures or parks was once thought to be the main reason for desertion, but only a handful of the deserted medieval villages, notably Doddershall with twenty-four houses put down and 120 people leaving, were said to have suffered a major loss of houses in the inquisition into such practices held in 1517.[10] The decay of the corn growing economy and social cohesion in villages could have been a major cause of desertion. Traces of medieval ploughing in open fields later turned over to pasture can still be seen in the form of the ridge and furrow found near many village sites (Fig. 5.6).

Although most archaeological investigations have focused on deserted villages, and thus, inevitably, on the north of the county, it is clear that some hamlets and villages in the south, like Great Hampden, suffered similarly from

FIGURE 5.6
The individual curving strips of medieval ploughing show as ridge-and-furrow, adjacent to the village of Padbury.

FIGURE 5.7
Cruck buildings at Swanbourne (top) and Haddenham (bottom). The walls of the Haddenham building are constructed from 'witchert', the local form of cob.

shrinkage and de-population. Further research may shed more light on the extent to which dispersed settlements in the Chilterns experienced the same fate as the villages north of the Chiltern edge.

There are many small domestic buildings dating from the late medieval period still standing within Buckinghamshire villages. Most are cruck-framed, a building style which had been used in the construction of houses belonging to wealthier peasants since the late thirteenth century. (Cruck frames consist of two curved timbers which reach from the ground and meet at a point at the top of the house. The roof sits on these timbers which bear its full weight thus allowing the walls to be constructed of lighter materials.) Long Crendon has more cruck houses than any other settlement in England but they occur throughout the county with over ninety-five known examples (Fig. 5.7).[11] Many others undoubtedly lie hidden behind the stone or brick structures of later centuries, as research in association with the Whittlewood project, notably at Akeley, has shown.[12]

The excavations of the Milton Keynes villages produced much evidence of the construction and development of peasant houses there. For example, at Great Linford, the rubble foundations of what had once been timber-framed houses with wattle and daub panels, built in the thirteenth or fourteenth centuries, survived with modification into the seventeenth (Fig. 5.8).[13]

The Milton Keynes excavations also produced a mass of evidence for peasant possessions and trade links. The richness of the metal finds (mostly buckles and other dress accessories) and the diversity of the pottery sources tell of the spending power of the peasantry and the extensive trade connections of a county

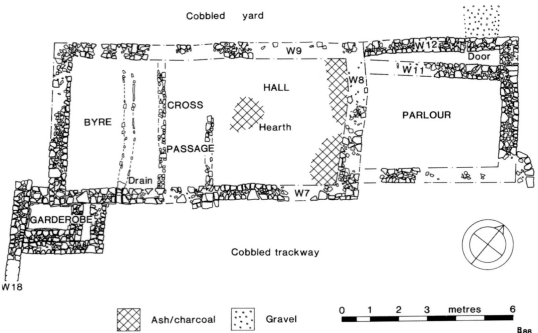

Cobbled yard

BYRE

CROSS

PASSAGE

HALL

Hearth

Drain

GARDEROBE

W9

W8

W7

W12

Door

W11

PARLOUR

W18

Cobbled trackway

Ash/charcoal   Gravel

0 1 2 3 metres 6

FIGURE 5.8
The plan of a mid-late thirteenth century farm-house excavated at Great Linford. The easternmost room was a subsequent addition. The walls, built of unmortared limestone rubble, probably stood to a height of 60cm and formed a base for a timber-framed structure.

FIGURE 5.9
Medieval objects in the County Museum: 1. belt end-plates. 2. buckle. 3, ampulla – all from Great Linford; 4. flute from Stanton Low. 5. tally stick from Bernwood. 6. spur from Great Linford. 7. bone spindle whorl from Aylesbury (not to scale).

with a dozen small towns in the later middle ages, and relatively easy contact with London. Figure 5.9 shows some of these objects together with others collected from around the county and deposited with the county museum.

Forests and deer parks

Royal forests were areas where only the king was allowed to hunt 'the beasts of the chase', primarily deer, and where special laws applied to protect both the animals and their environment. Although woodland was an important part of the forests generally they also contained substantial amounts of arable land and many settlements. There were three royal forests in Buckinghamshire – Salcey and Whittlewood, both partly in Northamptonshire, included several parishes in the north-east and north-west, whilst Bernwood, at its maximum extent at the end of the twelfth century, covered over 90,000 acres in the west between the rivers Thame and Great Ouse. Whaddon Chase, although not strictly a royal forest, having been granted by the king to one of his followers in 1242, was subject to similar restrictions.

Apart from royal forests, deer parks were established by lords throughout medieval England, particularly in woodland areas. As well as being status symbols, their purpose was to provide a securely enclosed area for the keeping of deer, usually fallow deer, to supply the lord with venison. The larger parks were, in effect, private hunting grounds, but deer in smaller parks were probably culled by a keeper on demand. Fifty-six medieval deer parks within the county are known from documentary sources but topographical and field name evidence suggests that there were many more.[14] Only the parks at Oakley and Long Crendon, both within Bernwood, were recorded in Domesday Book but parks at Lavendon and Newport Pagnell were known to have been in existence by the twelfth century. Most seem to have been created in the thirteenth and early fourteenth centuries and they were generally fairly small, the forty acres emparked at Little Linford in 1278 being typical. The land emparked was generally enclosed by a ditch and external earth bank topped with a wooden paling fence. Traces of such earthworks can still be seen at Olney, Newton Blossomville, Bradenham and elsewhere.[15]

Manors

The administrative organisation of land and people was based on the manor, a unit the primary purpose of which was to extract revenue from both for the benefit of the lord. This system had its origins before the Norman Conquest and, although evidence for buildings found at the few manorial sites excavated can usually be dated to the twelfth century or later, there are signs of earlier activity on some sites – for example, at Bradwell where it was established that ninth or tenth century wooden structures had been replaced by a stone house in the thirteenth century.[16] Lords in Buckinghamshire ranged from the king, through bishops and the aristocracy, to minor gentry and, increasingly, as time went on, Oxford colleges. Their manorial centres took many forms and, although most were manor houses, some originated as castles, as at Weston Turville, whilst others were religious houses or monastic granges, as at Gorefields and Shipton Lee.[17] All were involved in exploiting the land, however, as evidenced by the dovecotes, fishponds, mills and rabbit warrens often found near to the centres and which, together with the arable fields, meadows and wastes, made up the manor.

Manor houses were often surrounded by moats, the building of which reached its peak between about 1200 and 1325, a period of growth and prosperity when lords and wealthy freemen were investing in their establishments. Although moats could and did serve many purposes, their main role seems to have been as status symbols and their proliferation was largely due to fashion. Over 160 moated sites are known in Buckinghamshire but their geographical distribution is very uneven. The highest densities are found along the northern edge of the Chilterns and immediately below the scarp, where many parishes such as the Kimbles and Dinton with Ford have in excess of four each.[18] This probably reflects the existence of a lot of small manors in the area but might also indicate prosperous tenants developing social pretensions. Few moated sites are recorded in the Chilterns away from the northern edge, but there are a number of medieval earthwork enclosures, perhaps related to small woodland settlements. Limited excavations at some of these such as Fillington at West Wycombe and Bray's Wood at The Lee, indicate that the buildings within them were of manorial status. However, documentary evidence suggests that they were probably occupied by wealthy tenants rather than manorial lords.[19]

FIGURE 5.10
Earthworks of the moated manor site of Vaches, Aston Clinton. The main moat is water filled. There are other earthworks to the right, perhaps ancillary buildings and enclosures.

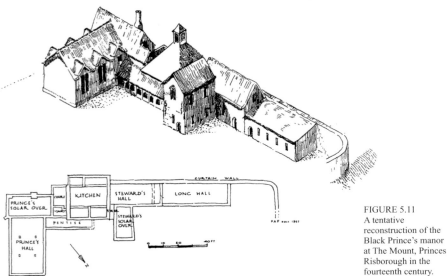

FIGURE 5.11
A tentative reconstruction of the Black Prince's manor at The Mount, Princes Risborough in the fourteenth century.

Some manorial sites continue in occupation to the present day, although traces of the medieval buildings rarely remain. Survivals include the fourteenth century manor house at Milton Keynes, the oldest known domestic building in the city, and the fifteenth century Little Loughton manor house which survives as a farm-house.[20] It is on manors held by the church, however, where most building work has been preserved, notably at Denham, where Westminster Abbey held a manor. Here the remains of three early fourteenth century timber aisled halls can be found which originally formed the main manor house, a sub-manor house and probably a steward's house.[21]

Many manorial centres, particularly in the north and centre of the county, have long been abandoned. The reasons for this are many – for example: at

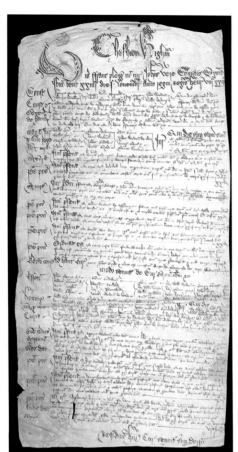

FIGURE 5.12
A roll from the manorial court of Chesham Higham, held 24 November 1530. It records the routine business of the court such as the swearing in of the jurors and their appointment of local officers, in this case a constable for Chartridge. Transactions in land are recorded and breaches of manorial custom, such as the abduction of animals from the pound and the cutting back of hedges, are dealt with.

Castlethorpe the manor was destroyed along with part of the village when the land was laid to pasture in the fifteenth century; the moated site at Broughton, near Aylesbury, was probably abandoned in the sixteenth century when two manors were consolidated; and at Aston Clinton the moat was filled in and the site of the original manor cleared during the nineteenth century to make way for the kitchen garden of the grander eighteenth-century house constructed nearby.[22] The site of another manor at Aston Clinton, known as Vaches Manor, survives only as an earthwork (Fig. 5.10). The royal residences in Buckinghamshire all fall within the category of abandoned sites. The king held seven manors in the county in 1086 and documentary sources indicate that royal residences existed at Aylesbury and Brill, although the exact location of neither is known. Excavations in 1955 at Princes Risborough almost certainly revealed traces of the large manorial complex, held by the Black Prince, within a moat close to the church (Fig. 5.11) but at Fulmer the substantial hall found was probably the predecessor of that built by Edward II in 1323–4.[23]

Documentary sources, such as accounts and the surviving records of manorial courts (Fig. 5.12), have supplied much of our knowledge of individual manors and how they operated and surprisingly few manorial sites have been investigated archaeologically. Of those that have, Bradwell and Whaddon are the most informative. At Bradwell some of the walls of the manor house, which was centrally located within a rectangular moat, were uncovered. The house, which went out of use in the fourteenth century, was found to have been a high quality building of lime-stone rubble faced with dressed stone, with a tiled roof and at least one decorated tile floor. A stone barn and two stone dovecotes were located nearby. The finds, including imported pottery and a chess piece, suggest that it was the home of a wealthy person.[24] At Whaddon the excavations revealed a hall and seven other buildings, including a kitchen, a barn, a smithy and several workshops, grouped around a cobbled yard. The group almost certainly formed a manorial complex which seems to have been occu-pied from the twelfth to the fourteenth century, although the smithy may have continued in use for longer, providing a service to the villagers.[25] In the far south of the county, excavations on meadowland in a bend of the River Thames, near Dorney, revealed that between the late eleventh and early thirteenth centuries some of the land had been used in connec-tion with a specialist horse-breeding enterprise belonging to the manor of Dorney.[26]

Markets and fairs

No fairs or markets in Buckinghamshire are recorded in Domesday Book, which is known to be incomplete in this respect, but the tolls of £10 recorded for Ayles-bury almost certainly related to a sizeable market there. There are records of nine markets and six annual fairs being held in the county before 1200 but the following century and a half saw a rapid rise in their number as lords, wishing to profit from the tolls and have an outlet for the sale of produce from their demesnes, rushed to acquire grants from the Crown. By 1350 there were grants for fifty-two fairs and thirty-four markets although, in practice, some of these may never have been held.[27] Many markets, such as those at High Wycombe, Aylesbury (Fig. 5.13), and Buckingham, continue to be held in what was the medieval market-place and evidence of long defunct markets remains in several villages such as Whitchurch and Great Horwood.

The timing of the fairs indicates that it was mainly agricultural produce that was bought and sold there – fifteen were held in September, when livestock would have been sold ahead of winter, and sixteen in July and August, when wool would have been traded. Other higher value goods, such as pots and pans, would also have been available but it was the weekly markets that would have supplied most of the day to day needs of the local population. Most markets were to be found in the north-east and the south of the county, with very few in the Chilterns and none at all in an area in the west of the county between Buck-

FIGURE 5.13
Many of Buckinghamshire's markets continue to be held in the medieval market place for example: (top) Aylesbury market in 1947; (bottom) High Wycombe market in 2009.

ingham to the north and Brill to the south. There could be several explanations for this – markets were often absent near to relatively large centres and the presence of Buckingham, Brill and Aylesbury could have inhibited their foundation. Alternatively, demand could have been low in what was predominantly a woodland area and markets across the border in Oxfordshire, such as those at Bicester and Thame, could have been meeting the needs of the population.

The numbers of both markets and fairs were reduced by about one half with the crises of the late fourteenth and fifteenth centuries. By 1500 fairs were still being held in twenty-two places, six of which had lost their market. Only fifteen markets survived, nearly all of them in places with some pretension to urban status.[28]

Towns

Buckingham and Newport Pagnell were the only towns in the county recorded in Domesday Book but Aylesbury's important minster church and large market almost certainly mean that it too was an urban centre by this time. Little is known about the early development of Newport Pagnell, whose name shows that it had been a trading centre before the Norman Conquest, or of Buckingham, as its defensive significance decreased and it evolved into a fully-fledged town. Archaeological investigations in Aylesbury have revealed little about the eleventh century town but there is copious evidence for activity from the mid twelfth century onwards.[29] This includes signs of the digging of a boundary ditch probably dividing Church Street into burgage plots which were long, narrow plots stretching back from the street-front, typically found in towns. The apparent increase in activity coincides with documentary evidence

FIGURE 5.14
Excavations on the west side of Marlow High Street before redevelopment. The chalk walls of a cellar can be seen.

which suggests that at this time that Aylesbury began to take over many of the functions of a county town from Buckingham. The topography of the medieval town remains obscure as no further boundary features were recovered and very few buildings have been located, however its form may still have been influenced by the prehistoric hill-fort within which it was sited. An excavation at High Street, Marlow (Fig. 5.14), the first in the town centre, has hinted that it may also have been an early urban centre, with the site showing signs of continuous, non-domestic occupation from the tenth century to the present. The High Street was confirmed as a major medieval street which had probably been about four metres wider than it is currently, the subsequent encroachment testifying to later growth.[30]

Most of the county's towns developed in the thirteenth and fourteenth centuries when lords, as well as founding markets, established new towns where tenants could hold land for fixed rent and without labour services. None of these 'new' towns seems to have been founded on green-field sites, but they were, rather, developments of existing settlements. The street plan of Olney shows clearly that development there in the thirteenth century was in the form of new burgage plots laid out in a regular plan to the north of the market square, which linked it to the existing village centre. At Wendover, the parish church was left isolated as the success of the borough founded about half a mile away attracted new settlement to it.[31] Limited excavations have shed some light on the early development of other towns. The focus of settlement in Chesham appears to have been St Mary's church, until the fourteenth century, when the first evidence of buildings fronting the High Street appears.[32] Areas quite close to the centres of Winslow and Princes Risborough were shown to have been peripheral to the main settlements in the thirteenth and fourteenth centuries, suggesting that these places did not expand significantly in their early years.[33] Other investigations have been less successful. At High Wycombe, which had become a prosperous town by the thirteenth century, excavations, in the business quarter of the town, revealed that no deposits of medieval date survived there, all having been destroyed by later activity.[34]

There were no large-scale, specialised industries associated with any of Buckinghamshire's towns, other than production of pottery at Brill and simnel bread for the London markets at High Wycombe, and it seems that a position on a busy main route was crucial to successful development. Olney, Newport Pagnell, Stony Stratford and Buckingham are all located where main roads cross the Ouse, and Great Marlow occupies a similar position on the Thames. Princes Risborough, High Wycombe, Amersham and Wendover are each situated at one of the ends of the two main routes through the Chilterns and, although Aylesbury lies close to where Akeman Street crosses the River Thame, its success was probably due more to its being ideally situated as a place of exchange for goods and provisions from the clay vales, the heavily wooded Chilterns, and the rich lands at the foot of the Chiltern scarp. Excavations in the town have confirmed its role as a marketing centre for the local area but have failed to find much evidence of longer distance trade.[35] In contrast, items found from one site in Olney testify to successful long-distance trading there, the assemblage including a Norwegian ragstone whetstone, lava querns (stones from a hand-mill), of possible German origin, and an Anglo-Gallic token.[36]

The period from about the middle of the fourteenth century to well into the sixteenth was a time of decline in many towns, as the effects of the population crisis caused by the Black Death began to be felt. Written records start to survive in some quantity from this period which help to shed some light on how Buckinghamshire's towns fared, perhaps the most informative of which are the records of the subsidies which were raised at various times to finance wars with Scotland and France. Although there are problems with these records they can probably be safely used to indicate broad comparative trends. The 1446 lay subsidy returns for the county indicate that, on the whole, the the towns were getting less relief for 'poverty and decay' than the countryside, and three towns – High Wycombe, Marlow and Brill – got no relief at all. Apart from these three towns, the relief granted seems to be largely inversely proportional to the wealth of the town, which may indicate that it was the smaller towns suffering the most decay and that a group of bigger, more successful, towns was beginning to emerge.

Archaeological evidence for this period paints a complex picture. Near Kingsbury, in Aylesbury, the digging of new pits, probably for cess, slowed down from the mid fourteenth century and had stopped altogether by the fifteenth, although this is a phenomenon seen in many towns and was probably due to the introduction of night cartage after the Black Death.[37] Excavations in other Buckinghamshire towns have been limited in number and small in scale, but results from them show that in the north there is evidence of early decline – for example trial trenches in Buckingham revealed signs of contraction from the mid-fourteenth century, not reversed until the seventeeth, and at Olney an industrial site near to the town centre seems to have been in decline before the Black Death.[38] At Chesham and Marlow there are few indications of decay, although a building on Chesham High Street shows signs of having been abandoned for a short period in the early fifteenth century.[39]

By the time of the 1524 subsidy the effects of the increasingly dominant London markets can clearly be seen, with the towns in the south of the county showing much higher rates of growth than those in the north. This is particularly true of High Wycombe, which had become a significant trading centre for London cornmongers. Aylesbury also seems to have experienced rapid growth and, with a probable population of between about 1300 and 1700 inhabitants, was the biggest town in the county. It was still small in national terms, however, and probably lay somewhere between fifty-eighth and eighty-third in the list of largest towns in England.[40]

Before the sixteenth century none of the county's towns had formal borough charters confirming their right to manage their own affairs through a mayor and council, although such institutions were known to have existed in High Wycombe by 1285. There is documentary evidence for the earlier existence of municipal institutions in Buckingham and Newport Pagnell, but their influence seems to have been minimal and most towns, including Aylesbury and Marlow, remained under the control of their lords with little sign of corporate life. It is possible, however, that, in some cases, the religious guilds which were known to have existed in most Buckinghamshire towns did, however, have some role in their governance.

Few medieval buildings survive in Buckinghamshire towns, a number having been demolished in development in the 1960s and 1970s, although their footprints are often preserved in today's town plans. The islands of buildings in the Market Square in Buckingham, the pattern of small streets in part of High Wycombe and the narrowing of the High Street in Marlow all testify to medieval encroachment onto what were originally open spaces.

One of the oldest remaining structures in the county is the cellar under the King's Head in Aylesbury (Fig. 5.15), dated to the late thirteenth or early fourteenth century, which was used as a tavern and had a staircase leading up to shops, at ground floor level.[41] More evidence survives from the fifteenth century, a time of much re-building often financed by wealthy merchants or important townspeople. The King's Arms in Amersham, for example, retains parts of the original fifteenth century hall house and at Beaconsfield a wing of the former

FIGURE 5.15
View of the King's Head, Aylesbury, in the
summer of 1962, when the buildings in
front were demolished. Its fifteenth-century
window which opens onto a medieval hall
can be clearly seen.

FIGURE 5.17
The Chantry Chapel, Buck-
ingham, which originated in
the twelfth century as the
hospital of St John. It was later
to become the Royal Latin
School.

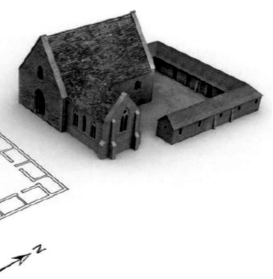

FIGURE 5.16
A reconstruction of the hospital of St
John the Baptist, High Wycombe,
next to its thirteenth-century plan.

Crown Inn dates from the same period.[42] In Aylesbury Ralph Verney, one time
steward of the manor and Lord Mayor of London, acquired the King's Head and
the plot next door and had a grand hall constructed, whilst in Buckingham a
family of wealthy lawyers who held much property in the town built Castle
House, a stone-built courtyard house.[43]

Institutional buildings, such as hospitals (Figs. 5.16 and 5.17) and
almshouses, were built in most towns and fifteenth century timber-framed guild
houses survive in Aylesbury and possibly, in part, at Fenny Stratford. That at
Aylesbury, which now forms part of the county museum, was investigated and
recorded during renovations in 1990, when it was revealed to have been a
substantial building with a large two-storey jettied range, fronting the street,
with a smaller single-storey wing behind. Although the carvings and mouldings
that survive demonstrate that the building was of high quality, it had no heating

of any form. One large upstairs room could only be reached from outside and this was probably a room used for meetings and fraternity dinners.[44]

Monastic houses, hermitages and hospitals

Domesday Book records only one minster church in Buckinghamshire, at North Crawley, but there is evidence to suggest that up to half a dozen others existed, most notably at Aylesbury, Buckingham and Wing.[45] There is no record that any of these developed into fully fledged monasteries, along Benedictine lines, as the reform movement spread across the country in the tenth and eleventh centuries, although this may have been the intention behind the gift of Wing church to the Benedictine foundation of St Nicholas at Angers.[46] In total, sites of only eighteen monastic houses are recorded in Buckinghamshire and none with a foundation date before the late eleventh century. The earliest was probably Tickford Priory, near Newport Pagnell which was founded c.1100 as a dependency of the Cluniac Abbey of Marmoutier, and was intended for sixteen monks.

The twelfth century saw a rapid increase in the number of monasteries in England due both to the increasing desire amongst lords to found houses, and the establishment of new orders concerned with a return to monastic ideals and a more ascetic way of life. There is a noticeable concentration of small houses founded in this period in north Buckinghamshire, on the fringes of what was then the heavily wooded area along the Northamptonshire border. By the middle decades of the twelfth century, religious houses of various orders had been established at Luffield, Bradwell, Lavendon, Snelshall and Biddlesden and most, if not all, must have been involved in woodland clearance. Grants of woodland to such houses would have suited both the patrons, who were gifting only marginal land for development, and the orders, who preferred sites that were both remote and free from manorial restrictions. Of this group, only Bradwell Abbey has been the subject of much modern investigation which has shown that the chapel, once thought to have been seventeenth century, was constructed in the early fourteenth century. It was the centre of the, possibly long-standing, healing cult of Our Lady of Bradwell and was found to contain an important series of medieval wall paintings depicting pilgrims approaching a place of healing.[47]

The wealthiest of Buckinghamshire's abbeys – Missenden and Notley (Figs. 5.18 and 5.19) – were mid twelfth century foundations of the Arroasian order (a branch of the Augustinian order) and both lay in the centre of the county. Missenden, one of the earliest and largest of the Arroasian houses in the country with at least twenty six canons, lay in the heavily wooded Chilterns and came to hold much cleared land. The documentary records are good and remains of monastic buildings survived until 1985 when they were largely destroyed by a fire. Little is known of the history of Notley Abbey, its early records having been lost, and, although about two thirds of the original ranges survive with few external alterations, no modern comprehensive archaeological or architectural study has been produced.

No further religious foundations were made in the northern half of the county until the middle of the thirteenth century, when there was a flurry of activity within the area forming the royal forest of Bernwood, the exact extent of which

FIGURE 5.18
Fifteenth-century roof
timbers of the dormitory
at Missenden Abbey:
arch-based trusses,
destroyed by fire in
1985.

FIGURE 5.19
An engraving of 1730
of the ruins of Notley
Abbey.

was under dispute. An Augustinian priory was established at Chetwode in 1245 and the canons there served the royal chapel at Brill as well as the local churches. The priory was dissolved shortly after being annexed to Notley in 1460 but the chancel of the priory church remains in use as the parish church. Four of the five hermitages known from anything other than place-name evidence or single, late documentary references also lay within Bernwood. (The fifth – Coddimoor hermitage – lay in what was then the royal forest at Whaddon.) The only other foundation of the mid thirteenth century in the north of the county was that of the Augustinian priory at Ravenstone, close to Yardley Chase. There are no standing remains and little is known about the priory, which was in royal owner-ship for much of its life.

The monastic houses in the south of the county were founded somewhat later than those in the north, the earliest being Medmenham, a Cistercian house subsidiary to Woburn Abbey, which was established in 1204 on the site of what

FIGURE 5.20
Pier at Medmenham
Abbey underpinned with
brickwork: a survival
from the abbey's church.

may have been an earlier Christian structure close to the River Thames (Fig. 5.20).[48] The only female houses in the county, the Benedictine priory at Little Marlow founded in 1218, and the Augustinian abbey at Burnham founded in 1266, also lay close to the Thames. Much survives of the monastic buildings at Burnham, which were built within a pre-existing moat and may have occupied the site of an earlier manor house.[49]

There were two small houses of the military orders in the county. The Knights Hospitallers founded a commandery in c1180 at Hogshaw and the Knights Templars had a preceptory at Bulstrode. Little is known about either but walls interpreted as the remains of related buildings have recently been discovered at both sites.[50]

The only urban monastic house in the county was the small Franciscan Friary established in Aylesbury towards the end of the fourteenth century. The approximate size and location of this is known from documentary sources[51] but the site has yet to be identified archaeologically. Most towns had hospitals, however, which were known to have existed at Buckingham (Fig. 5.17), Aylesbury, High Wycombe (Fig. 5.16), Newport Pagnell, Stony Stratford, Great Marlow and Wendover.

Churches

The century or so after the Norman Conquest saw the continuation and acceleration of the shift from the early established minster churches which served quite large areas, to local churches and the consolidation of the parochial system. It seems likely that most of what became the county's parish churches had been founded by the end of the eleventh century but only four are recorded in Domesday Book and, apart from the probable minster church of Wing, only a few surviving buildings have visible late Saxon or early Norman elements.

Documentary evidence provides information on the date of foundation for some churches – for example, it is clear that a chapelry of Aylesbury existed at Quarrendon by the early twelfth century when a writ confirmed the acquisition of burial rights from the mother church.[52] The status of the new churches depended largely on their acquisition of such rights and the graveyards of minster churches probably shrank as burials were diverted to them. Excavations at the possible minster churches of Aylesbury and Wing do, indeed, seem to indicate that parts of both cemeteries had stopped being used for burials and that there had been secular encroachment onto cemeteries by the late twelfth or early thirteenth century.[53]

Small churches became established as more permanent features, as lords continued to endow them with land and to re-build them, a movement which originated in the south and east of the country in the early decades of the

A Changing Church

The church of St James the Great, Hanslope, from the south, showing how the building developed in the medieval period (Fig 5.21). The oldest parts of the building date from shortly after 1160, when William Mauduit, chamberlain of the Exchequer and lord of Hanslope, applied to the Bishop of Lincoln for permission to build a new one on the present site. The initial building seems to have consisted of a nave and a square-ended chancel and much of the latter remains (see inset). The south aisle was added in the middle of the thirteenth century when the manor passed, through the female line, to the Beauchamp earls of Warwick who extended the church and made improvements to existing structures. In the fifteenth century the earls wanting a church that reflected their growing wealth and status, extended what was already a very large church adding a clerestory, tower and porches.

eleventh century and spread outwards. Most building work in Buckinghamshire, however, dates from the late thirteenth to the fifteenth centuries when many churches were extended or improved. Aisles were added to almost all churches at the beginning of the period and often later enlarged. In the following centuries clerestories (high level windows lighting the nave), chapels and towers were built. The two hundred or so churches in Buckinghamshire with medieval fabric have thus largely been built piecemeal (see Fig. 5.21), with very few that can be said to be predominantly of one date – notable exceptions being Stewkley (twelfth century) and Hillesden (fifteenth century).

Improvements were often funded by lords but, increasingly, also by wealthy traders or merchants, who often chose to be buried and commemorated in the churches they had patronised. The resulting monuments can still often be seen – for example, wooden effigies at Clifton Reynes (Fig. 5.22) and brasses at

FIGURE 5.22
Wooden effigies dating from 1331, in the church of St Mary, Clifton Reynes. They depict Ralph Reynes, who died in 1310, and his wife Annabel.

FIGURE 5.23
Early fourteenth-century wall painting of St George in All Saints Church, Little Kimble.

FIGURE 5.24
A fifteenth-century mould for making souvenir badges of John Schorne, found in Edlesborough in 1986. It depicts him preaching beneath a canopy with his devil-trap, a thigh boot on his right in photo. Although no badges from this mould are known to survive, many similar ones have been found around North Marston and also at Canterbury, Salisbury and London, where his cult seems to have been particularly popular.

Thornton and Taplow, where the earliest civilian brass in England is to be found. Buckinghamshire churches are particularly rich in wall paintings – those at Radnage date from c.1200 but the most notable survivals are from the fourteenth and fifteenth centuries, such as those found at Little Kimble (Fig. 5.23), Chalfont St Giles, Little Missenden and Broughton (Milton Keynes).

Aisles and chapels were frequently dedicated to saints, sometimes to those forming the focus of long-standing local cults, such as St Rumbold at Buckingham. The shrines of saints were not the only focus of popular devotion, however, and, despite the increasing formalisation of religion, there is evidence that folk religion continued in the county often under a Christian guise. The sites of four medieval 'holy wells' are known, with a further forty possible sites identified, and documentary evidence attests to thirteenth century well worship at High Wycombe and Linslade. At North Marston the shrine erected over the tomb of John Schorne, the rector there who died in 1314 and who was popularly believed to have trapped the devil in a boot and created a miraculous holy well, continued to attract pilgrims from a wide area until the Reformation (Fig. 5.24).

Defensive structures

The sites of twenty three motte and bailey castles and four ringworks are known

within Buckinghamshire, although unidentified mounds and place-names, such as Castle Fee recorded in the fourteenth century in Aylesbury, indicate that there may have been more. Buckingham is probably the only castle in the county constructed as part of the eleventh-century programme of building Norman strongholds to control the newly conquered kingdom. Parts of it survived into the eighteenth century before being demolished and some evidence may still remain within the substrata of the mound now occupied by the parish church. Excavations in 1877 recovered masonry and a fireplace and, more recently, the remains of a large wall or early medieval embankment, perhaps forming part of the castle bailey, were located.[54]

The remainder were manorial centres or strongholds erected in the centuries after the Norman Conquest and mostly abandoned by the end of the thirteenth century. Some may have had military functions but most provided prestigious residential and domestic facilities for the heads of important local lordships. They were located in two main areas: along both edges of the Chilterns and in the north-eastern part of the county on both sides of Watling Street. Bolebec (Whitchurch), Wolverton and Castlethorpe (Fig. 5.25) were the centres of Buckinghamshire baronies. The only motte to be excavated in the county, at Weston Turville, was found to have been originally over six metres high with a surrounding ditch of similar proportions to that at Bedford Castle. By the end of the thirteenth century the castle had been transformed into a moated manorial enclosure.[55]

The only complete medieval fortified building in the county is the fourteenth-century gatehouse with encircling moat at Boarstall.

FIGURE 5.25
Aerial photograph of Castlethorpe showing the curving inner defence of of the castle. In the background are the banks of its outer defence.

Crafts, trade and industries

Buckinghamshire is rich in the raw materials needed for pottery and tile production – clay, wood, and water – and medieval kilns have been found at many sites in the county. Most seem to have been small, rural production sites supplying the local market and the potting was almost certainly a part-time occupation combined with small-scale agriculture. Some sites produced both pottery and tiles as at Ley Hill, Latimer, where a fifteenth-century pottery kiln was discovered built into a disused roof tile kiln (Fig. 5.26).[56] Tile-making was a seasonal occupation and it is likely that potting was also. At Denham, for example, the potters appeared to live elsewhere and the site may only have been used in the summer months.[57]

At Olney Hyde, however, where a deserted medieval settlement and pottery production centre were identified in 1957, excavations revealed a house/workshop close to the kilns. The site, which contained at least fourteen kilns, produced roof tiles and a wide range of pottery, much of which was was wheel-thrown and well-made. Small fingerprints found on some items showed that children had assisted in its manufacture. The kilns were probably in operation from the mid twelfth century to the early fifteenth when they closed and the village was deserted.[58]

The most successful of the county's clay-based industries, and the only ones with any significance outside their immediate localities, were the pottery industry based at Brill, and nearby Boarstall, and the tile workshops of Penn. Much has been learnt about the Brill-Boarstall industry since four thirteenth and fourteenth-century kilns were excavated in 1953.[59] Documentary sources indicate that pottery production had probably begun in the area by the second half of the twelfth century, and that there were ten kilns in operation by 1254. The industry seems to have reached its zenith in the late thirteenth and early fourteenth centuries, when the vast amounts of pottery found in excavations demonstrate that it was a large-scale production site for cooking pots, pans, skillets, herring dishes and glazed jugs (Fig. 5.27). All were of good quality, wheel-thrown and well fired. The cooking pots and pans were distributed over an area within about a twenty mile radius of Brill, but the more highly decorated glazed jugs, some of exceptional quality, seem to have been marketed over a much larger area, and were to be found in gentry households across England.[60]

It has been suggested that at least part of Brill's success was due to it being the location of a favourite royal hunting lodge in the thirteenth century. The requirements of the royal household may have stimulated the initial demand for goods – for example, jugs and pitchers would have been required for decanting the wine that was known to have been delivered from Southampton in wooden barrels – but the king's visits were too infrequent to explain the continued success of the industry. Although pottery production continued at Brill throughout the medieval period and beyond, its popularity outside the local area had begun to decline by the mid fourteenth century due to the general economic slump and competition from kilns located in Hertfordshire, Northamptonshire and elsewhere.

The tile workshops at Penn were probably the most extensive and successful in England between c.1350–c.1380 'with a near monopoly on the supply of vast

FIGURE 5.26
Late medieval kilns at
Ley Hill, Latimer. The most
obvious feature are the curved
walls of a pottery kiln on the
left, however this was built
within an earlier tile kiln
whose rectangular outline,
also built of tile, can be seen.

FIGURE 5.27
Medieval jugs made at Brill
found in excavations in
Aylesbury.

FIGURE 5.28
Floor tiles made at
Tylers Green, Penn in the
fifteenth century: designs
depicting repeating
patterns (top) and animals
(bottom).

quantities of decorated floor tiles and roof tiles for royal palaces and major ecclesiastical and secular buildings all over London and the south-east' (Fig. 5.28).[61] As in the case of Brill, an early established industry seems to have expanded rapidly, largely as a result of royal patronage, in this case in the form of the supply of roof and floor tiles to the building works at Windsor Castle, where Penn tilers were kept occupied for over eight years. Tiles were supplied to other royal sites, such as Westminster Palace and the Tower of London, and to other places around Penn, or close to the navigable parts of the Thames. The last reference to decorated floor tiles occurs in 1388, by which time the market had probably become saturated, but the production of roof tiles continued.

Woodland industries were vital to the economy of the Chilterns, and evidence of the management of resources can be seen in the surviving wood-banks, originally built to protect coppiced trees from grazing animals, and in areas of ancient coppicing and pollarding. Some of the wood was grown for timber, which was in great demand for construction, but much was grown for fuel, the latter being sold both within the county and in London. There is also documentary evidence of small-scale woodworking taking place. The most important archaeological evidence for wood-working, however, comes from Whaddon, in the north of the county, where a late fourteenth century turner's workshop, forming part of the manorial complex, was excavated. Lathe turned bowls at all stages of production were found, supplying much information about both the woodworking process and the range of vessels produced.[62]

The cloth trade was never very extensive in the county although attempts were made to attract the industry to towns such as High Wycombe and Buckingham, where a 'Drapers Hall' had been built by 1473. Fulling mills are known to have existed at many places in the county – for example, that at Newton Blossomville owned by the prior of Ravenstone in 1378, and the High Wycombe borough records contain many references to weaving, fulling and dyeing.

The existence of tanning and leather working is mainly known from documentary sources but traces of the industry, possibly dating to the medieval period, have been found in excavations in or near to towns for example at Walton, near Aylesbury, High Wycombe and Marlow.[63] There is also some evidence for metal working in the county, for example smithies have been found at Whaddon and Brill and traces of iron smelting and possibly copper working at Olney.[64]

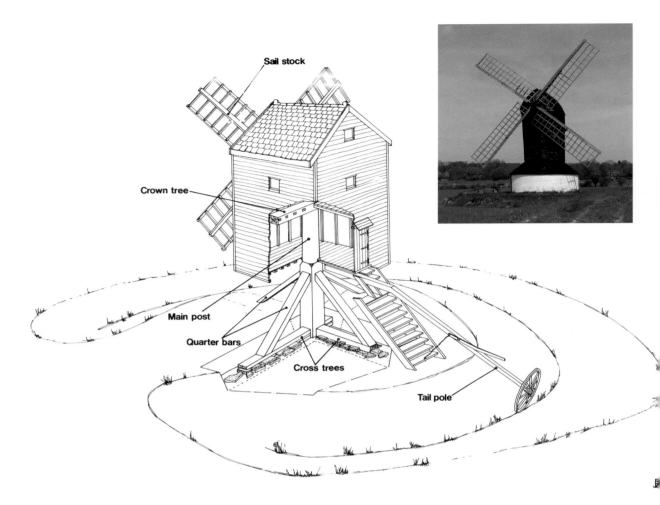

Sail stock

Crown tree

Main post

Quarter bars

Cross trees

Tail pole

FIGURE 5.29
A reconstruction of the medieval post-mill at Great Linford and, inset, the post-mill at Pitstone. Although the latter probably dates from the seventeenth century (1623 is carved into the frame) the basic technology remained unchanged from the medieval period.

Virtually every manor in the county would have produced corn that required milling so it is not surprising that Domesday Book records 134 watermills in Buckinghamshire with at least another 118 added by 1500. The most valuable were situated along the Ouse, the Thames and the Colne but some areas, such as the north-central part of the county, recorded few mills, possibly because of the lack of suitable streams. Some grain from these areas would have been transported to other sites for milling but much must have been milled by hand or by animal power. Windmills were an early introduction to the county with one of the earliest in the country being recorded at Dinton by about 1180. Much is known about some of these early post-mills, both from the accounts kept of their construction – for example, that at Ibstone, built at great expense by Merton College in 1293/4 and from the excavation of the mound of a late thirteenth century windmill at Great Linford (Fig. 5.29).[65] Stone built tower mills began to replace post-mills by the end of the thirteenth century and that built at Turweston by Westminster Abbey is one of the earliest known examples in the country.[66]

A large number of other crafts and trades must have existed in the county ranging from the carpentry, masonry, tiling and thatching evidenced by standing buildings to the small scale fur production indicated by the finding of skeletons of skinned cats in Aylesbury.

Transport and Communications

The River Thames was the main route for shipping bulky goods, such as firewood, from the Chilterns and southern half of the county to London in the middle ages and there were important wharves at Marlow and Hedsor, the latter probably being used for the shipping of Penn tiles. Excavations at Hedsor in 1894–5 and 1968–9 revealed what is thought to have been part of the medieval wharf.[67] It is not known whether the Great Ouse was used for transporting goods but no wharves that were in use in the medieval period have been found, nor are there any surviving records of tolls being charged or collected. It is possible that the many mills known to have existed on the river made it virtually impassable.

Although river transport was in many cases cheaper, the overwhelming majority of journeys were made by road and, even where goods were shipped by river, at least part of the journey would have been overland – for example, in the fifteenth century a boar that was being delivered to the London house of the Earl of Wiltshire from Aylesbury was sent to Reading for shipping on via the Thames.[68] The road system was, therefore, vital to the economy of the county and its study crucial to an understanding of the development of trade, towns and settlement patterns. There is a surprising lack of archaeological evidence in respect of the use of the roads for carrying goods, an important exception being the find of a hoard of fifty-nine thirteenth-century copper alloy brooches at Hambleden. These were probably made in a London workshop and lost or hidden when being carried to High Wycombe or beyond for sale.[69] However, much relevant information will inevitably come from documentary sources as roads, many of which were never constructed but evolved over time and remained in use over many centuries, are not generally datable by excavation.

The earliest cartographic evidence for the existence of a national road system, centred on London, comes from the Gough Map, dating from c1360. This shows that three of the main roads radiating out from the capital – those to Bristol, Oxford and Carlisle – passed through Buckinghamshire. Other Roman roads – Akeman Street; the Ouse Valley roads linking Oxford and the south-west with Cambridge and East Anglia; and the road from Towcester to Dorchester-on-Thames which crossed the Ouse at Water Stratford – are known to have remained in use, and the Fleet Marston to Thornborough road continued to be the main route from Aylesbury to Buckingham until eighteenth-century turn-piking. There is virtually no evidence of the making of new roads in medieval England and it was probably the increasing traffic, particularly to and from London as its importance grew, that gave rise to the development of generally accepted routes between places, often based on more ancient trackways.

The routes that grew in importance can often be identified by the building of bridges, sometimes with a chapel or hospital attached – for example, the hospital of St John the Baptist which had been built on the bridge at Stony Stratford by 1306. Many medieval bridges in the county are known from documentary sources, one of the earliest being the bridge of Avice recorded at Barton

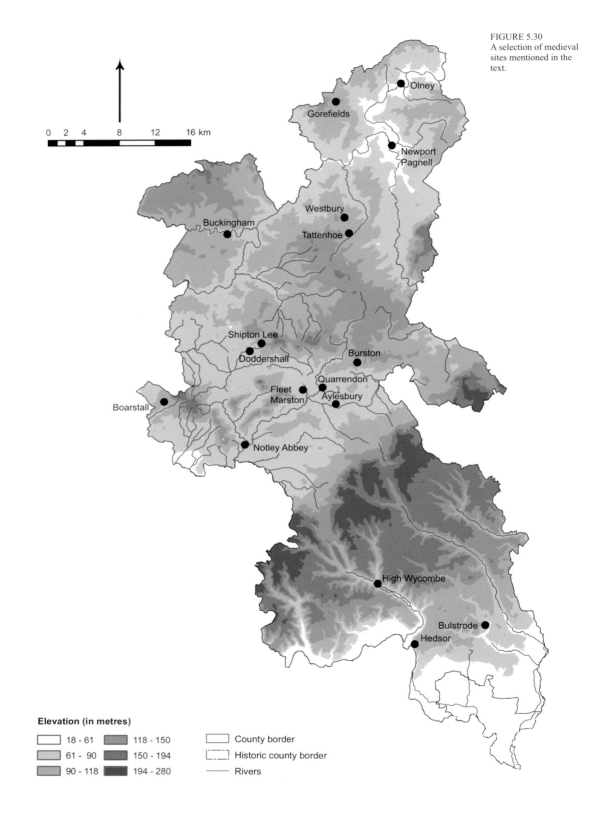

FIGURE 5.30
A selection of medieval sites mentioned in the text.

Hartshorn in 1225, but the only one to survive is the fourteenth-century bridge over the Twin at Thornborough. Rivers were not the only obstacles to travellers, however, and parts of the claylands north of the Chilterns were sometimes virtually impassable in wet weather. Causeways are known to have been constructed on well-used routes such as the one that Leland, in 1540, noted ran nearly all the way from Aylesbury to Wendover.[70]

In addition to longer distance routes, there must have been a myriad of local roads and tracks used for the movement of goods, by cart or pack animal, and by people as they went about their everyday business. Identification of such routes is notoriously difficult but, in the north of the county, many holloways have been located by aerial photographs and field surveys of deserted villages – for example that at Stowe, where the old road from Buckingham to Towcester was traced as a series of tracks, holloways and earthworks.[71] The roads and tracks in Padbury were studied by map and aerial survey in 1958.[72] This showed many roads leading out from the village to the open-fields with very few continuing to the parish boundary. In the north east of the county, work at Milton Keynes has identified many of the roads that were in use in the medieval period – for example the routes linking villages to the nearby market towns, known as Portway in every parish through which they passed, and roads linking villages on opposite sides of the rivers which generally crossed the river at mill sites.[73]

The pattern of roads in the Chilterns seems to have been very different, with the main arterial routes passing through the river valleys and many lesser used tracks linking dispersed settlements to the commons on higher ground. A study mapping the character of roads in a small section of the Chilterns has given an indication that roads and tracks used in the medieval period may have had much earlier origins, their alignment being cut across by the building of Akeman Street in the Roman period.[74] This gives some support to the theory of the survival of a pre-Roman, co-axial road network across the Chilterns and the north of the county.

Conclusion

England had changed considerably by the first decades of the sixteenth century. The population remained low after the crises of the fourteenth century, meaning that land and resources were concentrated in the hands of fewer people, and the grip of feudalism was weakening. Lords no longer farmed directly and some peasants had acquired large land holdings, becoming wealthy on the profits of pastoral agriculture. High wages fuelled the demand for goods available at markets or in towns and a group of wealthy merchants and tradesmen was beginning to appear. Evidence of these changes can be seen in the Buckinghamshire landscape – in the replacement of arable open fields in the north with the enclosures of wealthy graziers, in the deserted villages, and in the wave of new building in the towns.

An urban network was in place, consisting largely of towns which had grown up in the optimistic times of the thirteenth century and which had proved strong enough to survive the troubles of the fourteenth and fifteenth. The influence of the London markets was increasing and the south of the county, particularly the area around High Wycombe, was prospering more than the north where transport to the capital was more difficult and expensive.

A stone built church was present in virtually every parish, and most had had towers added or been enlarged, embellished or improved in other ways. Chapels of ease had been constructed to serve communities distant from the mother church and, in many cases, these had been raised to parish church status. The wave of enthusiasm for monasteries had passed, however, and several Buckinghamshire houses were dissolved before the Reformation, most of their estates going to endow Oxford colleges. The last religious house in the county, Burnham Abbey, surrendered to the king in September 1539.

Postscript

Sandy Kidd

The Battle of Bosworth Field (1485), and the subsequent accession of Henry Tudor to the English throne, marks the traditional end of the Middle Ages. For a book based on local landscape and material culture such an abrupt end is not appropriate but there is no doubt that the 'Tudor Age' was a time of fundamental change in English society, and in England's relationship to the world. The breaks between each of the chapters in this book have been defined by continental influences: the first migrations into what was to become the island of Britain; the adoption of farming; the Roman conquest; the Anglo-Saxon migrations and the Norman conquest. It therefore seems appropriate that the final chapter should end with Henry VIII's break with Roman Catholicism and the dissolution of those quintessentially medieval institutions, the monasteries. But this was not the only change as before the end of the fifteenth century the first English sailors had reached the New World, and in 1558 Calais, the last outpost held by England on the other side of the Channel, fell to the French. With the benefit of hindsight these events mark Britain's abandonment of medieval territorial ambitions in Europe and set her on a future course of worldwide imperial expansion based on sea-borne commerce and naval power.

Buckinghamshire was greatly affected by Britain's changing place in the world, and particularly its proximity to London. In the sixteenth-century economic forces drove ambitious men such as Sir Henry Lee to depopulate villages like Quarrendon on the outskirts of Aylesbury in order to graze cattle destined for the London market, and to build a mansion and ornamental garden; the 'peacock's tail' of the successful courtier. For the next three hundred years Buckinghamshire's landscape was to a great extent moulded by similarly powerful and wealthy aristocratic families who promoted the enclosure of the county's medieval open-fields and commons, leading to the depopulation or relocation of hamlets and villages, and the creation of great houses and country estates. New farms were built in what had formerly been open fields creating an agricultural landscape which survives to the present day across large parts of the county.

Buckinghamshire's lack of coal, metal ores and fast-flowing streams to power mills meant that it was not at the forefront on the industrial revolution. But as Buckinghamshire lay astride the main lines of communication from the capital to the industrial and commercial centres of the north and west it was crossed by two of the world's first inter-city railways – the London and Birmingham and Great Western. The arrival of the railways in the 19th and early 20th centuries provided easy access to the capital city thus stimulating the growth of Buckinghamshire's towns, a process that continues to the present day. The ending of the Catholic Church's monopoly of religious authority enabled the rise of non-conformist religious groups, who built numerous chapels and meeting houses. In recent times this religious diversity has been augmented by purpose-built mosques, and a Buddhist chanting hall reflecting the openness of Buckinghamshire society drawn from the process of 'globalisation' that began five hundred years ago.

Today our heritage is better understood and more widely appreciated than ever before, but that should be no reason for complacency. In a world of rapid change, with many diverse social, economic and environmental pressures, we can use our knowledge to protect the best of our past, and use this unique local knowledge of 'deep time' to celebrate and maintain those qualities which make Buckinghamshire special.

Notes

Chapter 1 – Earliest Buckinghamshire

1. Parfitt *et al.*, 2005
2. See Stringer, 2006, for an informative introduction to the subject.
3. Oakley *et al.*, (1977)
4. For a readable and detailed introduction to Quaternary climate change, please see Imbrie and Imbrie (1986).
5. Housed with Buckinghamshire County Council, Milton Keynes Council and for parts of the old county, Berkshire Archaeology.
6. Sherlock, 1960
7. White, 1997
8. Catt, 1978
9. Ibid
10. White, 1997
11. Sherlock, 1960
12. River terraces are formed by the accumulation of fluvial material along the sides of a river valley. These deposits would have been laid down when river levels were higher, before downcutting takes place. See Bridgland, 1994 for a more detailed account of this process.
13. BP = Before Present, with present defined as being 1950.
14. Green *et al.*, 1996
15. Wymer, 1999
16. There is a detailed discussion in Bridgland 1994.
17. Sherlock, 1960; Jukes-Browne & Osborne White, 1908
18. Wymer 1968
19. Shotton *et al.*, 1980
20. See Stringer (2006) for more information on the Bytham river.
21. Roberts, and Parfitt, 1996
22. Preece *et al.*, 2007
23. Gibbard *et al.*, 1986
24. Grid reference: SU 947840; Wymer, 1968
25. Grid reference: SU 945843; Wymer 1968
26. Wymer, 1999
27. Bridgland, 1994
28. Schreve *et al.*, 2002
29. See McNabb, 2007 for a more detailed discussion.
30. Wymer 1968
31. Grid reference: SU 958822; Wymer, 1968
32. Grid reference: TQ025802; Wymer, 1968
33. Lacaille, 1936; Wymer, 1968
34. Green *et al.*, 1996
35. Murton *et al.*, 2001
36. A *tufa* deposit is a sedimentary rock formed by the precipitation of carbonate in fluvial or lake water settings.
37. Murton *et al.*, 2001
38. Bridgland, 1994
39. Grid reference: SU 849879, Wymer, 1968

40. Grid reference: SU 861873, Wymer, 1968
41. Grid reference: SU 883884, Bridgland, 1994
42. Grid reference: SU 883585, Bridgland, 1994
43. Grid reference: TQ012801, Wymer, 1968
44. Wymer, 1968
45. Bridgland. 1994
46. Ibid
47. Sherlock and Noble, 1922
48. Wessex Archaeology, 2005
49. Lewis *et al.*, 1992
50. An interstadial is a short duration of warm conditions occurring between within a glacial period. This one was named after organic-rich lake deposits found at Low Wray Bay, Windermere, in the Lake District.
51. Mithen, 1994
52. Lowe and Walker, 1997; Barker, 2006
53. Barker, 2006
54. Momber and Campbell, 2005
55. Ingrouille, 1995
56. e.g. Chambers *et al.*, 1996
57. Birks, 1989
58. Parker and Robinson, 2003
59. Wessex Archaeology, 2005
60. Birks, 1989
61. Parker and Robinson, 2003
62. Richmond *et al.*, 2006
63. Sidell *et al.*, 2000; Wilkinson *et al.*, 2000
64. Lubbock, 1865
65. Peake, 1917
66. Jacobi, 1978
67. Gardiner, 2003
68. Jacobi, 1978; Smith 1992. Defined as the Maglemosian techno-complex.
69. A *microlith* is a small stone tool, made from flint (or sometimes chert), less than 5cm long. It is thought that several microliths would be mounted on bone or wood handles to form composite hunting or food-processing tools.
70. Smith, 1992
71. Hodder, 1983
72. Clark 1972, *Star Carr: A Case study in Bioarchaeology*
73. For example Healy *et al.*, 1992; Ellis *et al.*, 2003
74. Lacaille, 1963
75. Wymer, 1977
76. Lewis *et al.*, 1992
77. Wessex Archaeology, 2005, 2009
78. Numbered 2a, 2b, 5 and 6 in the excavation records.
79. Wessex Archaeology, 2009
80. Radiocarbon determination NZA-19005: Wessex Archaeology, 2005
81. Wessex Archaeology, 2009
82. Lewis *et al.*, 1992
83. Reynier, 2005
84. See, for example, Mithen, 1999; Myers, 2000; Kozlowski, 2003.
85. Simmons 1996
86. For example, Mellars, 1987; Simmons, 1996; Richard and Mellars, 1998
87. For example, Smith, 1992
88. For example, Simmons and Innes, 1996 (a) and (b)

89. Mellars and Wilkinson, 1980
90. Stainton 1989
91. Farley, 1983
92. Croft, and Mynard, 1993
93. e.g. Jacobi, 1973; Morrison, 1980
94. Smith, 1992
95. Conneller and Warren, 2006
96. Mithen, 1994; Price 1997
97. Meddens, 1996
98. e.g. Moffett *et al.*, 1989, Thomas, 1991
99. e.g. Parker *et al.*, 2002
100. e.g. on Hampstead Heath; Girling and Greig, 1985

Chapter 2 – Prehistoric Farmers

1. For the extensively referenced 'resource assessment' up to 2007 on which this chapter is largely based see Biddulph 2009 and Kidd, 2009.
2. See Cunliffe, 2008, 88–139
3. Renfrew, 1989
4. This view need not envisage deliberate genocide. Rather, it is possible to draw upon the work of Jared Diamond (1998, 195–214) looking at the impact of later contacts between indigenous peoples and European agriculturalists. Diamond points out that human crowd diseases such as measles, tuberculosis and flu are probably derived from pathogens found in cattle, pigs and other domesticated animals. By the time Europeans reached the New World they had developed resistance to these conditions whereas Native Americans who had never encountered them were exposed to their full force – it is estimated that Native Americans suffered up to 95% mortality in the contact period. Whilst we do not have direct evidence for such a plague effect at the Mesolithic/ Neolithic transition the conditions for it could have been present as Britain's Mesolithic population may have been isolated before farming reached Europe when the channel land-bridge was inundated (c 6500 BC), whilst Central European farmers lived along-side their domestic livestock in large longhouses which would have provided ideal locations for the transfer of pathogens.
5. Genetic studies of modern populations have given rise to wildly different estimates of Neolithic inputs to modern populations, ranging from 20% to 100%. Study of DNA profiles of ancient European hunter-gatherers and farmers is still developing, but research on mitochondrial DNA from early Neolithic females in Central Europe suggests that they did not have a strong genetic influence on modern populations; and by extension the studies support a Palaeolithic ancestry for modern Europeans (Haak *et al.*, 2005).
6. The Channel may not have been as wide as today as there were probably still sand-banks and islands forming an archipelago in the southern North Sea (Coles, 1998).
7. Parker *et al.*, 2002. The 'elm decline' in Britain is first recorded 4393–4357 BC and lasted just over a thousand years. It is attributed to a complex interaction of Dutch elm disease, climate change and human disturbance of natural woodlands, including the use of elm leaves as cattle-fodder.
8. Hey and Barclay, 2007
9. Allen, *et al.*, 2004, 85–91. These dates are amongst the earliest secure radiocarbon dates for cereal cultivation in Britain, the arrival of which is currently attributed to c 3950 BC–3630 BC (Brown, 2007).
10. Society of Antiquaries Newsletter 25/07/2008. See also the Wessex Archaeology web site: http://www.wessexarch.co.uk/blogs/news/2008/06/30/stone-age-house-found

11. Bradley, 2007, 69–77
12. Lewis *et al.*, 2006
13. I am grateful to Nick Crank at Milton Keynes Council for this information.
14. I have assumed a starting population of less than 200 hunter-gatherers at a density of 1 per 10km^2 growing with the adoption of agriculture at rates of 1–4% per annum until reaching early agriculturalist capacity of c 5 per km2, giving a population of 9–10,000. Population densities and growth rates are based on Renfrew, 1987, 124–133 and Diamond, 1998, 45. For comparison, the recorded population of Buckinghamshire in the Domesday Book (AD 1086) was 5095 households (representing perhaps c 25,000 individuals), almost all of whom were engaged in peasant agriculture bringing about 50% of land under arable cultivation.
15. Land snail shells survive well in the largely alkaline and neutral soils of the Chilterns and north Bucks clay vale. They are most useful for distinguishing between open grassland or wooded environments using particular indicator species although other environments such as wetland environments can also be recognised. Obvious limitations in comparison with pollen studies are that particular plant species cannot be identified and that the catchment area for a sample will usually be very localised and possibly not representative of the wider area (e.g. snails of wet shady ground found in a ditch).
16. Bonner and Parkhouse, 1997. Unfortunately no radiocarbon dates were obtained for this rather imprecisely dated clearance episode.
17. Possible flint mines are recorded on Pitstone Hill and at High Wycombe, in the former case the distinctive annular earthwork of the spoil heap appears to be respected by the later prehistoric Grim's Ditch suggesting an early date. Prehistoric mines probably took the form of 'bell-pits' with a narrow opening dropping vertically into a larger cavern from where horizontal shafts would follow seams of good quality flints. Horizontal shafts (known as 'adits') could also have been dug into a slope to follow a seam.
18. Schofield and Humble, 1997. 333 lithic scatters were assessed of which 49 had no Neolithic/Bronze Age component whilst 166 were solely of these dates, the remainder were multi-period. Scatters vary tremendously in size with many just being represented by a handful of artefacts whilst more prolific sites produce hundreds or even thousands of worked flints. Since early 1990s another major fieldwalking survey has been carried out in the Whittlewood area of north Buckinghamshire.
19. The traditional interpretation is expounded in Hepple and Doggett, 1994 and its critique in Harrison, 2003.
20. In an ambitious paper published in 1993, Ted Bull drew attention to a "bi-axial" pattern of roads and trackways surviving to the present day across the Chilterns and north Buckinghamshire which he suggested pre-dated the Roman road network and might be Bronze Age, or even Neolithic, in origin akin to co-axial field systems recognised elsewhere (Bull, 1993). Subsequently, similar networks have been noted in the Hertfordshire Chilterns extending into Buckinghamshire (Williamson, 2002). Partial support for the 'Bull hypothesis' comes from the Buckinghamshire Historic Landscape Characterisation Project (Green and Kidd, 2006) which identified extensive "co-axial fields" surviving in the Buckinghamshire Chilterns into modern times, mostly between Aylesbury and Chesham. For medieval strip parishes see Hepple and Doggett, 1994, 61–65
21. Masefield, 2008
22. By the late 1990s 136 pit alignments had been recognised in Northamptonshire (Kidd, 2004).
23. Although there are no signs of defences at Walton itself, Aylesbury hillfort lies only a short distance to the north, an association which may be more than coincidence.
24. Another recently excavated site at All Souls Farm, Wexham, shows a similar Iron Age hiatus between a circular Bronze Age enclosure and a sizeable Roman settlement (Steve Ford, pers comm).
25. R.J. Williams in Croft and Mynard, 1993, 5–10

26. e.g. Coldharbour Farm, Bonner and Parkhouse, 1997.
27. It has also been suggested that Danesfield Camp at Medmenham occupied a strategic position on the frontier between the Atrebates and the Catuvellauni; but the pottery from the site need be no later than c 100 BC (Keevill and Campbell, 1991).
28. It is noticeable that the distinctive Late Iron Age 'Belgic' cremation burials typical of the Catuvellaunian/Trinovantian areas of Bedfordshire, Hertfordshire and Essex are yet to be found south of the Chiltern scarp whilst distinctive 'saucepan pots' typical of Hampshire are occasionally found in the Chilterns.
29. See Booth P, Dodd, A. Robinson, M. and Smith, A. 2007, p. 365–371.
30. Earlier Trinovantian coins are rare in Northamptonshire and there is a distinct, if imprecisely dated, later middle Iron Age culture, defined by the reoccupation of Hunsbury hillfort (Northampton), numerous enclosed farmsteads and a distinctive local decorated-pottery style apparently copying southwestern 'Glastonbury Ware'. (Kidd , 2004)
31. The largest known late Iron Age coin find in Britain, from Leicestershire, comprised 17 individual hoards containing in all over 5000 Iron Age silver and Roman Republican coins and also a Roman cavalry parade helmet – it is interpreted as a ceremonial meeting place of the Corieltavi.
32. Of 364 Celtic coins from Buckinghamshire recorded on The Oxford Celtic Coin Index 73.1% are attributed to the Catuvellauni/Trinovantes (Essex/Hertfordshire), 14.6% to the Atrebates (Berkshire/Hampshire/Sussex), 2.2% to the Dobunni (Gloucestershire/Somerset), 2% to the Cantii (Kent) 0.8% to the Durotriges (Dorset), 0.5% to the Corielatavi (Leicestershire/Lincolnshire) with the remainder being either Gaulish or Mediterranean imports or unidentifiable. *http://www.finds.org.uk/CCI/index.php*. Note that the coin index does not include all the finds from the much-dispersed Whaddon Chase hoard.
33. Although a mixed group of hand-made and wheel-turned pottery from Cippenham, Slough has been given a rather broader date range of *c*. 50 BC to AD 40 (M. Lyne in Ford, S. 2003).
34. Stontium isotope analysis of tooth enamel from seven cattle at the Gayhurst barrow is consistent with local origins for five beasts,but the other two had been born further afield then brought to the local area in their first or second years, well before they were slaughtered. One of the two non-local animals probably came from an area of chalk geology, perhaps the Chilterns, whilst the other probably originated in western Britain. The non-local animals were most likely obtained through long-distance trade networks in order to maintain the health of herds by obtaining fresh bloodlines rather than being specific funerary gifts (Towers *et al.*, in press).
35. A similar conclusion was reached by a study of British Iron Age diets based on stable isotope composition of burials and other evidence. Diets were found to be high in animal protein with significant cereal consumption but little sign of non-domesticated animals or plants or fish. (Jay and Richards, 2007).
36. Green 2004
37. The full publication of this important project by Oxford Archaeology is eagerly awaited. Some interim reports have been published by Tim Allen and colleagues in *South Midlands Archaeology* and elsewhere. For references see Biddulph 2009 and Kidd 2009. An excellent education pack is available.
38. Childe and Smith, 1954
39. Hey, Dennis and Mayes, 2007
40. For full excavation report see Chapman, 2007
41. Cotton and Frere, 1968; Green, 1981
42. Allen, Hayden and Lamdin-Wymark, 2009
43. Farley, pers comm
44. Williams, 1993a
45. Farley, 1983

Chapter 3 – Roman Buckinghamshire

1. Branigan 1987
2. Ashcroft 1940
3. Scott 1993, 25
4. Cocks 1921
5. Lyne 2006, 2
6. Branigan 1967, 138
7. Williams & Zeepvat 1994, 207–208
8. Allen 1986
9. Kidd 2004, 107–108
10. Woodfield 1977, 384–399
11. Webster 1980, 118
12. Farley *et al.*, 1981, 53
13. Branigan 1987, 37
14. Neal 1987
15. Waugh, Mynard & Cain 1974
16. Morris *et al.*, 1970
17. Cox 1997
18. Johnson 1975
19. Yeoman & Stewart 1992
20. Green 1970, 58
21. Woodfield 1989
22. Neal 1987; Collard 1988; Hunn *et al.*, 1995
23. Parkhouse 1997
24. Scott 1993, 29–30
25. Zeepvat 1993, 10
26. Woodfield *in* Mynard 1987, 52–59
27. Zeepvat *in* Mynard 1987, 79–81
28. Zeepvat *in* Mynard 1987, 90–96
29. Williams *et al.*, 1996
30. Mynard 1987, 82–90; Zeepvat 1988
31. Mynard 1987, 97–104
32. Scott 1993, 27
33. Green 1965
34. Scott 1993, 29
35. *ibid*, 30
36. *ibid*
37. Mynard 1987, 30–31; 39–40 respectively
38. Roundell 1862
39. Scott 1993, 31
40. *ibid*
41. Ashcroft 1938; 1939; 1940; Branigan 1969
42. Stone 1859
43. Branigan 1971
44. CVAHS 1985
45. Hartley 1959
46. Perring and Brigham 2000, 156
47. Cocks 1921; Farley 1983
48. Ford *et al.*, 2001, 79–123
49. Thatcher 2006
50. RPS 2005, xii
51. Allen 2005

52. Ford 2004
53. Coleman *et al.*, 2004
54. Zeepvat 1991, 23
55. Branigan 1967, 147
56. Taylor 1975
57. Williams & Zeepvat 1994
58. Branigan 1971
59. Cocks 1921
60. Ford 2000
61. Mynard 1987, 37–39
62. *ibid*, 32–34
63. Williams *in* Mynard 1987, 43–45
64. Zeepvat *et al.*, 1994
65. Neal *et al.*, 1990
66. Booth *et al.*, 2007, 24–26
67. Petchey 1978
68. Morris & Wainwright *in* Holgate 1995
69. McOmish *et al.*, 2001, 91–92
70. Green 1965
71. Scott 1993, 30
72. Bucks Historic Environment Record, 02399000
73. *pers. comm.* R Tyrrell
74. Farley *et al.*, 1988
75. Parkhouse 1997, 155–162
76. Toynbee 1964, 156
77. Storer 1863
78. Williams & Zeepvat 1991, 321
79. Hunn *et al.*, 1995, 53
80. Green 1983
81. Toynbee 1964, 81, plate XVII
82. Henig 1992, 158
83. Green 1976, 196–197
84. Petchey 1979, 35–39
85. Liversidge 1954
86. MK Historic Environment Record, 1367000
87. Zeepvat *in* Mynard 1987, 18
88. Anon 1923
89. Hey 2005, 31
90. Dunnett 1971, 145
91. Davis & Bull 2003, 30
92. Atkins & Rees 2008
93. *Recs Bucks* 47.1, 2007, 222
94. Johnson 1975, 3–56
95. Allen 1979; Cox 1997
96. Coleman *et al.*, 2004
97. Waugh 1972
98. Zeepvat 2003
99. Farley & Wright 1979, 81–97
100. Neal 1987
101. Collard & Parkhouse 1993, 66–75
102. Chapman *et al.*, 1999, 17–30
103. Farley 1973, 329–335
104. Branigan & Niblett 2003, 57

105.   Wessex Archaeology 2007
106.   Marshall 1995; Booth 1999; Taylor 2004
107.   Woods *et al.*, 1981, 369–395
108.   Corder 1943; Tarrant & Sandford 1972
109.   Oakley *et al.*, 1937
110.   Stainton & Stanley 1987
111.   Allen & Mitchell 2001, 27
112.   Zeepvat 1997
113.   Edwards & Wells 2006
114.   Thatcher 2006, 28–29
115.   Head 1964, 228–231
116.   Marney 1989
117.   Allen 1986
118.   Zeepvat 1994
119.   Lowndes 1870
120.   Hunn & Farley 1995, 113–126
121.   Farley 1999
122.   Rivet 1969
123.   *Recs Bucks* 36, 1994, 179
124.   Booth *et al.*, 2007, 313–314
125.   Coleman *et al.*, 2004, 14–17
126.   Henig 1984, 129–131

Chapter 4 – Saxon Buckinghamshire

1.   The version used here is *The Anglo-Saxon Chronicle*, trans GN Garmonsway 1954.
2.   Views differ as to the meaning of Thame/Thames; it may mean 'dark river' (Ekwall 1960) or simply 'flow' (Owen 2007).
3.   EPNS 1925
4.   The difficulties of defining ethnic identity by archaeological means have only been clearly acknowledged in recent decades, see for example Lucy 2002, 72–87.
5.   Myres 1977, 287
6.   Neal 1987
7.   Williams and Zeepvat 1994
8.   Allen 1986
9.   Branigan 1971and 1973
10.   Cocks 1921
11.   Farley 1976; Dalwood *et al.*, 1989; Parkhouse 1995; Ford, Howell and Taylor 2004; Stone 2009
12.   Croft and Mynard 1993; Thorne 2005; Preston 2007: Hancock 2008
13.   Masefield 2008
14.   It has been suggested that in Northamptonshire and East Anglia that there was a retreat from claylands during the early Saxon period. The original hypothesis has been refined to take into account the subtleties of local soil variation in Williamson 2008,127–8.
15.   EPNS 1925
16.   Jones and Page 2006
17.   Ibid 52–53
18.   Page 1996, 220–1
19.   Farley 1997
20.   PAS record
21.   Farley 1992
22.   Ivens, Busby and Shepherd 1995

23. Parkhouse and Bonner 1997
24. Ivens, Busby and Shepherd 1995
25. Foreman, Hiller and Petts 2007, 33–4
26. Allen 2005, 25
27. Parkhouse and Bonner 1997
28. Masefield 2008
29. Hancock 2009
30. HER records
31. However, a burial recently found not far away has been dated to the medieval period (information from S.Kidd).
32. Farley 1987
33. Hunn, Lawson and Farley 1994
34. Ivens, Busby and Shepherd 1995
35. Masefield 2008
36. Hancock 2009
37. Stevens 1884
38. Geake 2002 has a useful discussion of 'late' burials.
39. Astill and Lobb 1989; Pine 2003
40. Williams 1993
41. Williams 1993
42. Williams and Zeepvat 1994
43. Allen 1986
44. Ford and Taylor 2001
45. Phillips 2005
46. Masefield R 2008
47. Allen 2000, 25
48. Preston *et al.*, 2007
49. Gill 2008
50. Hancock 2008
51. Ford 2008
52. Williams 1993
53. Ibid
54. Ivens, Busby and Shepherd 1995
55. Farley 1976; Dalwood 1989; Parkhouse 1995; Ford 2004; Stone 2009
56. Phillips 2005
57. HER record
58. Bull 1978
59. Ford 2008
60. Foreman, Hiller and Petts 2002
61. EPNS 244–5
62. Preston 2003
63. Astill and Lobb 1989
64. Preston 2007
65. Thorne 2005
66. Farley 1980
67. Ford 2000
68. Allen *et al.*, 2006
69. Love 1996
70. Bailey 1994
71. Durham 1978
72. Farley 1986
73. Farley 1979: Allen 1983
74. Bailey 1989

75. Kidd 2004
76. Gem 2003
77. Holmes and Chapman 2008
78. Taylor and Taylor 1980–4
79. Stockerand Went 1995
80. Mynard 1994
81. The topic has recently been considered by Bailey 2003.
82. Pevsner, Williamson and Brandwood 1994
83. Parkhouse 1998
84. The edition used here is Morris 1978
85. Bailey 2004 discusses the transfer of ownership in Buckinghamshire as a whole.
86. Adkins and Petchey 1984.
87. Reed 1979, 181–4
88. Reed 1979, 178–181
89. Baines 1981
90. Mynard and Zeepvat 1992
91. Pine 2003
92. Ivens, Busby and Shepherd 1995
93. Mynard 1994, 121–150
94. Zeepvat *et al.*, 1994
95. Mynard and Zeepvat 1992
96. Mynard 1994
97. Thorne 2005. Finds from the site included a smith's hoard.
98. Page and Jones R, 2006, 87–8
99. Enright 1996
100. HER records, except Ashendon, see Slatcher 2004.
101. Foreman, Hiller and Petts 2002
102. Oosthuizen 2005
103. Jefferys 1770
104. CMAG 1978
105. Baines 1993
106. Hill 1969
107. Carroll and Parsons 2007
108. Baines 1986
109. Blackburn, Bonser and Conte 1993
110. EPNS 1925, 48–8
111. Carroll and Parsons 2007
112. BRO D-X131/1
113. Collard 1988
114. Baines 1988
115. VCH 3, 70
116. BCC and EH 2009
117. Harrison 2003; Masefield 2008; Bailey 2009
118. Reed 1979, 180
119. Bailey 2009
120. Thacker 1920
121. Woodfield 1989
122. EHD, 1955
123. Baines 1986
124. EHD, 1955
125. Recognisable Viking burials are surprisingly rare in England as a whole. See Richards 2002 for a discussion.
126. Evison and Mynard 1997

127. HER records
128. Arbman 1940–3, taf 14
129. BCM Acc No 1905. 37. 1
130. See Archaeological Notes from Buckinghamshire County Museum, 1996 *Recs Bucks* 38, 259.
131. Information from PAS
132. See Williams 1997 for a detailed study of these objects.

Chapter 5 – Medieval Buckinghamshire

1. See Roberts and Wrathmell 2000; Reed 1979, 88–104
2. Lewis, *et al.*, 2001
3. Lewis *et al.*, 2001; Parker and Boarder 1991
4. Mynard and Zeepvat 1992
5. Jones and Page 2006
6. Slatcher *et al.*, 2004; Bailey 2005
7. Jones and Page 2006
8. Ivens *et al.*, 1995; Slatcher *et al.*, 2004
9. Everson 2001
10. Dyer 2005
11. Alcock 1981
12. Jones and Page 2006
13. Mynard and Zeepvat 1992
14. Cantor and Hatherly 1977; Pevsner and Williamson 1960, 51
15. Pevsner and Williamson 1960, 51
16. Mynard 1994
17. Yeoman 1986; Mynard and Ivens 2002; Kidd 2006
18. Lewis *et al.*, 2001, 114–117
19. Parker and Boarder 1991; Secker 2005
20. Croft and Mynard 1993, 25
21. Pevsner and Williamson 1960, 52; Chenevix-Trench and Fenley 1979
22. Reed 1979, 152; Archaeological Solutions Ltd 2004, 47; Gulland 2003, 197
23. Pavry and Knocker 1957; Farley 1982a
24. Mynard 1994, 2–60
25. Griffiths 1979
26. Foreman *et al.*, 2002
27. Letters 2006
28. Reed 1978, 574–5
29. Bonner 1996, 3–4, 85; Allen and Dalwood 1983, 5, 53
30. BCAS 1996
31. Reed 1993, 51; Reed 1979, 110
32. Armour-Chelu 2001, 19
33. Network Archaeology Ltd 2003, 7; John Moore Heritage Services, 2002, 12
34. Bourn 2000, Moore 2001
35. Allen and Dalwood 1983, 55; Bonner 1996, 86
36. Thorne and Walker 2003, 88
37. Allen and Dalwood 1983, 53
38. Dawson 2002, 14, 22; Laws 2002, 5–12;Thorne and Walker 2003, 88
39. Armour-Chelu 2001, 20
40. Taylor-Moore 2006, 45–6
41. National Trust 1993
42. Preston 2001; Pevsner and Williamson 1960, 175–6

43. Rouse 1977; Elvey 1977; Pevsner and Williamson 1960, 51–2
44. Chenevix Trench and Fenley 1991
45. Bailey 2003, 64–5
46. Gem 2005, 68–9
47. Mynard *et al.*, 1994; Ivens 2004
48. Farley 2001
49. Sister Jane Mary *et al.*, 1985
50. Archaeological Services and Consultancy Ltd 2003; Moore 2002
51. Little 1942, Hanley 1976
52. Morris 1989, 146
53. Allen and Dalwood 1983, 53; Holmes 2005, 52–54
54. Hindmarch 2002
55. Yeoman 1986
56. Farley and Lawson 1990
57. Farley and Leach 1988
58. Mynard 1984, 56
59. Jope 1954. Reports have been published covering subsequent excavations: Jope and Ivens 1981; Ivens 1981; Ivens 1982; Farley 1982b.
60. Mellor 1994
61. Green 2005
62. Griffiths 1979
63. Dalwood *et al.*, 1989; Bourn 2000; BCAS 1996
64. Griffiths 1979; Jope 1954; Thorne and Walker 2003
65. Roden 1966, 52; Mynard and Zeepvat 1992, 104–5
66. Watts and Langdon 2004
67. Keen 2000
68. Elvey 1965, 334
69. Babb, 1997
70. Toulmin Smith 1964, 112
71. Riley 2001, 12
72. Beresford and St Joseph, 254–7
73. Croft and Mynard 1993, 25–6
74. Chiltern Historic Landscape Characterisation project

Bibliography

Adkins R A and Petchey M R 1984 The Secklow hundred mound and other meeting place mounds in England. *Archaeological Journal* 141, 243–251

Alcock N W 1981 *Cruck Construction. An Introduction and Catalogue*. CBA Research Report 42, London

Allen D 1979 Two Roman cremation burials from Great Brickhill. *Records of Bucks* 21, 29–34

Allen D and Dalwood C H 1983 Iron Age occupation, a Middle Saxon cemetery, and twelfth to nineteenth century urban occupation: excavations in George Street, Aylesbury, 1981. *Records of Bucks* 25, 1–59

Allen D 1983 Iron Age occupation, a Middle Saxon cemetery and twelfth to nineteenth century urban occupation. Excavations at George Street, Aylesbury 1981. *Records of Bucks* 25, 1–60

Allen D 1986 Excavations at Bierton, 1979: A late Iron Age 'Belgic' settlement and evidence for a Roman villa and a twelfth to eighteenth century manorial complex. *Records of Bucks* 28, 1–120

Allen T and Lamdin-Whymark H 2000 The rediscovery of Taplow hillfort. *South Midlands Archaeology* 30, 22–28

Allen T and Mitchell N 2001 Dorney, Eton Rowing Lake. *South Midlands Archaeology* 31, 26–30

Allen T, Barclay A and Lamdin-Whymark, H 2004 Opening the wood, making the land. The study of a Neolithic landscape in the Dorney area of the Middle Thames Valley. 82–98 in *Towards a New Stone Age: aspects of the Neolithic in south-east England*. (Eds.) Cotton J and Field D. Council British Archaeology Research Report Series 137. York

Allen T 2005 Dorney, Eton Rowing Course excavations 2003: sixth interim report, *South Midlands Archaeology* 35, 23–30

Allen T, Lamdin-Whymark H and Maricevic DI 2006 Taplow, Taplow Court (Phase 2), Cliveden Road. *South Midlands Archaeology* 36, 19–21

Allen T, Hayden C and Lamdin-Whymark, H 2009 From Bronze Age enclosure to Anglo-Saxon settlement. *Archaeological excavations at Taplow hillfort, Buckinghamshire, 1999–2005*. Oxford Archaeology Thames Valley Landscapes Monograph No 30. Oxford

Anon 1923 Roman remains at Radnage, *Records of Bucks* 11, 242–243

Anon 2006 Taplow, in Archaeological Notes. *Records of Bucks* 46, 199

Arbman H 1940–3 *Birka: Untersuchungen und Studien. I. Die Gräber*. Vols I and II. Stockholm

Archaeological Services and Consultancy Ltd, 2003 *Watching brief and salvage recording: Claydon Road, Hogshaw*. unpublished report

Archaeological Solutions Ltd 2004 *Business/Science Park, Aston Clinton Major Development Area, Aylesbury Buckinghamshire. Archaeological desk-based assessment and earthwork survey*. unpublished report

Armour-Chelu R 2001 128 High Street, Chesham, Buckinghamshire. *Archaeological excavation on the site of supermarket development and associated parking*. unpublished report

Ashcroft D 1938 Notes. *Journal Roman Studies* 28, 185

Ashcroft D 1939 Notes. *Journal Roman Studies* 29.2, 10–11 and 228–229

Ashcroft D 1940 Report on the excavation of a Romano-British villa at Saunderton. *Records of Bucks* 13, 398–426

Astill G G and Lobb S J 1989 Excavation of Prehistoric, Roman and Saxon deposits at Wraysbury, Berkshire. *Archaeological Journal* 146, 68–134

Atkins R and Rees G 2008 *An Iron Age and Roman Settlement at Broughton Manor Farm,Milton Keynes, Buckinghamshire. Post-Excavation Assessment and Updated Project Design.* CAM ARC report 968. unpublished

Babb L 1997 A thirteenth-century brooch hoard from Hambleden, Buckinghamshire. *Medieval Archaeology* 41, 233–6

Bailey K A 1989 Osyth, Frithuwold and Aylesbury *Records of Bucks* 31, 37–48

Bailey K A 1994 Early Saxon territorial organisation in Buckinghamshire and its neighbours. *Records of Bucks* 36, 129–143

Bailey K A 2003 The Church in Anglo-Saxon Buckinghamshire c 650–c1100. *Records of Bucks* 43, 61–76

Bailey K A 2004 Who was Who and Who became Whom: Buckinghamshire landowners 1066 and 1086. *Records of Bucks* 44, 51–66

Bailey K A 2005 Early medieval Stewkley: settlements and fields. *Records of Bucks* 45, 93–114

Bailey K 2009 Evidence for Anglo-Saxon routeways and Icknield Way in Buckinghamshire. *Records of Bucks* 49, 239–244

Baines A H J 1983 The boundaries of Monks Risborough. *Records of Bucks* 23, 76–101

Baines A H J 1984 The Danish wars and the establishment of the Borough and County of Buckinghamshire. *Records of Bucks* 26, 11–27

Baines A H J 1985 The development of the Borough of Buckingham. *Records of Bucks* 27, 53–64

Baines A H 1986 The origins of the Borough of Newport Pagnell. *Records of Bucks* 28, 128–137

Baines A H J 1988 St Wulfstan in Buckinghamshire. *Records of Bucks* 30, 43–52

Baines A H J 1993 Bernwood: continuity and survival on a Romano-British estate. *Records of Bucks* 35, 19–30

Barker G 2006 *The Agricultural Revolution in Prehistory.* Oxford University Press. Oxford

BCAS 1996 *Interim report on an archaeological excavation at the Brewery Site, High Street, Marlow, Buckinghamshire.* Report 384. unpublished report

Beresford M W and St Joseph J K S 1958 *Medieval England – An Aerial Survey.* Cambridge

Biddulph K 2009 Neolithic and Earlier Bronze Age. p21–35 in *An Archaeological Research Framework for Buckinghamshire; collected papers from the Solent-Thames Research Framework.* Buckinghamshire Papers 15

Birks H J B 1989 Holocene isochrone maps and patterns of tree-spreading in the British Isles. *Journal of Biogeography* 16, 503–540

Blackburn M A S, Bonser M J and Conte, W J 1993 A new type of Edward the Confessor for the Newport mint. *British Numismatic Journal* 63

Bonner D and Parkhouse J 1997 A prehistoric and Saxon site at Rislip Farm, Soulbury. *Records of Bucks* 39, 140– 148

Bonner D 1996 Investigations at the County Museum, Aylesbury. *Records of Bucks* 38, 1–89

Bonner D and Parkhouse J 1997 Investigations at the Prehistoric Site at Coldharbour Farm, Aylesbury in 1996. *Records of Bucks* 39, 73–139

Booth P 1999 Pink grogged ware again. *Study Group for Roman Pottery Newsletter* 27, 2–3

Booth P, Dodd A, Robinson M and Smith A 2007 *Thames through Time. The Archaeology of the Gravel Terraces of the Upper and Middle Thames. The early historical period: AD 1–1000.* Oxford Archaeology. Thames Valley Landscapes Monograph 27

Bourn R 2000 *The Courtyard, Frogmoor, High Wycombe. Archaeological desk based assessment.* unpublished report

Bradley R 2007 *The Prehistory of Britain and Ireland.* Cambridge University Press. New York

Branigan K 1967 The distribution and development of Romano-British occupation in the Chess Valley. *Records of Bucks* 18.2, 136–149

Branigan K 1969 The Romano-British villa at Saunderton reconsidered. *Records of Bucks* 18.4, 261–276

Branigan K 1971 *Latimer: A Belgic, Roman, Dark Age and early modern farm*. Chess Valley Archaeological and Historical Society

Branigan K 1973 Latimer – some problems of archaeological interpretation. *Records of Bucks* 19, 340–343

Branigan K 1987 *The Catuvellauni*. Alan Sutton, Gloucester

Branigan K and Niblett R 2003 *The Roman Chilterns*. Chess Valley Archaeological and Historical Society

Bridgland D R 1994 *The Quaternary of the Thames*. Geological Conservation Review Services, Nature Conservation Committee. London, Chapman and Hall

Brown M 2001 *Ivinghoe Beacon, Ivinghoe, Buckinghamshire*. English Heritage Survey Report AI/17/2001

Buckinghamshire County Council with English Heritage 2009 *Princes Risborough Town*. draft report

Buckinghamshire County Museum Archaeological Group 1978. Buckinghamshire Windmills. *Records of Bucks* 20, 516–524

Bull E J 1978 A medieval settlement area adjacent to Pitstone church. *Records of Bucks* 20, 646–655

Bull E J 1993 The Bi-Axial Landscape of Prehistoric Buckinghamshire. *Records of Bucks* 35, 11–18

Cantor L M and Hatherly J 1977 The Medieval Parks of Buckinghamshire. *Records of Bucks* 20, 430–50

Carroll J and Parsons DN 2007 *Anglo-Saxon mint names. Part 1: Axbridge to Hythe*. English Place Names Society, extra series 2

Catt J 1978 in White M J 1997 The earlier Palaeolithic occupation of the Chilterns (Southern England): re-assessing the sites of Worthington G Smith. *Antiquity* 71, 912–31

Chambers F M, Mighall T M and Keen D H 1996 Early Holocene pollen and Molluscan records from Enfield Lock, Middlesex, UK. *Proceedings of the Geological Association* 107, 1–14

Chapman A, Jones C, Holmes M and Prentice J 1999 Gayhurst Quarry (SP853446). *South Midlands Archaeology* 29, 17–20

Chapman A 2007 A Bronze Age Barrow Cemetery and Later Boundaries, Pit Alignments and Enclosures at Gayhurst Quarry, Newport Pagnell, Buckinghamshire. *Records of Bucks* 47(2), 81–211

Chenevix-Trench J and Fenley P 1979 A base-cruck hall in Denham, *Records of Bucks* 21, 3–10

Chenevix Trench J and Fenley P 1991 The County Museum buildings, Church Street, Aylesbury. *Records of Bucks* 33, 1–43

Chess Valley Archaeological and Historical Society 1985 A report on excavations at Bury Farm, Amersham, *Records of Bucks* 27, 119–128

Childe V G and Smith, I 1954 Excavation of a Neolithic Barrow on Whiteleaf Hill, Bucks. *Proceedings of the Prehistoric Society* 8, 212–30

Clark J G D 1972 *Star Carr: A Case Study in Bioarchaeology* Addison-Wesley. Reading, USA

Cocks A H 1921 A Roman-British homestead in the Hambleden valley, Bucks *Archaeologia* 71, 141–98

Coleman L, Havard T, Collard M, Cox S and McSloy E 2004 Denham, The Lea. *South Midlands Archaeology* 34, 14–17

Collard M 1988 Magiovinium Roman town, Bow Brickhill. *South Midlands Archaeology* 18, 29–30

Collard M 1988 Archaeological investigation of 'The Old Churchyard', Olney, *Records of Bucks* 30, 165–169

Collard M and Parkhouse J 1993 A Belgic/Romano-British cemetery at Bledlow-cum-Saunderton, *Records of Bucks* 35, 66–75

Conneller C and Warren G 2006. *Mesolithic Britain*. Cambridge University Press

Cotton M A and Frere S S 1968 Ivinghoe Beacon Excavations 1963–65. *Records of Bucks* 18, 187–252

Coles B 1998 Doggerland: A speculative survey. *Proceedings of the Prehistoric Society* 64, 45–81

Corder P 1943 The Roman pottery at Fulmer. *Records of Bucks* 14.3, 153–63

Cox P W 1997 *Billings Field, Bicester Road (Quarrendon) Aylesbury, Bucks: An archaeological evaluation report*. unpublished report

Croft R A. and Mynard D C 1993. *The Changing Landscape of Milton Keynes*. Bucks Archaeology Society Monograph 5. Aylesbury

Cunliffe B W 1991 *Iron Age Communities in Britain* (3rd edition). London

Cunliffe B W 2008 *Europe between the Oceans 9000 BC – AD 1000*. Yale University Press. New Haven and London

Dalwood H, Dillon J, Evans J and Hawkins A 1989 Excavations in Walton, Aylesbury, 1985–1986. *Records of Bucks* 31, 137–221

Darvill T 1987 *Prehistoric Britain*. London, Batsford

Davis S and Bull R 2003 Milton Keynes, Monkston Park. *South Midlands Archaeology*. 33, 29–30

Dawson M 2002 *Archaeology desk based assessment and trial trench evaluation at the Grand Junction Hotel, Buckingham*. unpublished report

Dyer C 2005 *An Age of Transition? Economy and Society in the Later Middle Ages*. Oxford

Diamond J 1998 *Guns, Germs and Steel*, London. Vintage

Dunnett B R K 1971 Report on the trial excavation at Wards Coombe, Ivinghoe, 1971. *Records of Bucks* 19.2, 141–155

Durham B 1978 Traces of a Late Saxon church at St Mary's, Aylesbury. *Records of Bucks* 20, 621–6

Edwards Y and Wells M 2006 Common Wood earthwork enclosure: a footnote for 2006. *Chess Valley Archaeological and Historical Society Journal* (2006), 1–3

Ekwall E 1960 *The Concise Oxford Dictionary of English place names*. 4th edition Oxford

Ellis C, Allen M. J, Gardiner J, Harding P, Ingrem C, Powell A. and Scaife RG 2003. An Early Mesolithic Seasonal Hunting Site in the Kennet Valley, Southern England. *Proceedings of the Prehistoric Society*, 69: 107–136

Elvey E M 1965 Aylesbury in the fifteenth century – a bailiff's notebook. *Records of Bucks* 17, 321–335

Elvey E M 1977 The History of nos. 1 and 2 Market Hill, Buckingham. *Records of Bucks* 20, 301–7

Enwright D and Parkhouse J 1996 Archaeological investigations at Weston Underwood in 1994. *Records of Bucks* 38, 175–198

English Place Names Society 1925 *The place names of Buckinghamshire*. Vol.2. (Eds) Mawer A and Stenton F M. Cambridge University Press

Everson P 2001 Peasants, Peers and Graziers: the Landscape of Quarrendon, Buckinghamshire, interpreted. *Records of Bucks* 41, 1–45

Evison V I and Mynard DC 1997 A Saxon spearhead from Haversham, Buckinghamshire. *Records of Bucks* 20, 350

Farley M E 1973 A Roman burial at North Marston. *Records of Bucks* 19.3, 329–335

Farley M E 1976 Saxon and medieval Walton, Aylesbury, Buckinghamshire 1973–4. *Records of Bucks* 20, 153–292

Farley M E and Wright R 1979 An Early Romano-British inhumation cemetery at West Wycombe, Bucks. *Records of Bucks* 21, 81–89

Farley M 1979 Burials in Aylesbury and the early history of the town. *Records of Bucks* 21, 116–120

Farley M E 1980 Middle Saxon occupation at Chicheley, Buckinghamshire. *Records of Bucks*. 22, 92–104

Farley M E, Nash D and White R F 1981 A Late Iron Age and Roman Site at Walton Court, Aylesbury. *Records of Bucks* 23, 51–75

Farley M 1982a Excavations at Low Farm, Fulmer, Bucks: II, the medieval manor. *Records of Bucks* 24, 46–72

Farley M 1982b A medieval pottery industry at Boarstall, Buckinghamshire. *Records of Bucks* 24, 107–117

Farley M E 1983 The villa at Mill End, Hambleden, Buckinghamshire, and its neighbourhood. *Britannia* 14, 256–259

Farley M 1983 Archive Notes and finds. CASS 5276, Buckinghamshire County Museum. 417

Farley M E 1983 Mirror Burial at Dorton. *Proceedings of the Prehistoric Society* 49, 269–302

Farley M 1986 Aylesbury: Iron Age hillfort to medieval town. *Current Archaeology* 101, 187–9

Farley M. 1987 An Anglo-Saxon cemetery at Bourne End, Wooburn, Buckinghamshire, reinstated. *Records of Bucks* 29, 170–174

Farley M E, Henig M, and Taylor J W 1988 A hoard of late Roman bronze bowls and the mounts from the Misbourne valley, near Amersham, Bucks. *Britannia* 19, 357–366

Farley M 1992 The Cop round barrow at Bledlow, Buckinghamshire: prehistoric or Saxon? *Records of Bucks* 34, 11–13

Farley M 1997 Christians and pagans in Weedon, Buckinghamshire. *Records of Bucks* 39, 59–62

Farley, M, 1999 *The Prestwood, Bucks, Roman coin hoards.* unpublished report

Farley M 2001 *Medmenham Abbey, Medmenham, Bucks; results from some archaeological watching briefs.* unpublished report

Farley M and Lawson J 1990 A fifteenth-century pottery and tile kiln at Leyhill, Latimer, Buckinghamshire. *Records of Bucks* 32, 35–62

Farley M and Leach 1988 Medieval pottery production areas near Rush Green, Denham, Buckinghamshire. *Records of Bucks* 30, 53–102

Ford S 2000 The excavation of a Roman trackway and field system at Three Locks Golf Course, Stoke Hammond, Buckinghamshire 1994. *Records of Bucks* 40, 35–54

Ford S 2000 An evaluation and rescue excavation at the Westcroft District Centre, Milton Keynes, Buckinghamshire 1993. *Records of Bucks* 40, 23–33

Ford S and Taylor K 2001 Iron Age and Roman settlements, with prehistoric and Saxon features, at Fenny Lock, Milton Keynes, Buckinghamshire. *Records of Bucks* 41, 79–123

Ford S 2003 *Excavations at Cippenham, Slough, Berkshire, 1995–7*. Thames Valley Archaeological Services Monograph 3. Reading

Ford S 2004 *All Souls Farm Quarry, Wexham, Buckinghamshire: an archaeological* evaluation. Thames Valley Archaeological Services, unpublished report

Ford S, Howell I and Taylor K 2004 *The Archaeology of the Aylesbury-Chalgrove Gas Pipeline, and the Orchard, Walton Road, Aylesbury*. Thames Valley Archaeological Services Monograph 5. Reading

Ford S 2008 *An early/Middle Iron Age enclosure, Saxon halls and Roman features at Wexham Road, Wexham, Slough, Berkshire*. Site Code WRE07/55. Unpublished report by Thames Valley Archaeological Services, Reading

Foreman S, Hiller J and Petts D 2002 *Gathering the people, settling the land. The archaeology of a middle Thames landscape: Anglo-Saxon to post-medieval*. Thames Valley Landscapes Monograph 14, Oxford

Gardiner J 2003 *Resource Assessment: The Mesolithic in Hampshire.* unpublished report

Garmonsway G N (editor) 1954 *The Anglo-Saxon Chronicle*

Geake H 2002 Persistent problems in the study of conversion-period burials. in *Burials in Early Medieval England and Wales*. (Eds) Lucy S and Reynolds A. Society for Medieval Archaeology Monograph 17

Gem R 2003 *All Saints Church, Wing*. (pamphlet), R J L Smith and Associates, Much Wenlock, Shropshire

Gem R 2005 *The Church of All Saints, Wing, Buckinghamshire*, in *Excavation of a Late Saxon – Medieval Cemetery at the site of the former Victorian School, Wing, Buckinghamshire May – June 1999 (M. Holmes)*. unpublished report

Gibbard P L, Bryant I D and Hall A R 1986 A Hoxnian doline infilling at Slade Oak Lane, Denham, Buckinghamshire, England. *Geological Magazine* 123.1, 27–43

Gill L 2008 Broughton Barn, Broughton Northern Infill. *South Midlands Archaeology* 38, 20–1

Girling M A and Greig J R A 1985 A first fossil record for *Scolytus scolytus* (elm bark beetle): its occurrence in elm decline deposits from London and the implications for Neolithic elm disease. *Journal of Archaeological Science*, 12, 347–351

Green C 1965 A Romano-Celtic temple at Bourton Grounds, Buckingham. *Records of Bucks* 17.5, 356–66

Green C 1970 Upper Ouse valley: the Roman scene. *Wolverton Historical Journal* 1, 55–62

Green H S 1974 Early Bronze Age burial, territory and population in Milton Keynes, Buckinghamshire, and the Great Ouse Valley. *Archaeological Journal* 131, 75–139

Green H S 1981 The Dating of Ivinghoe Beacon. *Records of Bucks* 23, 1–3

Green M J 1976 A *corpus of religious material from the civilian areas of Roman Britain*. British Archaeological Reports 24, 196–7. Oxford

Green M J 1981 The miniature bronze scythe from Walton Court. in Farley, Nash and White *Records of Bucks* 23, 61–62

Green M J 1983 Isis at Thornborough. *Records of Bucks* 25, 139–141

Green M 2004 *The Gods of the Celts*. Sutton, Stroud

Green, Miles 2005 Medieval tile industry at Penn. *Records of Bucks* 45, 115–160

Green C P, Coope G R, Jones R L, Keen D H, Bowen D Q, Currant A P, Holyoak D T, Ivanovich M, Robinson J E, Rogerson R J and Young R C 1996 Pleistocene deposits at Stoke Goldington, in the valley of the Great Ouse, UK. *Journal of Quaternary Science* 11, 59–87

Green D and Kidd A 2006 *Buckinghamshire and Milton Keynes Historic Landscape Characterisation*. Buckinghamshire County Council

Griffiths R 1979 Rescue excavations of a medieval house at Whaddon, Buckinghamshire. *Records of Bucks* 21, 40–76

Gulland D 2003 Aston Clinton Manor House: from moated site to classical mansion, *Records of Bucks* 43, 195–207

Hancock A 2008 Bletchley, land at Stoke Road, Water Eaton. *South Midlands Archaeology* 38, 20

Hall R A 1975 An excavation at Hunter Street, Buckingham 1974. *Records of Bucks* 20, 100–133

Hanley H 1976 The Friarage, Rickfords Hill, Aylesbury. *Aylesbury Society Newsletter* 7, 5–6

Harrison S 2003 The Icknield Way: some queries. *Archaeological Journal* 160, 1–22

Hepple L W and Doggett A M 1994 *The Chilterns*. Phillimore, Chichester

Haak W, Forster P, Bramanti B, Matsumura S, Brandt G, Tänzer M, Villems R, Renfrew C, Gronenborn D, Alt K W and Burger J. 2005 Ancient DNA from the First European Farmers in 7500–Year-Old Neolithic Sites. *Science* 310, 1016–1018

Harrison S 2003 The Icknield Way: Some Queries. *Archaeological Journal* 160, 1–22

Hartley B R 1959 A Romano-British villa at High Wycombe. *Records of Bucks*.16.4, 227–257

Head, J F, 1964 A Romano-British site at Great Missenden. *Records of Bucks* 17.4, 228–231

Healy F, Heaton M and Lobb S J 1992. Excavations of a Mesolithic Site at Thatcham, Berkshire. *Proceedings of the Prehistoric Society*, 58: 41–76

Henig M 1984 A cache of bronze finger rings from Amersham. *Records of Bucks* 26, 129–131

Henig M 1992 Intaglio, in Yeoman and Stewart *Records of Bucks* 34, 158

HER Historic Environment Record; Buckinghamshire County Council, Milton Keynes Council or Berkshire Archaeology, as appropriate

Hey G 2005 Princes Risborough, Whiteleaf Hill. *South Midlands Archaeology* 35, 31

Hey G, Dennis C and Mayes A 2007 Archaeological investigations on Whiteleaf Hill, Princes Risborough, Buckinghamshire, 2002–6. *Records of Bucks* 47.2, 1–80

Hey G and Barclay A 2007 The Thames Valley in the late fifth and early fourth millennium cal BC: the appearance of domestication and the evidence for change. *Proceedings of the British Academy* 144, 399–422

Hill D 1969 The Burghal Hidage: the establishment of a text. *Medieval Archaeology* 13, 84–92

Hindmarch E 2002 *Church Hill, Buckingham, Buckinghamshire. An archaeological evaluation for Buckingham Town Council.* unpublished report

Hodder I 1983 *The Present Past: An introduction to anthropology for archaeologists.* New York, Pica Press

Holgate R (Ed) 1995 *Chiltern Archaeology, recent work. a handbook for the next decade.* The Book Castle, Dunstable

Holmes M 2005 *Excavation of a Late Saxon – Medieval Cemetery at the site of the former Victorian School, Wing, Buckinghamshire May – June 1999.* unpublished report

Holmes M and Chapman A 2008 A middle-late Saxon and medieval cemetery at Wing church, Buckinghamshire. *Records of Bucks* 48, 61–123

Hunn A, Lawson J and Farley M 1994 The Anglo-Saxon cemetery at Dinton, Buckinghamshire. *Anglo-Saxon Studies in Archaeology and History* 7, 85–148

Hunn A and Farley M 1995 The Chalfont St. Peter Roman coin hoard 1989. *Records of Bucks* 37, 113–12

Hunn A, Lawson J and Parkhouse J 1997 Investigations at Magiovinium 1990–91: the Little Brickhill and Fenny Stratford by-passes. *Records of Bucks* 37, 3–66

Hunn J R 1995 The Romano-British landscape of the Chiltern dipslope: a study of settlement around Verulamium. p76–91 in *Chiltern Archaeology, recent work. a handbook for the next decade.* (Ed) Holgate R. The Book Castle Bedfordshire

Imbrie J and Imbrie K P 1986 *Ice ages: solving the mystery.* Harvard University Press

Ingrouille M 1995 *Historical Ecology of the British Flora.* London, Chapman and Hall

Ivens R J 1981 Medieval pottery kilns at Brill, Buckinghamshire: preliminary report on excavations in 1978. *Records of Bucks* 23, 102–106

Ivens R J 1982 Medieval Pottery from the 1978 excavations at Temple Farm, Brill, *Records of Bucks* 24. 144–169

Ivens R, Busby P and Shepherd N 1995 *Tattenhoe and Westbury: two deserted Medieval settlements in Milton Keynes.* Bucks Archaeological Society Monograph 8

Ivens R 2004 Bradwell, Bradwell Abbey. *South Midlands Archaeology* 34, 28–30

Jacobi R 1978 The Mesolithic of Sussex. p15–22 in *The Archaeology of Sussex to AD 1500.* (Ed) Drewett P. CBA Research Report, 29

Jacobi, R. M. 1973. Aspects of the "Mesolithic Age" in Great Britain. p 237–65 in *The Mesolithic in Europe.* (Ed) Kozlowski S K. Warsaw

Jay M and Richards M P 2007 British Iron Age Diet: Stable Isotopes and Other Evidence. *Proceedings of the Prehistoric Society* 73, 169–190

Jefferys 1770 *Map of the County of Buckinghamshire surveyed in 1766–1768 and engraved by Thomas Jefferys*

John Moore Heritage Services 2002 *An archaeological investigation at Town Farm Barns, Market Square, Princes Risborough, Buckinghamshire.* unpublished report

John Moore Heritage Services 2006 *An archaeological recording action of land off Wotton End, Ludgershall, Buckinghamshire.* unpublished report

Johnson A E 1975 Excavations at Bourton Grounds, Thornborough 1972–3. *Records of Bucks* 20.1, 3–56

Jones R and Page M 2006 *Medieval Villages in an English Landscape: Beginnings and Ends.* Windgather Press, Macclesfield

Jope E M 1954 Medieval pottery kilns at Brill, Buckinghamshire: preliminary report on excavations in 1953. *Records of Bucks* 16, 39–42

Jope E M and Ivens R J 1981 Some early products of the Brill pottery, Buckinghamshire. *Records of Bucks* 23, 32–38

Jukes-Browne A J and Osborne-White H J (1908) *The Geology of the country around Henley-on-Thames and Wallingford.* HMSO

Keen L 2000 Windsor Castle and the Penn tile industry. in *Windsor: medieval archaeology, art and architecture of the Thames Valley.* (Ed) Keen L

Keevill G D and Campbell G E 1993 Investigations at Danesfield Camp, Medmenham, Buckinghamshire. *Records of Bucks* 33, 87–99

Kidd A 2004 Northamptonshire in the First Millennium BC. in *The Archaeology of Northamptonshire.* (ed) Mingle T. Northamptonshire Archaeological Society.

Kidd A 2004 Hillforts and churches: A coincidence of locations? *Records of Bucks* 44, 105–109

Kidd A 2006 The Cistercian grange at Grange Farm, Shipton Lee, Quainton. *Records of Bucks* 46, 149–56

Kidd A 2009 Later Bronze Age and Iron Age. 37–51 in *An Archaeological Research Framework for Buckinghamshire; collected papers from the Solent-Thames Research Framework.* Buckinghamshire Papers No 15

Kozlowksi S K 2003 *The Mesolithic: What do we know and what do we believe.* Papers presented at the 6th International conference on the Mesolithic in Europe, Stockholm. (Eds.) Akerlund A, Larsson L, Kindgren H, Knutson K, and Loeffler D. Oxbow Books. Oxford

Lacaille A D 1936 The Palaeolithic Sequence at Iver, Bucks. *The Antiquaries Journal* XVI, 420–443

Lacaille A D 1963 Mesolithic industries beside Colne Waters in Iver and Denham, Buckinghamshire. *Records of Bucks* 17.3, 143–181

Laws G 2002 *Stratford House, Buckingham, Buckinghamshire. Archaeological evaluation.* unpublished report

Letters S 2006 *Online Gazetteer of Markets and Fairs in England and Wales to 1516.* http://www.history.ac.uk/cmh/gaz/gazweb2.html. Accessed: 20 July 2006

Lewis C, Mitchell-Fox P and Dyer C 1997 *Village, Hamlet and Field. Changing Medieval Settlements in Central England.* 2nd edition Macclesfield

Lewis J, Brown F, Batt A, Cooke N and Barrett J 2006 *Landscape Evolution in the Middle Thames Valley. Heathrow Terminal 5 Excavations Volume 1, Perry Oaks.* Framework Archaeology Monograph I. Oxford and Salisbury

Lewis S C, Wiltshire P E J and Macphail R 1992 A Late Devensian/Early Flandrian site at Three Ways Wharf, Uxbridge: environmental implications. in *Alluvial Archaeology in Britain.* (Eds.) Needham S and Macklin G. Oxford Monograph 27. Oxbow Books. Oxford

Lister A and Sher A 2001 The origin and evolution of the woolly mammoth. *Science* 294, 1094–1097

Lister A M, Sher A V, van Essen H and Weid G 2005 The pattern and process of mammoth evolution in Eurasia. *Quaternary International* 126–128, 49–64

Little A G 1942 The Grey Friars of Aylesbury. *Records of Bucks* 14, 77–98

Liversidge J 1954 The Thornborough barrows. *Records of Bucks* 16.1, 29–32

Love R C (editor) 1996 *Three Eleventh Century Anglo-Latin Saints Lives.* Clarendon Press, Oxford

Lowe J J and Walker M J C 1997 *Reconstructing Quaternary Environments.* Longman Harlow

Lowndes C 1870 Note. *Records of Bucks* 4, 209

Lyne M 2006 The Pottery from All Souls Farm, Wexham, Bucks, *in All*

Souls Farm, Buckinghamshire, Archaeological Excavations 2005: Interim Report. unpublished report

Lubbock J L A 1865 *Pre-historic Times, as illustrated by Ancient Remains, and the Manners and Customs of Modern Savages.* Williams and Norgate. London and Edinburgh

McEwan R, McGregor D F M, Parish D; Robinson J E, Schreve D C and Smart P L 2001 A late Middle Pleistocene temperate-periglacial-temperate sequence (Oxygen Isotope Stages 7–5e) near Marsworth, Buckinghamshire, UK. *Quaternary Science Reviews* 20, 1787–1825

McNabb J 2007 *The British Lower Palaeolithic: stones in contention.* Routledge

McOmish D, Tuck C and Went D 2001 *West Wycombe Park: Buckinghamshire, Part II: The Earthwork Surveys.* English Heritage Archaeological Investigation Series. unpublished report

Marney P T 1989 *Roman and Belgic pottery from excavations in Milton Keynes 1972–82.* Bucks Archaeological Society Monograph Series 2. Aylesbury

Marshall G 1995 *Stowe Landscape Gardens: Roman pottery and kiln waste recovered from the Bourbon Fields (report no. stow/8).* unpublished report

Masefield R 2008 *Prehistoric and Later Settlement and Landscape from Chiltern Scarp to Aylesbury Vale. The archaeology of the Aston Clinton Bypass, Buckinghamshire.* BAR British Series 473. Archaeopress Oxford

Meddens F M 1996 Sites from the Thames Estuary wetlands, England and their Bronze Age Use. *Antiquity* 70 325–334

Mellars P 1987 *Excavations on Oronsay: Prehistoric Human Ecology on a Small Island.* Edinburgh University Press. Edinburgh

Mellars P A and Wilkinson M R 1980 Fish otoliths as indicators of seasonality in prehistoric shell middens: the evidence from Oronsay (Inner Hebrides). *Proceedings of the Prehistoric Society* 46, 19–44

Mellor M 1994 A synthesis of Middle and Late Saxon, medieval and early post-medieval pottery in the Oxford region. *Oxoniensia* 59, 17–217

Mithen S J 1994 The Mesolithic Age. In *The Oxford Illustrated Prehistory of Europe.* Oxford University Press. Oxford

Mithen S J 1999 Mesolithic Archaeology, Environmental Archaeology and Human Palaeoecology. *Quaternary Proceedings* 7, 477–483

Moffett L, Robinson, M A and Straker V 1989 Cereals, fruit and nuts: charred plant remains from Neolithic sites in England and Wales and the Neolithic economy. p 243–61 in *The beginnings of agriculture.* (eds) Milles A, Williams D and Gardener N. British Archaeological Reports, International Series 496

Momber G and Campbell C 2005 Stone Age Stove under the Solent. *Nautical Archaeology* 34, 148–149

Moore J 2001 *An archaeological evaluation at The Courtyard, Frogmoor, High Wycombe.* unpublished report

Moore J 2002 Hedgerley, Knights Rest, Moat farm Barns, HedgerleyLane, Gerrards Cross. *South Midlands Archaeology* 32, 16

Morris J (ed) 1978 *Domesday Book: 13 Buckinghamshire.* Phillimore, Chichester

Morris R 1989 *Churches in the Landscape.* London

Morris C Hargreaves G H and Parker R P F 1970 A Roman road through south Buckinghamshire. *Records of Bucks* 18.5, 367–385

Morris M and Wainwright A 1995 Iron Age and Romano-British settlement, agriculture and industry in the upper Bulbourne valley, Hertfordshire: an interim interpretation. p68–75 in *Chiltern Archaeology recent work. a handbook for the next decade.* Holgate R (Ed). The Book Castle, Dunstable

Morrison A 1980 *Early man in Britain and Ireland.* Croom Helm London

Moulins D de 2006 The weeds from the thatch roofs of medieval cottages from the south of England. *Vegetation History and Archaeobotany.* 16, no 5

Mudd A 2006 The Roman site at Hill Farm, Haversham: excavations and watching brief 2002–2004. *Records of Bucks* 46, 1–18

Murton J B, Baker A, Bowen D Q, Caseldine C J, Coope G R, Currant A P, Evans J G, Field M, Green C P, Hatton J, Ito M, Jones R L, Keen D H, Kerney M P, McEwan R, McGregor D F M, Parish D, Robinson J E, Schreve D C and Smart P L 2001 A late Middle Pleistocene temperate-periglacial-temperate sequence (Oxygen Isotope Stages 7–5e) near Marsworth, Buckinghamshire, UK. *Quaternary Science Reviews* 20, 1787–1825

Myers A M 2000 *An Archaeological Resource Assessment and Research Agenda for the Mesolithic in the East Midlands, East Midlands Archaeological Research Framework: Resource Assessment and Research Agenda for the Mesolithic.* 1–36

Myers J N L 1977 Zoomorphic bosses on Anglo-Saxon pottery. *Studien zur sachsen-forschung.* Hildesheim

Mynard D C 1984 A medieval pottery industry at Olney Hyde. *Records of Bucks* 26, 56–85

Mynard D C (editor) 1987 *Roman Milton Keynes,* Bucks Archaeological Society Monograph Series 1. Aylesbury

Mynard D C and Zeepvat R J 1992 *Great Linford.* Bucks Arch Soc Monograph 3

Mynard D C 1994 *Excavations on Medieval Sites in Milton Keynes*, Bucks Archaeological Society Monograph Series 6. Aylesbury

Mynard D C and Ivens R J 2002 The excavation of Gorefields: a medieval nunnery and grange at Stoke Goldington, Buckinghamshire. *Records of Bucks* 42, 19–101

Mynard D C, Woodfield P and Zeepvat R J 1994 Bradwell Abbey, Buckinghamshire research and excavation 1968 to 1987. *Records of Bucks* 36, 1–61

National Trust 1993 *The King's Head, Aylesbury. An historic building survey 1992/3.* unpublished report

Neal D S 1987 Excavations at Magiovinium, Buckinghamshire, 1978–80. *Records of Bucks* 29, 1–124

Neal D S, Wardle A and Hunn J 1990 *Excavation of the Iron Age, Roman and Medieval Settlement at Gorhambury, St Albans.* English Heritage Archaeological Report 14. London

Needham S P 2002 *Treasure Annual Report 2000.* p12–15. Department of Culture, Media and Sport London

Network Archaeology Ltd 2003 *Land to the rear of 10 High Street, Winslow, Buckinghamshire.* unpublished report

Oakley K P 1937 The Palaeolithic Sequence at Iver, Bucks. *The Antiquaries Journal* XVI, 420–443

Oakley K P, Vulliamy C F and Clive Rouse E 1937 The excavation of a Romano-British pottery kiln site near Hedgerley, Bucks 1971. *Records of Bucks* 13, 252–80

Oakley K P, Andrews A, Keeley L H and Clark J D 1977 A reappraisal of the Clacton spearpoint. *Proceedings of Prehistoric Society* 43, 13–30

Oosthuizen S 2005 New light on the origin of open-field farming. *Medieval Archaeology* 49, 165–193

Owen H W and Morgan R 2007 *Dictionary of place names of Wales.* Gomer Press, Llandysul, Ceredigion

Page M and Jones R, 2003 Medieval settlement and landscape; the Whittlewood project; interim report 2002–3. *Medieval Settlement Research Group Annual Report,* 27–36

Page W 1905–1927 *The Victoria County History of the Counties of England: A History of Buckinghamshire*: Vols I-IV

PAS. Information from Buckinghamshire County Museum's Portable Antiquities Survey Officer

Page R I 1996 *Chronicles of the Vikings: Records, Memorials and Myths.* University of Toronto Press

Parfitt S A, Barendregt R W, Breda M, Candy I, Collins M J, Russell Coope G, Durbidge P, Field M H, Lee J R, Lister A M, Mutch R, Penkman K E H , Preece R C , Rose J, Stringer C B, Symmons R, Whittaker J E, Wymer J J and Stuart A J 2005. The earliest record of human activity in northern Europe. *Nature* 438, 1008–1012

Parker A, Goudie A, Anderson A, Robinson M and Bonsall C 2002 A review of the mid-Holocene elm decline in the British Isles. *Progress in Physical Geography* 26, 43–69

Parker R F and Boarder A W F 1991 A medieval settlement site at Fillington Wood, West Wycombe. *Records of Bucks* 33, 128–39

Parker A G and Robinson M A 2003 Palaeoenvironmental investigations on the Middle Thames at Dorney, UK. p18–19 in *Proceedings of the Alluvial Archaeology of North-West Europe and Mediterranean, December, 2000*. (Eds.) Howard A J, Macklin M G, Balkema A A and Passmore D G. Netherlands

Parker A G, Goudie A S, Anderson D E, Robinson M A and Bonsall C 2002 A Review of the mid-Holocene elm decline in the British Isles. *Progress in Physical Geography* 26, 1–45

Parkhouse J 1995 Buckinghamshire County Museum Archaeological Service Fieldwork in 1994. *South Midlands Archaeology* 25, 24–27

Parkhouse J and Smith N 1996 An Anglo-Saxon cemetery at Bottledump Corner, Tattenhoe, Milton Keynes. *Records of Bucks* 36, 103–119

Parkhouse J 1997 A hoard of Late Roman pewter from Fleet Marston. *Records of Bucks* 39, 155–162

Parkhouse J and Bonner D 1997 A prehistoric and Saxon site at Rislip Farm, Soulbury. *Records of Bucks* 39, 140–148

Parkhouse J, Roseff R and Short J 1998 A Late Saxon cemetery at Milton Keynes Village. *Records of Bucks* 38, 199–221

Pavry F H and Knocker G M 1957 The Mount, Princes Risborough, Buckinghamshire. *Records of Bucks* 16, 131–178

Peake A E 1917 A Prehistoric site at Kimble S. Bucks. *Proceedings of the Prehistoric Society, East Anglia* II Part 3, 437–58

Perring D and Brigham T 2000 Londinium and its hinterland: the Roman period, 119–170 *The Archaeology of Greater London: an assessment of archaeological evidence for human presence in the area now covered by Greater London*. MoLAS Monograph, London

Pevsner N and Williamson E 1960 *The Buildings of England – Buckinghamshire*. Penguin Books

Pevsner N, Williamson E, Brandwood GK 1994 *The Buildings of England: Buckinghamshire*. Penguin Books

Petchey M R 1978 A Roman field system at Broughton, Buckinghamshire. *Records of Bucks* 20.4, 637–45

Petchey M R 1979 A Roman patera from Olney. *Records of Bucks* 21, 35–39

Phillips M 2005 Excavation of an early Saxon settlement at Pitstone. *Records of Bucks* 45, 1–32

Pine J 2003 Excavation of a medieval settlement, Late Saxon features and a Bronze Age cremation cemetery at Loughton, Milton Keynes. *Records of Bucks* 43, 77–126

Pine J 2003 Late Bronze Age occupation, Roman enclosure and early Saxon occupation at Waylands Nursery, Welley Road, Wraysbury, Berkshire, 1997. in *Prehistoric, Roman and Saxon sites in Eastern Berkshire*. (ed) Preston S. Thames Valley Archaeological Services Monograph 2. Reading

Preece R C, Parfitt S A, Bridgland D R, Lewis S G, Rowe P J, Atkinson T C, Candy I, Debenham NC, Penkman K E H, Rhodes EJ, Schwenninger J L, Griffiths H I, Whittaker, J E and Gleed-Owen C 2007 Terrestrial environments during MIS 11: evidence from the Palaeolithic site at West Stow, Suffolk, UK. *Quaternary Science Reviews* 26 9–10, 1236–1300

Preston J 2001 *The Kings Arms, High Street, Old Amersham, Buckinghamshire. Building Recording and Investigation*. unpublished report

Preston S *et al.*, 2007 Bronze Age occupation and Saxon features at the Wolverton Turn enclosure, near Stony Stratford, Milton Keynes. investigations by T. Schadla-Hall, Philip

Carstairs, Jo Lawson, Hugh Beamish, Andrew Hunn, Ben Ford and Tess Durden, 1972 to 1994. *Records of Bucks* 47 1, 81–117

Price T D 1997 The first farmers of southern Scandinavia. p 346–62 in *The origins and spread of agriculture and pastoralism in Eurasia*. (ed) Harris D. UCL Press London

Reed M 1978 Markets and fairs in medieval Buckinghamshire. *Records of Bucks* 20, 563–585

Reed M 1979 *The Buckinghamshire Landscape*. Hodder & Stoughton

Reed M 1979 Buckinghamshire Anglo-Saxon charter boundaries. in *The Early Charters of the Thames Valley*. Leicester University Press

Reed M 1993 *A History of Buckinghamshire*. Chichester

Renfrew C 1989 *Archaeology and Language*. Penguin, London

Reynier M J 2005 *Early Mesolithic Britain: Origins, development and directions*. Archaeopress Oxford

Richards C and Mellars P A 1998 Stable Isotopes and the seasonality of the Oronsay middens. *Antiquity* 72, 178–84

Richards J 2002 The case of the missing Vikings. Scandinavian burial in the Danelaw, in *Burials in Early medieval England and Wales*. Eds. Lucy S and Reynolds A. Society for Medieval Archaeology Monograph 17

Richmond A, Rackham J and Scaife R 2006 Excavation of a prehistoric stream-side site at Little Marlow, Buckinghamshire. *Records of Bucks* 46, 65–101

Riley H 2001 *Stowe Park, Stowe, Buckinghamshire*. Survey report English Heritage Archaeological Investigation Report series AI/21/2001. unpublished

Rivet A L F 1969 *The Roman villa in Britain*. London

Roberts B K and Wrathmell S 2000 *An Atlas of Rural Settlement in England*. London

Roberts M B and Parfitt S 1999 *Boxgrove: A Middle Pleistocene hominid site at Eartham Quarry, Boxgrove, West Sussex*. English Heritage

Roden D 1966 Field systems in Ibstone, a township of the south-west Chilterns during the later middle ages. *Records of Bucks* 18, 43–57

Roundell H 1862 Roman foundations discovered at Tingewick. *Records of Bucks* 3, 33–50

Rouse E C 1977 The wall paintings at Nos. 1 and 2 Market Hill, Buckingham. *Records of Bucks* 20, 293–300

RPS Group Plc 2005 *Archaeological investigations for the A41 Aston Clinton bypass, Buckinghamshire: analysis of excavations at the Woodlands Roundabout, Lower Icknield Way and Tring Hill sites including watching brief results*. Highways Agency unpublished report

Schofield J and Humble J 1997 *The Evaluation of Surface Lithic Scatters and Stray Finds*. English Heritage MPP/CAS Project, unpublished report

Schreve D C, Bridgland D R, Allen P, Blackford J J, Gleed-Owen C P, Griffiths H I, Keen D H, and White M J 2002 Sedimentology, Palaeontology and Archaeology of Late Middle Pleistocene River Thames Terrace Deposits at Purfleet, Essex, UK. *Quaternary Science Reviews* 21, 1423–1464

Scott E 1993 *A Gazetteer of Roman villas in Britain*. Leicester Archaeology Monographs 1, Leicester

Secker D 2005 A survey of earthworks and structural remains at Bray's Wood, The Lee. *Records of Bucks* 45, 65–73

Sherlock R L 1960 London and Thames Valley. 3rd Edition HMSO. London

Sherlock R L and Noble A H 1922 *The geology of the country around Beaconsfield*. Memoir of the Geological Survey of England and Wales

SPB J M, Miller D D and Miller D M 1985 The Manor and Abbey of Burnham. *Records of Bucks* 27, 94–106

Shotton F W, Goudie A S, Briggs D J and Osmaston H A 1980 Cromerian Interglacial Deposits at Sugworth, Near Oxford, England, and Their Relation to the Plateau Drift of the Cotswolds and the Terrace Sequence of the Upper and Middle Thames. *Philosophical*

Transactions of the Royal Society of London. Series B, Biological Sciences 289(1034), 55–86

Sidell J, Wilkinson K, Scaife R and Cameron N 2000 *The Holocene Evolution of the London Thames.* Museum of London Archaeology Service, Monograph 5. London

Simmons I G and Innes J B 1996(a) Prehistoric charcoal in peat profiles at North Gill, North Yorkshire Moors, England. *Journal of Archaeological Science* 23, 193–197

Simmons I G and Innes J B 1996(b) Disturbance phases in the Mid-Holocene vegetation at North Gill, North York Moors: Form and Process. *Journal of Archaeological Science* 23, 183–191

Simmons I G 1996 *The Environmental Impact of Later Mesolithic Cultures: The Creation of Moorland Landscape in England and Wales.* Edinburgh, Edinburgh University Press

Sister Jane Mary SPB, Miller, D D and Miller D M 1985 The Manor and Abbey of Burnham. *Records of Buckinghamshire* 27, 94–106

Slatcher D and Samuels J 2004 Multi-period activity at Main Street, Ashendon: excavations in 1999. *Records of Bucks* 44, 1–20

Smith C 1992 *Late Stone Age Hunters of the British Isles.* London, Routledge

Smith R A 1905 Anglo-Saxon Remains. in *Victoria County History.* 1905, 195–205

Stainton B 1989 Excavation of an early prehistoric site at Stratford's Yard, Chesham, *Records of Bucks* 31, 49–74

Stainton B and Stanley C 1987 A Romano-British pottery kiln at Springwood, Gerrards Cross. *Records of Bucks* 29, 160–169

Stenton F M 1943 *Anglo-Saxon England.* Oxford

Stevens J 1884 Remains found in an Anglo-Saxon tumulus at Taplow. *British Archaeological Journal* 40, 61–71

Stocker D and Went D 1995 Evidence for a pre-Viking church adjacent to the Anglo-Saxon barrow at Taplow, Buckinghamshire. *Archaeological Journal* 152, 441–454

Stone P 2009 *Saxon and medieval activity at Walton Street, Aylesbury, Buckinghamshire.* Draft report Archaeological Solutions Ltd (copy in Buckinghamshire HER)

Storer W P 1863 Some notes concerning Olney. *Records of Bucks* 2, 188–198

Stone J S 1859 Notes on ancient foundations in the parish of Ellesborough. *Records of Bucks* 2, 53–56

Stringer C 2006 *Homo Britannicus. The Incredible Story of Human Life in Britain.* Penguin Books

Tarrant N and Sandford A 1972 A Romano-British kiln at Fulmer. *Records of Bucks* 19, 174–88

Taylor C C 1975 Roman settlement in the Nene Valley: the impact of recent archaeology p 179 in *Recent work in rural archaeology.* (Ed.) Fowler P J. Bath

Taylor H M and Taylor J 1980–84 *Anglo-Saxon Architecture.* Cambridge University Press

Taylor J 2004 The distribution and exchange of pink, grog tempered pottery in the East Midlands: an update. *Journal of Roman Pottery Studies* 11, 66

Taylor-Moore K 2006 *The comparative development of Aylesbury and Buckingham up to c.1550.* MA dissertation University of Leicester. unpublished

Thacker F S 1920 *The Thames Highway.* (Ed) Munk L. 2 Vols 1968 reprint. David and Charles

Thatcher C 2006 *Roman Settlement at Grendon Underwood, The Hardwick to Marsh Gibbon Gas Pipeline, Buckinghamshire: Archaeological Evaluation.* CCC AFU Report Number 909

Thomas J 1991 *Rethinking the Neolithic.* Cambridge University Press. Cambridge

Thorne A T and Walker C 2003 *Excavations at the former Cowper Tannery, Olney.* unpublished report

Thorne A 2005 Wolverton Mill. *South Midlands Archaeology* 35, 19

Thorne A 2005 Wolverton Mill. *Medieval Archaeology* 49, 357–8 (also see leaflet issued by Northants Archaeology)

Towers, J, Montgomery, J, Evans, J, Jay, M, and Parker Pearson, M, in press, An investigation of the origins of cattle and aurochs deposited in the Early Bronze Age barrows at Gayhurst and Irthlingborough. *Journal of Archaeological Science*

Toulmin Smith L (editor) 1964 *The Itinerary of John Leland in or about the years 1535–1543. Parts IV and V.* Fontwell

Toynbee J M C 1964 *Art in Britain under the Romans.* Oxford

Walton Rogers P 2007 *Cloth and Clothing in early Anglo-Saxon England.* Council British Archaeology Research Report 145. York

Watts M and Langdon J 2004 An early tower windmill? The Turweston 'post-mill' reconsidered. *History of Technology* 25, 1–6

Waugh H 1972 The Romano-British burial at Weston Turville. *Records of Bucks* 17, 107–114

Waugh H, Mynard D C and Cain R 1974 Some Iron Age pottery from mid and north Bucks, with a gazetteer of associated sites and finds. *Records of Bucks* 19.4, 373–419

Webster G 1980 *The Roman invasion of Britain.* Batsford, London

Wenban-Smith F F, Allen P, Bates M R, Parfitt S A, Preece R C, Stewart J R, Turner C and Whittaker J E 2006 The Clactonian elephant butchery site at Southfleet Road, Ebbsfleet, UK. *Journal of Quaternary Science* 21.5, 471–483

Wessex Archaeology 2005 *Preferred Area 4, Denham, Buckinghamshire. Archaeological Evaluation Report and Outline Mitigation Strategy.* Wessex Archaeology Ltd. unpublished report

Wessex Archaeology 2007 *Archaeological Investigations at Weedon Hill, Aylesbury, Buckinghamshire Archaeological Assessment Report.* unpublished report

Wessex Archaeology 2009 *Preferred Area 4, Denham, Buckinghamshire: Initial Statement of Results, Access Road and Extraction Phases 1A, 1B, 2A, 2B and 5 (Plant Site) Including Flint scatters 5 and 6 (Phase 1A) and potential worked wood deposit (Phase 1B.* unpublished Report 60482.01

White M J 1997 The earlier Palaeolithic occupation of the Chilterns (Southern England): reassessing the sites of Worthington G.Smith. *Antiquity* 71, 912–31

Whitelock D 1930 *Anglo-Saxon Wills.* Cambridge University Press

Whitelock D (editor) 1955 *English Historical Documents c.500–1042*

Wilkinson N, Scaife R G and Sidell E J 2000. Environmental and sea level changes in London from 10 500 BP to the present: a case study from Silvertown. *Proceedings of the Geologists Association* 111, 41–54

Williams D 1997 *Late Saxon stirrup-strapmounts; a classification and catalogue.* Council British Archaeology Research Report 111

Williams R J 1993a *Pennylands and Hartigans. Two Iron Age and Saxon sites in Milton Keynes.* Bucks Archaeological Society Monograph Series No 4. Aylesbury

Williams R J 1993b Prehistoric Landscape, in *The Changing Landscape of Milton Keynes.* (Eds) Croft R A and Mynard D C. Bucks Archaeological Society Monograph Series No 5, 5–10. Aylesbury

Williams R J, Hart P J and Williams A T L 1996 *Wavendon Gate. A Late Iron Age and Roman settlement in Milton Keynes.* Bucks Archaeological Society Monograph Series No10. Aylesbury

Williams R J and Zeepvat R J 1994 *Bancroft. A Late Bronze Age/Iron Age Settlement, Roman Villa and Temple-Mausoleum.* Vol 1: Excavations and building materials; Vol 2 Finds and environmental evidence. Bucks Archaeological Society Monograph Series No 7, Aylesbury

Williamson T 2002 *Shaping Medieval Landscapes. Settlement, society, environment.* Macclesfield

Williamson T 2008 *Sutton Hoo and its landscape; the context of monument.* Windgather Press/ Oxbow

Woodfield C 1977 A Roman military site at Magiovinium? *Records of Bucks* 20.3, 384–99

Woodfield C 1989 A Roman site at Stanton Low, on the Great Ouse, Bucks. *Archaeological*

Journal 146, 135–278

Woods P Turland R and Hastings R 1981 A Romano-British pottery at Biddlesden, Bucks, 369–395 in *Roman Pottery Research in Britain and North-West Europe.* (eds) Anderson A S and Anderson A C. British Archaeology Reports 123, Oxford

Wymer J 1968 *Lower Palaeolithic Archaeology in Britain.* Humanities Press Inc.

Wymer J 1999 *The Lower Palaeolithic Occupation of Britain.* Wessex Archaeology and English Heritage

Wymer J J (editor) 1977 *Gazetter of Mesolithic Sites in England and Wales.* Council for British Archaeology Report 22. London

Yates D T 1999 Bronze Age field systems in the Thames Valley. *Oxford Journal of Archaeology* 18(2), 157–170

Yeoman P A St. J 1986 Excavations at the motte, Weston Turville Manor, 1985. *Records of Bucks* 28, 169–178

Yeoman P A and Stewart I J 1992 A Romano-British villa estate at Mantles Green, Amersham, Buckinghamshire. *Records of Bucks* 34, 107–18

Zeepvat R J 1987 Romano-British settlement in the upper Ouse and Ouzel valleys. p 6–18 in *Roman Milton Keynes* (Ed.) Mynard D C, Bucks Archaeological Society Monograph Series 1. Aylesbury

Zeepvat R J 1988 Another Roman building at Wymbush? *Records of Bucks* 30, 111–16

Zeepvat R J 1991 *Roman Milton Keynes.* Milton Keynes Archaeological Unit, Milton Keynes

Zeepvat R J 1993 Roman landscape, in *The changing landscape of Milton Keynes.* (Eds) Croft R A and Mynard D C Bucks Archaeological Society Monograph Series 5. Aylesbury

Zeepvat R J 1994 A Roman coin manufacturing hoard from Magiovinium, Fenny Stratford, Bucks. *Britannia* 25, 1–19

Zeepvat R 1997 *The Roman settlement at Cow Roast, Hertfordshire:updated project design and assessment report.* Hertfordshire Archaeological Trust. unpublished report

Zeepvat R J 2003 A Romano-British cremation burial from Wellwick Farm, Wendover. *Records of Bucks* 43, 47–59

Zeepvat R J, Roberts J C and King N A 1994 *Caldecotte, Milton Keynes: excavation and fieldwork 1971–1991.* Bucks Archaeological Society Monograph Series 9. Aylesbury

Zeepvat R J, Roberts J S and King N A 1994 *Caldecotte, Milton Keynes. Excavation and fieldwork 1966–9.* Bucks Archaeological Society Monograph Series 9. Aylesbury

Some Sites To Visit In Buckinghamshire

The list includes a small selection of the county's early historic sites that are always accessible, with the exception of Wing and Stewkley churches which are normally open during the day, and Buckingham Chantry Chapel. For other churches see J. Hunt *Buckinghamshire's Favourite Churches* (2007). A number of medieval and Tudor buildings are often accessible such as Dorney Court, Boarstall Tower, and Long Crendon Courthouse; see also the National Trust handbook and website and check with local tourist information offices. Many other archaeological sites and early buildings and sites are visible from footpaths. A most useful work for exploring any village is N.Pevsner and E Williamson's *The Buildings of England; Buckinghamshire* (Penguin 1994) which list many earthworks as well as buildings. The best maps for footpaths are the Ordnance Survey 'Explorer' Series.

Prehistoric

Boddington Hill, near Wendover: hillfort, the ramparts are well-preserved in woodland.

Bulstrode Camp, Gerrards Cross: interior and part of hillfort ramparts accessible from Camp Road.

Cholesbury Camp, Cholesbury: hillfort; impressive ramparts accessible.

Danesborough hillfort: some well-preserved lengths of rampart in woodland. Access by footpath from Bow Brickhill or Apsley Heath.

Grims Ditch: several stretches of this Iron Age boundary can be seen from Chiltern footpaths, in particular in Great and Little Hampden parishes, see OS maps.

Ivinghoe Beacon: hillfort and several Bronze Age barrows. The hillfort ramparts are clearest on the north side.

Pitstone Hill: a good length of Grims Ditch and a possible flint mine

Pulpit Hill, Great Kimble: hillfort within woodland.

Seven Ways Plain, Burnham Beeches: an unusual plateau fort.

West Wycombe: the parish church lies within a hillfort.

Whiteleaf Hill, Princes/Monks Risborough: the restored Neolithic barrow can be seen, also a Bronze Age 'cross-ridge' dyke.

Roman

Bancroft villa; the plan of the excavated Roman villa is laid out on the ground in North Loughton Valley Park.

Thornborough Barrows: can be seen from the A421; parking by old Thornborough Bridge

Saxon

Taplow: the mound which contained the princely burial is within Taplow's old churchyard beside Taplow Court.

The Black Hedge: a living Saxon boundary separating Monks and Princes Risborough **

The Secklow Mound: preserved within Milton Keynes city centre behind the central library. The mound marks the meeting place of Secklow Hundred

Wing Church: fine Saxon apse; crypt open only by arrangement with churchwardens.

Medieval

Buckingham Chantry Chapel, Market Hill; see National Trust for opening times.

Castlethorpe; medieval castle motte and earthworks of bailey.

Desborough Castle, Cressex, High Wycombe: an impressive earthwork, probably a defended manor site.

Hardacanute's Moat, Burnham; medieval moated site in Burnham Beeches.

High Wycombe Castle: motte in grounds of Wycombe Museum, Castle Hill House, Priory Avenue.

Pitstone Windmill; built in the late sixteenth century but similar to medieval mills. Interior occasionally accessible also.

Quarrendon, near Aylesbury; medieval village, moat, remains of chapel and Tudor earthwork; part accessible from footpaths.

Ridge and furrow; evidence of medieval cultivation ridges can be seen from footpaths all over central and north Buckinghamshire. Much however has been ploughed flat in recent years.

Thornborough Bridge: the county's only medieval stone bridge, parking nearby.

Stewkley Church: the county's finest Norman building.

Wolverton medieval village earthworks and motte (castle mound): adjacent to Holy Trinity church, Old Wolverton.

Useful Contacts
Relevant to The Historic County of Buckinghamshire

Historic Environment Records

Buckinghamshire County Archaeological Service
Planning, Environment & Development, County Hall, Aylesbury HP20 1UY
Email smr@buckscc.gov.uk
Web http://www.buckscc.gov.uk/bcc/archaeology/Archaeology.page?
Unlocking Buckinghamshire's Past http://ubp.buckscc.gov.uk/

Milton Keynes Archaeological Service
Conservation & Archaeology, Spatial Planning, Milton Keynes Council, Civic Offices, 1
Saxon Gate East, Central Milton Keynes, Bucks MK9 3EJ
01908 252599
Archaeology@milton-keynes.gov.uk
conservation@milton-keynes.gov.uk
http://www.milton-keynes.gov.uk/archaeology

Berkshire Archaeology
3rd Floor, Central Library, Reading, Berkshire RG1 3BQ
info@berkshirearchaeology.org.uk
www.berkshirearchaeology.co.uk

Central Bedfordshire Council (for Linslade)
Historic Environment Information Officer, Heritage and Design Team, Central Bedfordshire Council. PO Box 1395, Bedford MK42 5AN
0300 300 6027

Museums with archaeological material

Buckinghamshire County Museum
County Museum, Church Street, Aylesbury HP20 2QP
museum@buckscc.gov.uk
01296 331441
Contains displays on the county's archaeology and looks after the principal collection of
objects and archives relating to excavations in Buckinghamshire and Milton Keynes

Reading Museum
Town Hall, Blagrave Street, Reading RG1 1QH
mail@readingmuseum.org.uk
http://www.readingmuseum.org.uk/
Reading museum holds some Buckinghamshire finds from the Thames and also archaeological material from Slough District Council area.

British Museum
Great Russell Street, London WC1B 3DG
http://www.britishmuseum.org/

Holds some Buckinghamshire objects and normally has the Taplow Saxon burial finds on
display.

Oxford Museums
Both the Ashmolean Museum and the Oxford University Museum of Natural History hold
some Buckinghamshire material.

For Listed Buildings advice contact individual Conservation Officers at each District Council Office.

Portable Antiquities Scheme

Finds Liaison Officer, Museum Resource Centre, Tring Road, Halton, Aylesbury
HP22 5PN
01296 624519.
http://finds.org.uk

Archaeological and Historical Societies.

County Society
Buckinghamshire Archaeological Society, c/o County Museum, Church Street, Aylesbury, Bucks HP20 2QP
http://www.bucksas.org.uk
bucksas@buckscc.gov.uk

Founded in1847, maintains a library (staffed Wednesdays) and some archival material; holds meetings, runs excursions, publishes *Records of Bucks* and other papers and books, has sub-groups concerned with Natural History and buildings.

Other Societies
Many societies have links with the BAS website (above) also see the CBA South Midlands website (below). In addition all local societies in the Milton Keynes area are noted in the Milton Keynes Heritage Association website: http://www.mkheritage.co.uk/

Local Studies Libraries

Centre for Buckinghamshire Studies (for both reference works and archives)
County Hall, Walton Street, Aylesbury HP20 1UU
01296 382250
www.buckscc.gov.uk/archives

Milton Keynes Local Studies Library: 555 Silbury Boulevard,
Saxon Gate East, Central Milton Keynes
MK9 3HL
01908 254160
mklocal@milton-keynes.gov.uk
http://www.milton-keynes.gov.uk/library_services

High Wycombe Library
5 Eden Place, High Wycombe, Bucks HP11 2DH
01296 382587 (Centre for Bucks Studies for Local History information)

Slough Library:
Slough Borough Council, High Street, Slough SL1 1EA
www.slough.gov.uk

Other local organisations with an archaeological remit

Council for British Archaeology, South Midlands Group:
http://www.cba-southmidlands.org.uk/

(for the national CBA organisation with many useful links see:
http://www.britarch.ac.uk)

Index

By Diana Gulland